Born in Kiel in 1900, Walter Poller grew up in the working-class movement. His maternal grandfather was one of the founders of the German Social Democratic Party and his father worked all his life – and suffered imprisonment – for the same cause.

At 19 Walter Poller was the youngest editor in Hamm – Westphalia. Since then his travels as a journalist have taken him over most of the world. The rise and fall of the Nazi State he foresaw as early as 1932; a year later he was organising illegal resistance groups. After being arrested several times, he was convicted of treason against Hitler's Reich and condemned to four years with hard labour. This sentence completed, he was sent to Buchenwald.

WALTER POLLER

Medical Block, Buchenwald

The Personal Testimony of Inmate 966, Block 36

GRAFTON BOOKS

A Division of the Collins Publishing Group

LONDON GLASGOW
TORONTO SYDNEY AUCKLAND

Grafton Books
A Division of the Collins Publishing Group
8 Grafton Street, London W1X 3LA

Published by Grafton Books 1988

First published in Great Britain by
Souvenir Press Ltd 1960

Copyright © Verlag das Segel 1960

ISBN 0-586-07375-2

Printed and bound in Great Britain by
Collins, Glasgow

Set in Plantin

TO THE DEAD!
TO THE LIVING!

Contents

CONTENTS

Illustrations

Two plans of the camp: the first, drawn from memory by the author; the second, a copy of the original official plan discovered later in the Bavarian State Archives. Close study of the latter resulted in a startling discovery.

The infamous whipping-block.

Inmates massed for roll-call.

One of the rare pictures of the camp hospital.

A lampshade and other items made from human skin.

A body impaled on the wire.

Typical groups of inmates.

The quarry, scene of nightmares for many a survivor.

The instructions heading inmates' letter-forms, followed by a selection of pictures which add a postscript more eloquent than any words. NOTE: Several of the photographs in this section were taken after the author had himself left Buchenwald.

Introduction to the English Edition

I WROTE this book in April and May, 1945, directly after the collapse of the Third Reich, from the meagre notes—disguised for safety's sake—which I had jotted down during the first months after my release from the concentration camp in 1940. It was not my intention to release the book immediately for publication. I knew that the contents could have also become a manual of Evil and was afraid that in the forthcoming difficult years it could foster new irrational premises and obscure objective standards. My intuition told me that this report in its intended sense could not fulfil its purpose until, from an inner need and in the fullness of time, this blackest of chapters in history could fruitfully be overcome.

Fifteen years have passed since the first edition appeared. Today it has become an imperative duty to conquer the sinister past, not only in Germany and Central Europe but throughout the whole world. The public cannot and will not weaken in this respect. The reader will easily recognise that this book was written in order to break down doors which were closed to many and which might even have remained closed today. They are those doors through which each man must pass if he wishes to lead a decent human life and to strive for a better humanity.

As I wrote it there loomed behind me the shades of the 238,379 prisoners who passed through the Calvary of Buchenwald and of the 56,545 men and women who were murdered there. May this book prove a foundation stone for a better future!

WALTER POLLER

London, 6th December, 1960.

Introduction

THE reader is first justified in his desire to know who intends to give the report embodied in this book. He would naturally like to know the reason for the writer being sent to a National Socialist Concentration Camp.

A few facts about myself, then. I am the son of a moulder, and was born in Kiel in 1900. My father was actively engaged in a leading role in Trade Unions and various other political organisations of German workers.

I was educated first at an elementary school and then a secondary school; then had to leave for financial reasons, after obtaining the so-called "One Year's Certificate". I had joined the Arbeiter-Jugend (Workers Youth) movement during my schooldays, and it was in this group that my interest in literature and politics, aroused early in my life, was strengthened until it became the deciding factor for me.

From the time I left school until the day I was drafted into the army, I was engaged as an apprentice in the editorial office of the Workers' Newspaper in Kiel. At the age of nineteen I was promoted to the management of a workers' newspaper in Westphalia, work I carried out until the day I was taken into protective custody for the first time, with two long interruptions spent in studying and travelling abroad.

On 1st March, 1933, I was to have been introduced as a Town Councillor for the town in which I had been living for many years, thus being able to represent my party on the Town Council. To prevent my doing so, I was arrested, ostensibly for my own "safety". In accordance with the formal legal provisions of the time, I was put in a small cell in the state police station, where I remained for eight days.

Two or three days after my release from custody, during the afternoon, a roving band of about twelve youths, mostly wearing SA uniforms with swastika armlets, burst into the editor's room, stealing or destroying nearly all the contents. I was manhandled and forced to leave my place of work.

I was again taken into protective custody on 24th June of

that year, together with many political friends who were simultaneously arrested with me throughout the whole of Germany in an attempt to destroy the free German Workers' Movement. I was sentenced to fourteen days, and taken to a camp for people like myself. There, I experienced enough to realise that National Socialism was undoubtedly following the footsteps of Italian Fascism, the brutal and inhuman methods of which I had got to know in Italy.

In the early hours of 1st November, 1934, I was arrested in my rooms by five members of the Gestapo, on an indictment for "Attempted High Treason". My crime was that I had organised a movement against National Socialism, mainly with the assistance of members of my own party. Only two of the pamphlets edited by me, however, came into the hands of the Gestapo, and these through the police informer Maczek, from Wiescherhöfen, near Hamm (Westphalia).

My hands were shackled and I was locked in a barred cell in the basement of the Dortmund police station Steinwache. Here, I was subjected to numerous interrogations. Seventeen of these were attempts to force me into a confession of my crime by beating me both with sticks and rubber truncheons, on my back, buttocks, shins and abdomen. I had determined not to betray any of my political friends, and kept to my word.

On 28th July, 1935, the third Senate of the People's Court sentenced me to four years' penal servitude on a charge of attempted high treason, taking into account the eight months I had already spent in remand.* The public prosecutor proposed my deprivation of civil rights, but the court rejected this.

This sentence of penal servitude was the only one I received in my life, nor did I receive any disciplinary sentence during my imprisonment or during the time I spent in the concentration camp.

* The sentence was in the meantime officially cancelled. After the collapse of the "Thousand Year Reich" I received a copy of the written sentence from the legal authorities, prepared from the documents with which I was not acquainted during the Nazi regime. The sentence, particularly in its legal phrasing, revealed what the Nazi lawyer Parisius stated clearly in his speech on the fourth anniversary of the People's Court of Justice: "Its task was not to speak of justice but to destroy the opponents of National Socialism."

I was in prison at various places—Münster, Neusustrum, Börgermoor, Plötzensee (because of lack of accommodation the famous "Plötze" was turned into a penitentiary for some time), Oslebshausen, Celle and Moorlager Lührsbockel in the Lüneburger Heath.

On 28th November, 1938, my term of imprisonment was to have come to an end. Instead, without any explanation, I was taken into police custody and transferred to the prison in Celle, to the "White House", a place which became well-known through Hermann Löns. From there, I was transferred back to the Dortmund police station Steinwache.

After a few days, I was handed a back-dated order for protective custody. I was given a formal interrogation, and an equally formal medical examination, which consisted of the police doctor looking at me for two seconds.

On 17th December a police official secretly told me that within the next few days I would be transported to what was called "a camp for re-education". I left the Dortmund police station Steinwache on 18th December, and four days later arrived at the concentration camp known as "Buchenwald".

WALTER POLLER

MEDICAL BLOCK, BUCHENWALD

It is the 24th day of April, 1945. The time is eleven in the morning—a moment when I begin the realisation of a plan I have long contemplated . . . to write a report of my experiences in the concentration camp known as "Buchenwald", which is on the Ettersberg, near Weimar.

This is so moving a moment for me that I feel I must, before writing anything at all, make the following oath:

I swear by my own life and by all that I love and for which I consider worth living, that I will write the whole truth, and nothing but the truth, of what I saw and experienced there. I swear before myself and before mankind that I will not write a single word, consciously or carelessly, to distort that truth, to exaggerate it, or only partly to justify it; nor will I omit a word, consciously or carelessly, which could give the same effect.

I swear this oath and certify it with my signature.

Walter Poller

Neuschönningstedt, April 24th, 1945.

PART ONE

1. In the Police Prison of Halle

ON the 18th December, 1938, I found myself yet again pushed into the "Black Maria", the police transport which was to take the prisoners to Weimar. This was a city hallowed by the memory of Goethe and Schiller. I had often, in happier days, gone to see the Goethe house on the Frauenplan, or to the vault in which two simple sarcophagi have been placed; I had often entered the Schiller house with reverence, and had searched the local cemetery for monuments on which famous names have long been chiselled. I had walked to the simple cottage in which Goethe's wife had once lived, and about whom he, one of the very greatest of mankind, had written a four-line poem which was to become part of world literature:

> *Du versuchst, o Sonne, vergebens,*
> *durch düstere Wolken zu scheinen.*
> *Der einz'ge Gewinn meines Lebens*
> *ist, ihren Verlust zu beweinen.**

But now . . . the sun tried vainly to shine through the dark clouds, for it was veiled in black by cloudbanks of horror, the symbols of brutal power.

At this very moment the fury of Nazism tore unchecked across the whole of Germany. At the orders of the rulers of the State, places of worship fell prey to wanton flames, shops were looted, rooms were burgled of their contents, materials and foodstuffs were senselessly destroyed, and human beings, their faces made in the image of the Man of Nazareth, were clubbed to death like mangy dogs. These people were shot or stabbed, many thousands herded together by threats and merciless flogging, jeered at by abnormal beasts who treated them like

---

* You try, O Sun, in vain
  To shine through the dark clouds.
  My life's only gain
  Is to mourn her loss.

21

defenceless animals. It was the period of Jewish pogroms which were organised by the German State.

For me, too, the sun was veiled by dark clouds, for I knew that I stood before a door over the arch of which I seemed to see Dante's words written in letters of fire: "All hope abandon, ye who enter here!"

I knew something of what awaited me, but not everything. Protective custody, camps for political re-education, concentration camps! Gruesome and most unbelievable rumours had trickled through these places, but I was sufficiently trained, politically, to know that the unbelievable could be true—in this case, was true.

Now I was confronted with the truth in my own person, now I would see with my own eyes, hear with my own ears and feel with my own body, the effects of a National Socialist concentration camp.

Had I not already felt a thousand times in my life the tremendous difference between spiritual conception and personal experience?—for instance, when, in the observatory, I had first viewed the starry sky above me through the telescope?—or when the wonder of nature in its limitless complexity revealed itself to me for the first time under the microscope?—or as I stood on the edge of Vesuvius and felt the majestic heartbeat of the earth?—or in the Chiesa San Pietro in Vincoli before Michelangelo's gigantic "Moses"?

Even my strong mental picture of "The Last Judgement", with its details supplied by copies and reports and appreciations of this work of art, had not equalled the reality of my own experience when I had stood before the picture and had found everything I knew confirmed, with that something extra from my own spiritual conception.

So it was now to be with my personal experiences of a concentration camp about which I had only some hazy knowledge.

We were five days on our way to the camp, during which we were joined by other sufferers from all points of the compass.

In the police station at Halle we met a fellow-sufferer who had come straight from Buchenwald itself. Indeed, from him we heard the actual name of Buchenwald for the first time; for until then we had only vaguely known that we were going to a concentration camp near Weimar.

We besieged this man for information, but he told us nothing of importance, merely using general phrases which were true but gave no proper picture of Buchenwald.

I believed him to be a little dull-witted, but he was very active and extremely helpful in the preparation of our sleeping accommodation, which was on the floor. He was pale and nervous, yet not badly nourished, despite having already been three months in the camp. We found that he was now in transit to East Prussia for interrogation by the police.

Every time we put a question to him about Buchenwald he merely returned, "It is bad there; but you will see." It was not until later that we understood his reasons for not saying more. We knew then that he had not wanted the risk of becoming a "mangled corpse", as this process is called in the camp; that is, he did not want to be slowly and cruelly tortured to death. Understandably, then, he was silent in self-defence.

I rested on the mattress next to his during the night, and ceaselessly worried him with questions, although I learned very little, apart from the fact that he worked in a camp carpenter's shop.

"But why carpentry?" I asked. "Is there such a thing there also?"

"You have no idea," he returned; "there is everything there."

"What did you do?"

"I? I blackened the coffins."

"Coffins?"

"Yes."

"What else did you do?"

"Nothing else."

"Only blackened coffins?"

"Yes."

"The whole day?"

"Yes."

"How many per day?"

"Oh, about thirty; but I did not do all those on my own."

"Why not?"

"There were two more with me who also did nothing else."

"Were the coffins only for prisoners?"

"Of course. But they were all only quite simple boxes."

23

"Where are the corpses buried?"

"Don't know."

"How many people are there in the camp?"

"Oh, many. Twenty thousand, perhaps. But now the Jews have arrived, and that certainly makes it more."

"Were there no Jews in the camp before?"

"Of course, but these are the Jews from the November pogrom. More arrived every day. I mean those from barracks IA to VA."

"IA to VA?" I tried vainly to understand.

"Oh, leave off!" he cried impatiently. "You will see for yourself!"

"What other work is there in the camp?" I persisted.

"A lot, in the camp and outside," he answered wearily.

"Outside as well?"

"Yes, at the barracks, in the stone quarry and other places."

"Any beatings?"

"Let me alone!" he cried. "You will see it all!" After a few moments, he whispered, "I say, would you do me a favour?"

"If I can, of course," I answered promptly.

"My name is Marohn. Go along to the Kapo in the carpentry and tell him that I have given the two Marks to Hermann."

"Which two Marks?"

"The Kapo lent them to me but I could not pay him back again."

"Are you allowed money in the camp?"

"Of course. Each person may have up to ten Marks in his pocket. The Kapo gave me the money for safe-keeping."

"It was not lent?"

"Oh, leave off!" he said again. "You will see for yourself."

"Can we buy anything in the camp?" I asked, ignoring his plea.

"Yes; from the canteen. That is, if there is anything there."

"What can one buy?"

"Cigarettes and the like."

"May we smoke?"

"Sure. Only not now. We are now forbidden to smoke. However, the prohibition will probably be lifted for the holiday. But if you have any cigarettes you can smoke, anyway."

"Don't the guards keep a watch?"

"It's not like in jug. We all run around free. In the camp there are always only a few Scharführer, and at night no guard at all."

"How many Scharführer are there?"

"Many; but in the camp itself always only a few. Still, there are the pickets. They keep outside, where the work is done."

"Many of them?"

"Maybe a thousand. I don't know."

"Can one escape?"

"No, that won't work. They would shoot you."

"Does that happen?"

"Oh, you will see."

"Are there also lessons?"

"Lessons?"

"Yes; I mean, we are to be re-educated, so surely we must also receive lessons?"

"Re-education, my fellow? You must interpret that word quite differently."

"How differently?"

"You mean like education at school, with the teacher and so on, don't you?"

"Yes."

"No, that's not the sort of education they mean. There, there are only the twenty-five."

"Twenty-five?"

"Yes, on the arse. You have to lay yourself across the block and get twenty-five."

"Who does the beating?"

"The Scharführer."

"Does it hurt?"

"Sure; but let up! You will see for yourself!"

But I was still persistent. "Is everybody beaten?" I asked.

"No. Only if you are caught, and sometimes also when we have to count off and it is your turn to do this. But then, only five are given."

"Why only five?" I asked, although as yet all this was a little vague to me.

"Because there are far too many people to punish. If they

gave more, they would never finish. As it is, this punishment always takes up half a day or more."

"When do they count off?"

"If at times, they can't catch anyone, or no one is betrayed."

"Are there traitors?"

"Of course. So you be careful and keep your mouth shut. . . . Are you political?"

"Yes."

"Then you have it easier. The politicals hold together better."

"Are you also political?"

"No; I'm a black."

"What does that mean?"

"Work-shy."

"Why do you say a 'black'?"

"The politicals have a red badge, the work-shy a black one."

"Have you been released?"

"I don't know. I must first go up to East Prussia. Perhaps I will be released. I hope so."

"How long does one stay in the camp?"

"That differs a lot. Two years, three years, sometimes even longer. Some have been there since the beginning, but they mostly all have a job—as Kapo and so on."

"Kapo?" I queried.

"That's a foreman. The politicals are the best of those, although not always."

"Why the best?"

"They don't beat such a lot at work nor do they make reports so often."

"And the others do that?"

"Yes, almost all do. The greens are the worst."

"What are the greens?"

"They are the criminals."

"Are there others, too?"

"Only the bible-thumpers."

"Is there anything to read?"

"Let me sleep," he begged; but nevertheless answered:

"There are newspapers. You can order them if you have the money. But you will see for yourself."

This man Marohn was eventually taken back to the camp,

but did not return to the carpentry. Instead, he was allocated to the working party outside the camp. In the autumn of 1939, a complete wreck and terribly undernourished, he was brought in to the sick quarters, where I could only recognise him by his name. He died a few days after his admittance, and the cause of his death was put down to a general physical weakness.

* * *

The barred carriage of our train rolled its way along the tracks towards Weimar. Five and six prisoners were standing closely pressed together in the small one-man cells, while the narrow corridor between the cells was more than overcrowded.

The doors to the cells were kept open so that even that space could be put to more practical use. We could literally not move from the spot, only being able to move our heads. The air in the carriage was soon used up, so that it was so stuffy we breathed quickly and spasmodically. Perspiration broke out on our foreheads, in spite of the temperature being bitterly cold outside and the car itself unheated.

While we were in Halle we still had some room in the carriage, but soon many more prisoners joined up, while in Merseburg, Leipzig, Weissenfels and Naumburg new batches were continually packed into our carriage.

When at last we were taken out of the train at Weimar, I felt as if I had suddenly come into the light from the deepest dungeon in the earth, from a close and stuffy cave into the clear air of freedom.

For one moment I completely forgot my lot; yet only for one moment, one precious moment, for soon I saw the tight cordon of police awaiting us.

We were directed to the steps of a subway, where we had to stop while a police officer, surrounded by many others, addressed us.

"Whoever attempts to escape, or even does anything which indicates an attempt to do so, will be shot at once," he said. "It is not our practice to waste time. You must promptly do everything that is demanded of you. Any disobedience will be severely punished. You will soon find out what that means! And don't complain about your lot, because it is your own fault.

"You will now be transported from here in batches. Only those men may move who have been told to do so by a police official. All others must remain where they are."

As my turn came a policeman snapped a chain round my wrist and led me to a police car, which looked like one used for the flying squad. Its rows of benches were covered with rough tarpaulin, screened off on the sides. Policemen stood in the first and last rows of benches, the side seats also being occupied by their companions.

Suddenly a command rang out from in front. "Attention! Look this way! You will look straight ahead! Whoever turns his head sideways, even for a moment, or otherwise moves, will be shot at once!"

The new journey began. It took us over smooth roads, bumpy cobble stones, round sharp bends, and sometimes through cuttings and hollows.

We sat like idols in a temple. Nobody moved. Each prisoner was conscious of the revolvers and automatics pointed at him, in readiness to fire.

The car stopped at last. We were ordered out and lined up in rows of three. We found ourselves in a somewhat sloping square, one end of which was flanked by some woods arced in a semi-circle. Before us was a great massive trellised gate from which a wide and long well-built road led in a straight line to symmetrical buildings which blocked the road and, from where we stood, gave the impression of a big wall.

This road was the "Karacho Way", the buildings which looked like a wall was the camp entrance, its prison house to the left, the administrative buildings to the right.

Although we were still surrounded by policemen, on the other side of the trellised gate S.S. men of the Totenkopf units were gathering, all of them armed with carbines or automatics, the so-called "fat squirters".

Strong buildings lined the left of the Karacho Way, garages, a large petrol station and other buildings. On the other side were wooden barracks which stretched out a long way. As we found later, these held accommodation for guard personnel, the political department, the photo department, the barber's shop, the canteen for S.S. "other ranks", and so on.

As the man in charge of our transport handed us over to an

S.S. Scharführer, we were surrounded by S.S. men. The police themselves climbed back into their cars and drove off, no doubt to collect a new load of prisoners from Weimar.

I stood in the centre of our column. A command came: "Right-turn!"

A moment later the man behind us suddenly hit me with full force in the back, so thrusting me forward and compelling me to push the man in front of me. I could now see that the S.S. men were beating us, without discrimination, with rifle butts and rubber truncheons.

Our column of men began to run as shots rang out and bullets whistled by our ears. Closely pressed together, falling over each other, we ran in panic along the Karacho Way. Whoever fell was trampled on by those who followed, for blows rained down upon us, and we ran for our lives, one single, confused, turbulent horde.

No one knew where to go—we merely kept up with those in front and at our side, each clinging to the other, trying desperately to gain the centre of the column. The mind ceased to think. We knew only that we wanted to escape those blows and thrusts, to run from the whistling bullets. The column at last wheeled to the right and came to a halt before a wooden barrack.

By now, we hardly knew if we were on our hands or our heels. Beating us with fists and rubber truncheons and thrusting at us with their rifle butts, the S.S. men restored order again in the horde which had become so hopelessly confused and bewildered.

Those who, in the preceding panic, had been tramped down, now came limping along to join us, panting and bleeding, their clothes dirty and torn. Anyone who was not quick enough to move into line, however weak he felt, was treated to more punches and thrusts with the rifle butts.

Gradually silence returned to the column, although many were bleeding, all were panting, and no one was without fear and terror. By now we all knew why a carved direction board mounted above the trellised gate had the words "Karacho Way"! . . . for what we had just experienced we generally described by the words "with Karacho".*

* Karacho: slang for full speed.

2. The Camp

IN sections of about twenty, we were now taken into the barracks before which we had been standing. This was the Political Department. Almost along the whole length of the barracks there ran a wide corridor, from which various doors led into separate offices.

Some time elapsed before an S.S. man emerged from behind one of these doors and planted himself lazily in front of us. From a piece of paper in his hand, he roughly delivered the following address:

"You are not in a sanatorium here. You will have noticed that already! Those who have not yet grasped that fact will be made to understand, you can rely on that!

"We will now record your exact personal data. Each man will make his statements loudly and distinctly, to the last detail and strictly according to the truth. That goes for all statements you have to make, whether verbally or in writing. Anybody who disobeys will be sorry, because I can tell you right now that we have a whole bag of the trickiest penalties in store for you.

"So! Each order is to be obeyed immediately and without demur. That applies to this interrogation as well as to any in the camp. In the camp itself there will be various documents to fill in, and whoever does this incorrectly or insufficiently— for example, forgets to state any previous conviction, however trivial—will be punished.

"However, whoever adapts himself to camp discipline, and carries out immediately and without question everything demanded of him, will be left alone.

"The date of your release depends to a large extent upon yourselves. Here, we will make useful people of you or you will die. And dying here is not quite so simple as it sounds! You will soon grasp that!

"You will receive a letter-form in which you can inform your relatives that you have now arrived. Information about the camp is forbidden, and so are political statements of any kind. You will also be very brief and confine yourselves to the

30

most personal matters on any other letter-forms you may receive, for we have no time and no inclination to censor your twaddle and gossip.

"All political talk in camp, and all congregating there, are strictly forbidden. Anyone who observes another committing offences against the camp discipline or our orders must report the matter immediately to the camp management, or he will be punished.

"Those of you who have money on you may keep ten Marks of it. Every penny beyond that amount must be handed to the cashier. Anyone found even with one penny more will be punished.

"Everyone is to show the utmost industry at work; whoever is lazy will be punished; whoever does not work to the limit of his capabilities will only prolong the length of time of his internment.

"You are not convicts here," he concluded; "you are only 'under detention', and what that means you will soon learn, if you have not done so already! You are dishonourable and defenceless! You are outlawed! Yours is a serf's lot! . . . That's all."

We were standing in pairs in the long corridor, guarded by S.S. men armed with carbines, who sneered at us but did not touch us. I heard one of them observe to his colleague: "Detainees! A nice word, isn't it? Oh well, the dirty dogs will feel it for themselves."

"And how!" the other replied. "Say, how many kicked the bucket today? Weren't there fifty-eight?"

"No," returned the first man; "that was yesterday. So far, there are only forty-one."

These figures created cold horror in some of us, but most of us considered these remarks as being meant to frighten us. We learnt later they were not exaggerated. Only the next day I found that this high death rate was at least somewhere near the truth—and this, in a camp in which nearly all detainees were between the ages of seventeen and fifty, an age which, by all the laws of nature, normally has the lowest figures of mortality!

I was now one of the four men to enter the first office, being the third for interrogation. I saw innumerable office- and writing-desks, large filing cabinets, steel safes along the walls, typewriters, a large picture of Hitler and one of Heinrich Himmler. Scharführer and S.S. men were busy at their clerical work.

A Scharführer walked over to the typist whose job it was to record our personal data. He took up a folder, scrutinised us, and then called out a name. The detainee in front of me responded with, "Here!"

The Scharführer gave him a piercing look, walked up to him, and then punched him unexpectedly and with full force in the face, forcing him to stagger sideways.

The first man in our file was so frightened by this show of force that he could only faintly answer the questions put to him by the typist. The latter sprang to his feet, picked up a cane on the table beside him, and brutally slashed the man's face right and left, shouting, "Don't you know that you have to give your answers loudly and distinctly here?"

The rest of the proceedings continued without further incident. When my turn came to be questioned I staked everything on one card and shouted my name out in a sharply accentuated voice. For a moment the typist looked startled, having actually taken fright, and I began to think I had acted wrongly. But then he said, with a sour look, "It need not be as loud as all that!" and refrained from molesting me.

As soon as the recording of our personal data was completed, we were lined up in the Karacho Way, guarded by fewer S.S. men than before, but with a great show of carbines and fat squirters. These were held ready to fire and were quite enough to frighten us.

"Do you see that door down there?" one of the S.S. men demanded, and indicated the camp entrance we had already noticed from the trellised gate. This was a building two storeys high, with a watch-tower, above which flew a swastika flag. The wide entrance in the centre of the building was locked by a strong iron gate, in which a small door was now being opened, giving a view on to a wide square. The S.S. man continued: "Do you see that? Now with Karacho through there! Understand? Right turn! At the double!"

We tore along like madmen, each one wilder than the other. We were already so well "trained" that we did not notice that we were not being beaten and pushed this time; indeed, the S.S. men were standing quietly, having no need to drive us along like stubborn cattle.

There was a confused pushing and shoving as we came to the narrow camp entrance. We acted as if the devil were behind us. The tragic farce was that none of us wanted to go to the concentration camp, yet each of us now endeavoured to be the first to enter it!

Completely breathless, we came on to the square, to be received there by two detainees who were waiting for us.

These two men instructed us to stand in line. They wore old but clean army tunics of blue cloth, grey-green striped trousers and caps without peaks of the same colour, striped like the trousers. Both on the left chest of their tunics and on the seam of their right trouser legs at knee height a red triangle of cloth was sewn on, the longer point downwards; above this were narrow white strips of linen with a black number.

The men looked fresh and healthy, their bearing erect. Although not exactly good from a nutritional point of view, their general condition did not appear to be too bad.

One of them, turning to us, observed, "You were lucky today to get through the door so quietly."

Before us was a large square which sloped towards the back and was covered with yellowish-white and grey gravel. Along the left side ran a barbed wire fence about nine feet high, and behind this, but some distance away, stood several primitive wooden barracks, the first of which was marked IA in large letters. These were, in fact, the barracks 1A to VA in which over 12,000 Jews were still accommodated as a result of the last wave of pogroms. This we discovered later.

The lower end of the huge square, now completely empty, was bordered by a line of barracks, their flat roofs looking curiously squat. Smoke belched from the chimneys and indicated that they were inhabited. Beyond these flat roofs were tree tops, just visible in the dusk of the early winter evening. They seemed blue-grey in colour, but withered and extremely drab.

The right-hand side of the square had not yet been levelled, for tree stumps, rubble and heaps of sand indicated that a clump of woods had been cleared in order to extend the square.

Beyond this a high electrified wire fence seemed to enclose the whole camp, with concrete pillars standing in a straight line at regular intervals. In the background, in clearings cut into the woods, we could see high observation towers, in appearance like the old square mediaeval defence towers, the importance of which we were soon to learn.

We were now led across the square, down to the barracks, where, for the first time, we met quite another type of prisoner, not as clean and as properly dressed as the first two prisoners we had seen. These were dirty and wore ragged clothes covered with layer upon layer of crusted mud. The men were sluggish and stupid-looking, quite emaciated and of a greyish-yellow complexion, their clumsy and often defective boots covered with thick mud, their clothes hanging loosely around their bodies. Some of them had slung bread bags over their shoulders, and from these dented dixies hung. They all looked astonishingly and inexplicably alike as they swarmed and crawled in the spaces between the barracks.

By far the greater number of these creatures ignored us. How different it had been in the prison where I had previously been and where each new arrival had been critically examined. Even at the time when I had been in the camps on the moors the arrival of each new transport had created a sensation!

But now, hardly anybody appeared to notice us. Only occasionally did a prisoner pause as he quickly, almost shyly, studied our faces with a peculiarly reserved interest. If someone seemed to be too interested in us, or even blocked our way, one of our own leaders shouted, "Away, there!" and he immediately jumped aside, to disappear into the swarm of prisoners everywhere gathered together.

There did not appear to be any doubt that two types of prisoners existed in Buchenwald, the one forming something like an elite, the other the great mass. It was only peculiar to us that the great mass of prisoners complied so promptly with the orders given by the others.

A moment's thought showed me that this inert compliance was not peculiar. We newcomers were already acting in the same way. We had ourselves automatically complied with the orders of two fellow-prisoners. So far perhaps we did not act with the subservient and unconditional manner of the "seasoned" men, but who knew how we would degenerate in time?

After a few days, in fact, we learnt that there were more than two types of prisoners; indeed, there were a great variety of grades in the camp and, regardless of which type of prisoner gave the orders, we were prepared to obey them speedily and unconditionally. There may have been a difference between the order of a Scharführer and that of such an elite prisoner, but the difference was only one of degree. Indeed, I learnt this lesson myself within a few minutes of following our two leaders.

We came to the prisoners' clothing room. There, uniforms, underwear, boots, etc., were stacked on the shelves in large quantities. Those prisoners who worked in this room were comparatively well and clean, and almost all of them wore the red triangle.

We were now classified, the politicals being handed the red triangle, the work-dodgers and anti-socials the black triangle, the Jehovah's Witnesses the violet, the criminals the green, the homosexuals the pink. In addition to their ordinary triangle, the Jews received a yellow one, to be crossed with the other colour and thus form the Star of David.

Nearly every prisoner behind the issuing table asked me what colour I had. Beside me stood a Black, who was given worse clothing than I had. When the boots were issued, I was about to be given a down-at-heels pair, when I was asked if I was a political; upon my replying that I was, a better pair of boots was substituted. Only we politicals, too, were asked if we had brought pullovers or woollen jackets with us, and those who had not were given these garments. All other categories of prisoners went without them.

It seemed obvious to me that some organisation existed in the camp, and for a moment I was naive enough to assume that the camp management had themselves made all the arrangements involved. But then I thought the idea so absurd, so completely contrary to my experience so far, that I was ashamed of it.

I had more reason to assume that there was more likely some political organisation in the camp, and this was logically based on a thousand good reasons and experiences. This conclusion I found to be correct, and long before I was myself accepted into that confidential circle where I could not only personally contribute my share of organisation in the concentration camp at Buchenwald but could also fulfil my duty in organised co-operation with people like myself.

I did, for the present, wonder why the politicals received preferential treatment at all. Were these Violets, Blacks, Greens not also human beings, the same poor wretches we Reds were? I thought this favouritism to be contradictory to all our principles, for my own experiences had shown that every true political person considers his neighbour first and himself afterwards. Who, then, gave whom the right here to organise this special favouritism to politicals?—what moral law supported such a discrimination between people?

It was clear to me that none of the prisoners handing out clothes knew me and my political opinions. Indeed, the comrade whom I had got to know in transit to this place was also placed in the "politicals" group and treated with exactly the same favouritism as I was, although he had himself told me that he had been a member of the N.S.D.A.P. (Nazi Party) and had embezzled party money.

With the garments we had been issued with under our arms, we moved on to another rather large barracks, where we were ordered to change our clothes, after first being examined for lice by another prisoner. We had to hand over all our personal effects, keeping back up to ten Marks in money, a pocket knife, a belt, soap, food, cigarettes and tobacco, and a pullover.

The politicals were separated from the others, and were asked about their political past, where they had lived, in which institution they had spent their previous imprisonment, and so on.

I met two acquaintances whom I had known in a previous prison. In spite of the fact that we did not really know each other well, our greetings were warm. One of them immediately interested himself on my behalf and took me down into the cellar of the barracks, where he asked one of the prisoners working there, "Where are the sacks for the politicals?"

The clothing sacks in which we had to cram our personal effects were spread out on long tables. The sacks for the politicals were a little apart from the others, and although they all looked alike, there must have been some difference between them, because my acquaintance himself picked one out and said, "Here, take this one."

"Why that particular one?" I asked.

"That is a low number, and Block 36," he answered.

"And what does that mean?"

"You will find out."

In this manner I became Prisoner No. 996 of Block 36!

I received an old blue uniform jacket, somewhat patched but clean and warm. My striped cotton coat was brand new, and my boots fitted well and were newly soled. My cap was without a peak and was striped like the coat, somewhat dirty but washable. The socks were well darned but a little uncomfortable to wear. The bread sack had been used but was clean.

Now we returned to the parade square, this time to assemble at the far end, near the barracks.

The early winter evening began to fall. It was cold and I was slightly shivering. There was a lively coming and going on the paths between the barracks; but in the dusk the faces of the prisoners were not easily visible.

The light from the windows of the barracks fell upon the paths, but a haze seemed to spread over everything. From one building came a song, from another the music of a concertina and from a third the sounds of quarrelling.

After standing on the parade square for some time, we were ordered to stand to attention on the command of a prisoner, and then another, stocky in appearance, came towards us in the dusk and stood us at ease. He wore a soldier's thick dark overcoat, around his sleeve being an armlet with some writing, although I could not read the inscription, owing to the fading light.

He delivered a somewhat pompous speech to us, and spoke of our behaviour. In the camp we would be pretty well left alone, but entry into strange barracks was forbidden. We were to work industriously until we collapsed from exhaustion. Everything ordered by the overseers—the man in charge of our room, the senior of our block, the Kapos, the Camp Supervisor and the Camp Senior—should be carried out at once and without argument.

No attempt to escape was to be made, he went on, such

an attempt being stupid in any case, as we would be fired at immediately, while the whole camp would have to suffer for our misdeeds.

Whoever had anything on his mind, he assured us, could come to him and, where he could help, he would do so. However, anybody who did not obey what he was told to do would receive his share of punishment. As to this, he could not enumerate the full range of punishments which were a daily occurrence in the camp. But he did want to tell us one thing: in this place nothing was not possible in the way of punishment, up to and including hanging, and the latter he would even carry out himself!

We should know right from the beginning, he told us, that he was one of the important people in the camp. Politics, he said, were forbidden, and that particularly concerned the politicals among us.

Within the camp, he continued, we would be almost without S.S. supervision, but then there were correspondingly more "informers" to make up for that fact. It would be best, therefore, if each man relied upon himself. Yes, we would soon find out whom we could trust and whom we could not.

Outside, he said, at work we would be guarded by S.S. men, whom no one could approach at nearer than five paces. Whoever passed a chain of guards, even through carelessness, would be shot at once, so he advised us not to approach them nearer than ten paces, even if we were ordered to do so.

Above all, he concluded, he advised us to carry out every order immediately and to keep strictly to the camp rules; otherwise one would very quickly become a mangled corpse . . . that meant, he explained, one's passage to the other world would not be a process from one day to the next but a slower one and all the more certain.

A second prisoner, wearing an armlet, came towards the speaker to stand beside him, and the first man became perceptibly less sure of himself. The words did not flow from his mouth as fluently as before, and after a few stuttered sentences he asked the new arrival if he wanted to add a few words. The newcomer shook his head. Whereupon we were told that we would be taken to our Blocks, where the man in charge of our room would tell us everything else we needed to know.

On our way back to the rows of barracks, I could not help wondering why the first prisoner had grown so uncertain of himself upon being joined by the second man, and could only assume that the latter had been his superior in some way.

The prisoners were allocated to their separate barracks, and the first one consisted of wooden shacks, one storey high and about thirty metres long. The entrance was in the centre of the building, from which three doors led off, the middle one leading into a very primitive washing-room with chipped enamel basins, dented cans and buckets, while the others led into the day-rooms, which were terribly confined and in which the prisoners seemed literally to sit on top of one another.

On our way further down the camp we passed a latrine set up between the barracks. It consisted of a deep open pit over which a primitive construction of tree trunks had been erected, and was not enclosed by any protective wall or anything of that kind. Numerous prisoners were waiting for a vacancy in the long queue, and it was obvious that all feeling of shame had long ago disappeared.

The way led further down into the camp. The paths between the barracks became increasingly worse, until they resembled a building site with ditches and holes, heaps of sand, rubble and stones lying about everywhere.

Only a few weeks later, when the thaw had set in, we were to wade stoically and indifferently along these roads through ankle-deep and gluey mud, and by then would no longer notice the water penetrating through our shoes. We would not even laugh when a prisoner got so stuck in the deep mud that we had to help him out. For in the interval between the present and the future we would have learned to throw ourselves bodily into the mire on the orders of a moody Scharführer. By then, such small "incidents" would be only part of the ordinary happenings of the day, and hardly worth noting.

At last we reached the stone barracks, which were two storeys high, not ugly in architecture, and apparently stoutly built. It was already too dark to notice details, but the light which came from the opposite barracks did serve to give an over-all impression which contrasted favourably with the wooden ones.

Block No. 36—that is, the stone barracks to which I had

been allocated—seemed to have only recently been completed, because building implements and material of all kinds still lay about. Then I noted that work was yet to be done on one or two parts of the barracks before it was completely finished.

3. Block 36

WE were received by the Senior of the Block, who distributed us to the individual rooms, of which there were four in the Block. I was sent to Room C, on the top floor.

In principle, the Block was arranged like that of the wooden barracks, with an entrance in the centre, and below, rooms A and B. A concrete double staircase led to the top floor and to rooms C and D.

Three doors led from the narrow passage into the wash-room and two rooms to the right and left. The washroom was modern and sensibly equipped, with a large round basin, at which about twenty men could wash at the same time, lava-tories and built-in footbaths, tiled floors and walls.

The day-rooms were equipped with new furniture, forms, stools and a loudspeaker connected to a microphone in the guardroom at the camp gate. The lighting was shrouded in suitable, not unpleasing big globes of milk glass.

I naturally saw hardly any of these things on the evening of my arrival, because the day-room was so overcrowded with men that only little of the equipment was visible. Later, how-ever, I had plenty of opportunity to see the day-room without prisoners in it, and I always had the impression that everything in it was practicable and hygienic, actually ideal, considering it was intended to be a dwelling for men who were not con-sidered to be human beings at all.

The dormitory, accessible through the living quarters by a door opposite the entrance, revealed the same practicability and cleanliness. Here, however, it was apparent that concentra-tion camp was an institution of a particular type; for the passages between the rows of beds were just narrow enough to squeeze through, but no more. The iron bedsteads were in four, sometimes five tiers, one above the other.

The impression of overcrowding was an immediate one. The prisoners in the top beds had to exercise some truly acrobatic contortions if they were to reach the "trap", and it was not easy to see how they made up their beds. Yet, if in the opinion of a Scharführer, a bed were badly made, this was reason enough to give a man camp punishment.

The "Olympic" man was at an advantage in this case, for his bed almost touched the ceiling. He could only get into it sideways and could not turn over in his sleep. Still, nobody bothered to examine his bed-making, which was sufficient compensation for him, considering how severe were the customary camp punishments.

The senior of the Block instructed one of the prisoners to take me along to the senior of Room C. I walked up the stone stairs, through the passage, past many prisoners, who hardly noticed me, and entered the room.

It was overflowing with prisoners wearing the red triangle, for Block 36 was a political one. The tables were all occupied, the prisoners who had found no chairs standing and walking about between them and in the passages.

Apparently the food had just been distributed, for most of the men were eating from their tin bowls. Many stood while they ate, while some had their full bowls on the table, ready to take a place at it as soon as someone else had finished his meal.

All were clean-shaven over their chins and heads. It is true that I could not see a single prisoner who looked really well fed, but nobody appeared to be starving. Most of the men had a healthy colour, and on the average their facial expressions were not so uniformly stupid as had been those of the men whom I had met at the first row of barracks. I had the impression that the politics were far more self-reliant and obviously resisting the fate which had overcome them. They had not yet lost faith in themselves.

But I felt it peculiar that here also nobody took any notice of me, everyone being self-absorbed or engaged with a companion.

The senior of the room was called Franz. Later on, I got to know him well. He was a young man who was always helpful,

41

extremely good-natured, and with a sure, quiet, energetic way of accomplishing unobtrusively what he considered to be in the best interests of his men.

He received me in a friendly manner and, without waiting for my questions, gave me the sort of information I wanted.

He handed me a tin bowl, a spoon and a mug. Any other crockery I needed, he told me, I would have to borrow from others. He showed me to a bed in the dormitory and told me how it had to be made and showed me exactly how the clothes had to be arranged on a stool overnight.

Then he referred me to the senior of a table, from whom I would receive my portions of food. At the moment, however, there was no vacancy at the table and no prospect of one, because places were allocated in order of arrival, and the room was already filled to six times its capacity. Still, now and again there was an odd seat vacant and I could make use of that, but of course I would have to give it up if its rightful occupier claimed it.

The senior told me he would, if necessary, willingly assist me in composing the letter which concerned my arrival, as well as the political questionnaire I had to answer.

This evening there was still the daily bread ration to come, besides the food portions, but tomorrow morning, after waking, there would be coffee. After that, the Block would form up and proceed to the square for roll-call. When the loudspeaker announced, "Newcomers to the gate", I would have to hurry there at the double and report to the labour supervisor, who would then detail me to a labour detachment. The Kapo would give me further instructions.

I was given a portion of bread and a small piece of rubber-like sausage by the senior of the table to which I had been allotted. He told me he would allot a locker for me later on, for at present the lockers were all full and so he would have to see where a corner could be cleared for me.

So I stood there, in one hand a dry chunk of bread, in the other a small piece of so-called liver sausage, with nobody troubling themselves about me any further. Being very hungry, I was not particularly aware of my loneliness. What was left of my bread I packed into my bread bag, not knowing where else to put it.

I was about to pack this away when Franz came up to me and said, "You must now sew on your triangles and numbers."

For this purpose, he took me to his table and gave me needle and cotton, but when he saw how clumsy I was, he took my jacket and himself sewed on the badges.

While doing this, he told me in a friendly consoling manner that he had to sew on the triangles for many newcomers, as none of them came into the camp without trembling or being excited in some way. I could repay him for his assistance, he added, by carrying out this little service for other newcomers.

When I was dressed in accordance with camp regulations, another man took charge of me, his job being haircutting and shaving. He had himself made a barber's chair, in a primitive but clever way, and even had an electric hair-cutting machine at his disposal. After my head had been shaven, making me fit for the camp, he said, "Have another look at your hair; you will never see it again," and then stuffed it into a sack.

This barber was Eduard Raderick, from Cranz on the Elbe, with whom I later became friends. He had been imprisoned since 1933 and now hoped to be discharged soon, especially as he was only an ordinary member of the K.P.D. (Communist Party), with little reason for keeping him in the camp for so long a time. I learnt later that he met his fate in 1944. He was not discharged from the camp, despite all efforts by his relatives, but was put on clearance work in bombed Duisberg, where he was afterwards shot by S.S. men.

I soon got into conversation with several prisoners, who thoroughly questioned me, although my own questions concerning conditions in the camp received evasive answers.

This surprised me. In the other prisons where I had been it had been customary for every new arrival to be minutely informed of what went on, without his having to ask questions. It did not, however, take me long to understand the reasons for caution in Buchenwald. One had only to pass on information to the wrong person, that is, an informer or traitor who thought he could ingratiate himself with the camp management, and one would pay for the error in cruel punishments, which frequently ended in death.

While we were in the course of lively conversation, someone gripped my shoulder and turned me round to face him. I saw a smiling face which I somehow seemed to recognise; yet I could not remember where I had seen it before.

He realised this fact, and said:

"Don't you know me?"

"No; not with the best of wills."

"Are you not Walter?"

"Yes."

"Are you not from Hamm?"

"That's right."

"And you don't know me?"

"Not that I can remember. Are you also from Hamm?"

"Yes; Widumstrasse."

"Widumstrasse?"

"Yes. Well? You still don't remember me?"

"No; I really don't."

"Schulenburg!" he exclaimed.

I recalled him instantly.

"Good gracious, Hännes, old boy! Yes, now I recognise you! Yes, that's you! Hännes Schulenburg! . . . How are things? Where do you come from? How long have you been here? Have you any other acquaintances here? What is it like in the camp?"

So thin that it was no wonder I had not recognised him in spite of having known him so well, Hans Schulenberg only smiled, without replying to my hurried questions. Instead, he said quietly and to the point:

"Have you a locker?"

When I gave him a negative answer, he cleared a small corner in his own locker where I could put my tin bowl, although four other men already shared it with him.

He spoke to the senior of his table, who finally agreed to my being accepted there, after a first reluctance. Then Hans said, "Come along; let us smoke a cigarette."

He took me into the washroom, smoking being forbidden in the day-room. Although it was not allowed even here, there was an implied agreement among the prisoners to permit this, yet everyone smoked at his own risk.

In a casual, companionable fashion, Schulenburg allowed me to smoke as much of his tobacco as I liked. He asked me whether I had any money of my own or would like some of his, and instructed me briefly in everything I had to do in order to get along in the camp in some comfortable measure. For instance, I would have to give any money I had above ten Marks to another prisoner for safe-keeping.

He proved to be a good comrade in every way, and remained so until the last hour. What he did for me was done in such a matter-of-fact way, with such utter unselfishness, that it seemed almost incredible to me that we had actually been political opponents.

And yet . . . were not those political ideals which had kept us in opposite camps basically of equal importance to humanity in trying to overcome conditions that were far worse? Did we have to go through the hell of Buchenwald before we could be united in an unconditional comradeship?

He had been schooled by the hardships of the concentration camp and so knew exactly what was in my mind, and what things were most important for me to know during this short hour of our first meeting.

"Go to sleep," he said, soon. "You will have a hard day tomorrow, and it is better if you rest yourself. You will still have plenty of time to talk about what we have at heart."

After I had crawled under my two thin blankets, I thought over the events of the day, as I had done every night for many years. Shortly, I began to realise that though Hans Schulenburg had given me many important hints, he had been extremely careful with his statements about the camp and had not answered many of my questions.

It was only later that I fully understood his reasons, after I myself had learnt to understand that the atmosphere of the camp was due to the force and cruelty which existed in it.

4. Morning Roll-call

IN winter, the night ended for us prisoners at five o'clock; in summer, the day started at four. We were assembled on the square for roll-call one hour after awakening. In winter, work went on until four or five p.m.; in summer, until six p.m.

Scale approx. 1:4000

(Drawn by Hans Geiser from a sketch by the author)

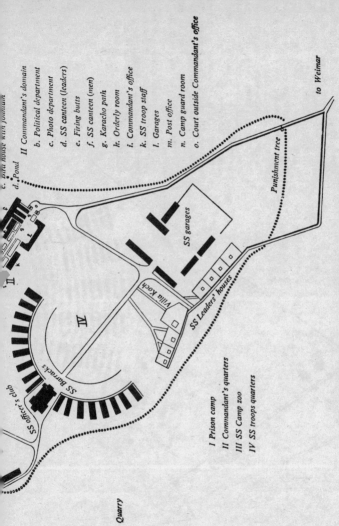

a. Bird house with fountain
b. Pond

II Commandant's domain
 b. Political department
 c. Photo department
 d. SS canteen (leaders)
 e. Firing butts
 f. SS canteen (men)
 g. Karacho path
 h. Orderly room
 i. Commandant's office
 k. SS troop staff
 l. Garages
 m. Post office
 n. Camp guard room
 o. Court outside Commandant's office

I Prison camp
II Commandant's quarters
III SS Camp zoo
IV SS troops quarters

SS officer's club

SS Barracks

Villa Koch

SS garages

SS Leaders' houses

Punishment tree

Quarry

to Weimar

BUCHENWALD CONCENTRATION CAMP

The plan on pages 48/49 was drawn by the author from memory. It corresponds in all its details with the original plan (copied here) which was discovered later in the Bavarian State Archives and is dated April 29th, 1938.

After a study of this original plan the author was able to establish the shattering yet irrefutable proof—long a matter of controversy—that the National Socialists had from the very start planned the concentration camp as a death camp. From the original plan it is evident that the building of a crematorium (see left) directly adjacent to the mortuary was intended. This despite the fact that within a few miles from Buchenwald—at Weimar, Eisenach and Gotha—three crematoria already existed, at which only a few corpses were burned once or twice a week.

The crematorium drawn in the S.S. plan here—in common with several other buildings—was never actually built. Later, in its place near the mortuary hut, a very primitive incinerator was installed.

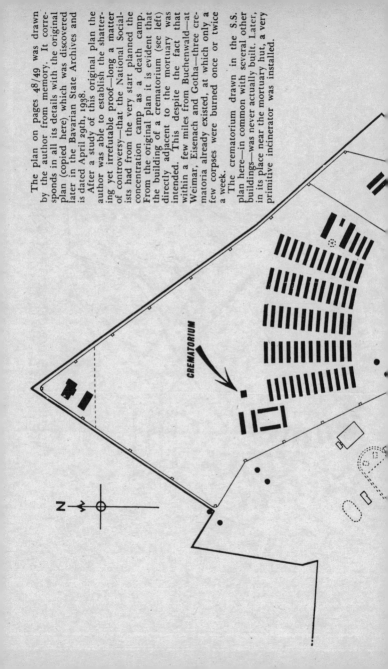

CREMATORIUM

N

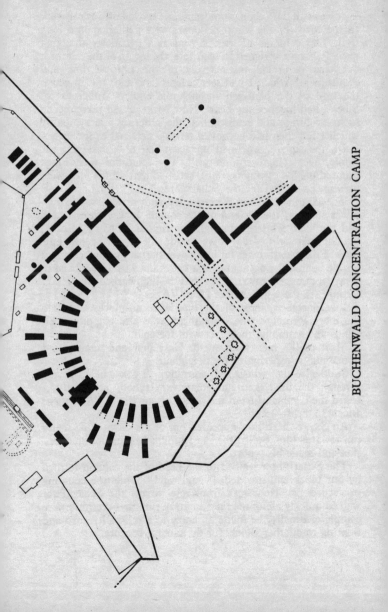

BUCHENWALD CONCENTRATION CAMP

It was still dark as, next morning, we moved off for roll-call. In the roads of the camp prisoners were gathering in a long trail. The columns of men moved at a peculiarly dragging pace, lethargic, resigned to their fate, the legion of the damned.

I was reminded instinctively of the film "Crime and Punishment" which I had seen a long time ago, and in which the trail of the banished through the endless wilderness of Siberia had touched my heart. Now I was myself marching in such a column, and realised that the suffering and sympathy which I felt then had become a terrible personal experience.

On the square, we lined up according to Blocks. On the whole, everything went off well. The senior of each Block counted off his members, until, satisfied that all his men were present, he waited for the Scharführer.

The large square was overcrowded with prisoners. We ourselves stood at the far end of the square. It was bitterly cold and the wind whistled through our clothes. It was still dark, but the first light of dawn was gradually appearing, the outlines of the watch-tower far away over the camp gate becoming visible behind the occupants of a Block lined up some distance away from us. On my right, behind the high barbed wire fence, I could see the big Barracks IA to VA.

Like ourselves, most of the men wore no gloves, although the more fortunate who wore them were also clapping their hands and stamping their feet with the cold.

Most of the men were silent. Only now and again did I notice one whispering to his neighbour.

Suddenly the whispered warning, "Look out!" passed through the lines, and immediately everybody stood still. I heard the command from the senior of our Block, "Attention! Block 36, eyes—left!"

An S.S. Scharführer appeared out of the dawn. Our senior ran towards him, pulled the cap from his head, stood to attention and made his report.

The Scharführer walked to the head of the column formed by our block and growled, "Count off!" While the counting proceeded like clockwork from row to row the Scharführer walked quickly along the lines to make sure that the rows were complete. Finally, he made an entry in a roll-call record and went on to another Block, for the same procedure.

50

The senior called "At ease!" whereupon movement returned immediately to the Block which until a moment ago had been as rigid as a rock. Feet were stamped, hands rubbed, arms swung, all movements strangely restrained, as if carried out contrary to strict orders.

For nearly an hour we stood on the square, the light constantly increasing, our limbs becoming increasingly stiffer. We breathed on our hands and rubbed our noses and ears to warm them.

Now I could see the Blocks in front of us more distinctly, and noticed that they too went through the same restrained movements, with stamping and rubbing of hands and swinging of arms. As far as my eyes could see there were only prisoners in striped clothing or old military overcoats—many hundreds, thousands, tens of thousands . . .

The huge loudspeakers distributed over the square crackled into wakefulness. Instantly everything grew still again, as if some gigantic manipulator of a puppet show had suddenly put down the strings of his dolls. I heard a tapping in the loudspeakers as the set was apparently tested.

Then came a command, hollow, resounding and excessively loud: "Camp—attention! Eyes—right!"

I could see nothing of the things happening up there at the gate, but I stood as rigid and as immovable as the rest. Had I been made to do so, I dare say I would have held my breath.

The loudspeakers crackled again; and then: "Eyes—front! Stand at ease!"

Immediately the restrained movement began again through the ranks of the Blocks. I heard somebody in front of me say, "Well, that worked out right again today. Damned cold. To the devil with the whole works!"

Again the loudspeakers crackled, "Newcomers, to the gate! Labour detachments, fall in!"

At once a lively movement seized the masses, and men ran about in seeming confusion, like a suddenly disturbed swarm of bees. Yet there was no real confusion, for within a few days I would soon observe how speedily and surely the tens of thousands re-grouped themselves.

I was told to hurry to the gate, for the commander of the

51

labour detachments, S.S. Hauptscharführer Bräuning, loved to attach newcomers who did not appear promptly at the gate to particularly heavy labour detachments, being dreaded by everyone because of his brutal blows and kicks.

I hurried across the square, only to find several newcomers already lined up near the microphone. I took my place in the second row on the advice of a fellow-prisoner, who told me that there I would not be in reach of the S.S. man's blows, though near enough to the front to push my way perhaps into a less dreaded labour detachment if I had to.

I need not have been so cautious, for Bräuning himself was on Christmas leave. His deputy told us to report at the gate again, with other newcomers, on the day after Bräuning's leave ended, before assigning us en bloc to the labour detachment "Garage Building".

We were taken in charge by a prisoner wearing an armlet with the word "Kapo" on it. He led us back to the square, and then to the place where his labour detachment had already fallen into line. This consisted of about a thousand prisoners.

While placing us in line, he warned us that when marching through the gate we should have to pay attention to our step and keep together. Anyone who did not do so could expect the worst and consider himself lucky to get away with a few thrusts with a rifle butt or some blows across the head, instead of a punishment of twenty-five strokes or gate-standing or a fresh-air party on a tree.

Some terribly emaciated men stood at the head of the column, dull, resigned, with hunched-up shoulders, shivering with cold and apparently so weak that they could only keep on their feet with the greatest effort.

One of them had certainly not washed himself for weeks. Slime ran from his nose and mouth, the latter constantly moving like that of a ruminant, saliva running down the deep wrinkles extending from the corners of his mouth to his pointed chin. What an "image of God"! I thought in disgust.

Later, when I became more familiar with the state of things in the camp, I found that this condition was a preliminary to the unavoidable last days of life; but now I was not in the know; at present, I knew nothing of the mass dying which

52

haunted the camp, the result of a cruel and deliberate policy of starvation.

The camp's band had lined up at the gate beside the microphone and its music now started up, loud, blaring, shrill and thundering like guns. Some sort of march was played, yet it was no march, no music at all—merely a great cacophony of noise meant to keep a horde of savages in step by an ecstatic delirium, with a hypnotic rhythm.

Our Kapo shouted the order, "Mark time—by the left— march!" and the column began to move. Assistant Kapos walked at our side, dealing out more or less severe kicks and blows to keep us in line. We marched in the direction of the gate and grouped ourselves into the long, seemingly endless trail of the great and small columns of men marching with us.

Through the din of the band we suddenly heard terrible and excruciating cries of pain, which came from a prisoner being thrashed on the bar-post at the gate.

We marched past the stock and, shortly before reaching the gate, the command came to pull off our caps from our heads. I have never been quite clear in my mind whether by so doing we were supposed to salute the swastika flag flying on top of the watch-tower or the S.S. men at the gate.

We marched through the gate, along the Karacho Way, and out through the second gate, our Kapo meanwhile several times ordering, "Caps off!" and then "Caps on!" as each S.S. officer had to be saluted in turn.

5. First Day's Labour

WE turned right, into the well-built road which ran through the wood. We could hear for a long time the noise of the camp's band behind us.

On the left of us were the new garage buildings to which we newcomers had been detailed for today. The brick-laying work had stopped, owing to the severe cold, but digging continued.

The column divided into smaller groups. I saw no guards or Scharführer anywhere. A few S.S. men were taking lorries and motor-cycles out of large, apparently newly completed garages, but they did not trouble us.

I was allocated to a column ordered to clear away a large pile of rubble. The prisoner who assigned the work to us, a kind of under-Kapo, walked away and left us to it.

The seasoned prisoners, already acquainted with the working conditions, started work immediately, hacking industriously with picks and shovels, without looking up or around.

To us newcomers, this prompt action was fascinating. We could not understand such zeal, for all supervision appeared to be missing. Yet the seasoned prisoners not only worked, but slogged and burrowed away to such an extent that we soon thought it best to follow their example; for, although we failed to understand why they worked so hard, we felt it must be in our own interest to show the same ardour they did.

Despite the Arctic cold and icy wind, we soon grew warm. We stared at the seasoned ones ceaselessly burrowing away, and we did the same. A newcomer said to an old prisoner, "I say, take it easy! Don't overdo it!" The other did not interrupt his work even for a second, merely retorting "Are you mad?"

We shovelled the rubble into small hods and took it to tip-up waggons standing on rails some fifty yards away, and there other men were as busy as bees removing a great mass of soil.

The work was heavy, but I felt equal to it. I was still reasonably well fed, my body hardened by my work in the last two and a half years on the moors of the Lüneburg Heath. I had also learned to work under supervision, so that I could preserve my strength and work continuously for hours without completely exhausting myself, despite the immediate threat of severe punishment if I were found not doing all I could.

Yet the speed of the work done here was much greater than in previous places, and I began to suspect the principal and important difference that existed between work in prisons and that in concentration camps.

In both cases the highest possible performance of work was the aim, in both labour being exploited to the utmost. But in the National Socialist prisons, labour was not unlimited, so that prisoners had to be kept in a condition making them capable of work; after finishing their term of imprisonment, most of the men had to be returned to the community, where they had still to be able to work.

In the concentration camp such limits no longer applied. Enough labour was available, and more than enough, streaming into the place in constantly increasing volume from an apparently inexhaustible reservoir.

And what kind of people were they who were available for labour in the concentration camp? The ruthless elimination of all people who opposed National Socialism or were otherwise in its way was an openly admitted principle, so that a human life meant nothing to the Nazis. With a frivolity incomprehensible to a normal human brain, they were prepared in principle to destroy human life—and not only prepared, but did it!

The labour performed by prisoners in concentration camps was to them, therefore, only a means with two objects in view —extermination of an opponent and at the same time a comfortable way of creating in their opinion an enjoyable existence for themselves, forcing the people placed at their mercy to die while working for them.

What did the death of an opponent matter to such people, prepared even to exterminate millions of people to force their own ends. They were so unimaginably vile, so incomprehensibly demoralised, so void of any human feelings, that they did not shrink from the most bestial cruelties, if to perpetrate them meant a special advantage or enjoyment.

The animal which is driven to the slaughter-house is rendered unconscious and then speedily killed. The human being, however, can still give good value before he dies. Should he die because of the terrible enforced labour, what does it matter!

In the case of Nazi Germany, there were enough, and more than enough, of such human beings available. The only question was how to squeeze everything, really everything, out of each prisoner, and then, in accordance with National Socialist conviction, torture, torment and harass him. According to National Socialist opinion, such people had deserved no better and were now only receiving their just deserts.

We dug, shovelled and carried hods unceasingly. Now and again the Kapo came along to inspect our work. His approach alone was sufficient to spur the seasoned prisoners to such efforts that they perspired despite the severe cold.

One of them, a Black, approached the Kapo in a shameless cringing way, to tell him that we newcomers were not doing our work properly. It was obvious that he was endeavouring to curry favour. Though the Kapo did not interfere with us, he did not reject the slimy customer, but confined himself to instructing us how we should perform our work. My fingers and hands began to ache in time, and I felt I was slackening.

There was a Kapo who was about twenty-five years old and wore the red triangle. He was the son of a building contractor, but completely uncommunicative as to the reason for his being at Buchenwald. I saw him suddenly rush at the double across to some S.S. men who beckoned him from a garage door. Cap in hand, he stood to attention, before disappearing into the garage with them. After an interval, he emerged, walked up to our column, and sharply and domineeringly ordered, "Come along!" He repeated the order to a second group of men working close by.

We followed him into the garage, which revealed itself as a spacious hall in which numerous lorries were sheltered, alongside motor-cycles and building material of all kinds.

We were confronted with a steam boiler, fifteen to twenty feet long and about three feet six inches high, which we were ordered to lift on to a lorry.

First, we pushed thick wooden levers under the boiler. Then, while some of us gripped the levers, others held the hooks and protrusions. With the utmost exertion, we succeeded in lifting the giant structure at one end, but still could not move it from the spot.

On instructions from the Kapo, we placed wooden rollers under the boiler, and found it possible to move it to the lorry. After several attempts, and with the greatest of effort, we finally succeeded in lifting one end on to the lorry.

We could lift the other end twelve, eighteen, perhaps

twenty-four inches, but our knees kept giving way as we panted and sweated, and further efforts were useless.

We began again for the fourth time, but, in spite of the Kapo's ravings, the task was still useless—we could not get the boiler above the dead point between lift and push.

"Don't drop it!" the Kapo shouted, as we tried once more and got the boiler to the dead point. He was in an ecstasy of fury, rather like an animal trainer of ungovernable temper who endeavours to force a stubborn animal into submission by using extreme brutality.

"I'll kill you if you drop that boiler!" he continued to roar. Then, beside himself with rage and bellowing like a mad bull, he kicked us with frenzy, dealing out blow after blow upon our bodies.

Yet, as the boiler grew constantly heavier, we had finally to gradually slide the uplifted end down to the ground again.

The Kapo tore round the boiler. "I'll get you, you lazy gang!" he shouted. "I'll teach you! You swine, you dogs, you filthy rogues, you!"

He gave the command to start again, but now an S.S. man intervened. "Fetch a few more of the rotters," he told the Kapo.

"That would be a fine thing!" retorted the Kapo; but as the S.S. man insisted, he went off to obey.

We rested a moment. We were stooped in body and scared in mind, and as we panted, we tried to gather together our exhausted energies.

The Kapo returned with six more prisoners. Longer levers were now pushed under the boiler in order to allow all the men to handle it. With extra help, we were now able to lift the giant, only to find some obstacle as we pushed it on the lorry.

Again the Kapo roared like a madman, again he lashed out at us, beating and kicking indiscriminately.

With the last strength of despair, we pressed and pushed and heaved, until slowly, slowly, the boiler glided on to the lorry.

No sooner was it in position than the Kapo roared, "Get back to your work, you howling apes!" We ran from the garage as fast as we could, eager to return to our previous work, hard as it was, for there at least we were not also maltreated.

I could not help noticing that the seasoned prisoners set about their work with greater vigour than before, troubled about nothing else. Charity began at home, and nobody said a word, all digging and shovelling and carting away as if the devil were behind them.

A Kapo came towards us as I was about to loosen with my pickaxe another lump of rubble from the frozen mass of rubbish, while the prisoner with whom I had been detailed to work shovelled the rubbish into the hod. Conscious of his approach, we worked like mad, watched by the Kapo.

Two other men moved off with their hods, and he bellowed, "Do you call that working? At the double, quick, quick!" They started to run without demur, not hesitating a second. "I'll teach you blockheaded so-and-so's how you must work here, you spineless lot! Get that hod filled in double quick time! Then get going with Karacho to the tip-up waggon and back. And keep it up like that all day long. If that heap has not disappeared this evening, then the whole detachment will go through the stocks. Do you understand?"

As my mate and I grabbed the over-loaded hod, we, too, carried on at the double, like defenceless automata, no longer thinking human beings, but mere machines.

Even now, after all this time, when I think back to that day I am still mystified why it did not occur to me to resist the order this Kapo obviously gave only because the S.S. man in the garage had forced him to call for the assistance of six more men than he had wanted to use. Of course I did not know then how cruelly at times people died who did not bow on the spot to the orders of an S.S. man or a Kapo.

For about half an hour the Kapo remained where he could see us, but even long after he had left, out of sight and raging at other labour columns, we still kept up the murderous speed of our work. It was not our will but our physical limitations that finally caused the pace to slow.

At twelve o'clock a distant siren announced a midday break of half an hour. We were so exhausted by then that we simply fell over, stretched ourselves on the cold ground, and could hardly eat the dry bread carried in our knapsacks. We welcomed the interval of rest as a gift from heaven.

The building site, so recently alive with swarming, crawling men, now seemed lifeless . . . But not quite, for here and there some prisoners remained working, being obliged to do so as a punishment by the Kapos for some misdemeanour.

I could see our Kapo walking across the site with measured tread, upright, fresh, playfully tossing from one hand to the other the stick with which he had so recently beaten heads and faces.

If he had been an S.S. man, I would have turned from him to gaze into space; but he was a prisoner like myself, wearing exactly the same clothes as I was, with exactly the same triangle. Only the Kapo armlet visibly distinguished him from me . . . and that brutality of his, that animal-like disposition, that terrible vileness, that incomprehensible demoralisation of character!

It was fortunate that I was still able to think a little. I had often enough met this type of man in the prisons, parasites among the prisoners, serving the guards, and known to us as toads. I had sometimes despaired of their humanity—until some such toad had reasoned with me, so that I could see that even under their slimy ragged coats there sometimes still endured decent-mindedness, a dignity of manhood and perhaps wonderful qualities of sacrifice which forced them to fight for their lives.

Our Kapo seemed to be one of those who did not deserve to be referred to as human beings; yet surely there were more decent-minded Kapos in the camp?—Hans Schulenburg, for example? Other prisoners who had not known me at all had assisted me. There was that man whom I had only known casually, yet to whom I was indebted for the number 996. The significance of this number was still unknown to me, but I thought it might indicate a number of importance and advantage to me.

The sound of the distant siren came again, and the midday break was over. Back again to the hard drudgery of murderously endless hours. From each quarter of an hour to the next the labour became increasingly harder.

At last a shrill whistle called the parade. Work for this day had come to an end. I felt a wreck, exhausted, bruised, at the end of my strength. With despair I saw that half of the heap of rubble still remained, although it was to have disappeared by now, according to the Kapo's orders.

6. The First Night

THE labour corps had lined up again, and the Kapos ascertained that the prisoners were all there. We could hear the camp band striking up in the distance before we began to march. The loudspeakers transmitted the din for miles. At an even pace, we marched back into the camp, the assistant Kapos watching the line and file and shouting, "Caps off!— Caps on!"

A hold-up occurred as we reached the iron gates. Another labour column, coming from the road to Weimar, marched into the Karacho Way in front of us, its prisoners also tired and worn out. I could see many half-starved figures, with faces all curiously alike, a fresh face, an upright bearing, sparkling eyes being very rare.

The column sang a song about the Frenchman who wanted to shoot an Alpine goat. They sang this mechanically, listlessly and without expression, because they had been ordered to sing.

The end of the column was composed of the "knockedups", men who had broken down during the day, some just managing to walk, others having to be carried. Each casualty was carried by four men at a time and according to his condition; that is, the clearer his senses the more carefully and cautiously they carried him—not the other way round at all.

At last we ourselves marched through the gate, above which, in large letters, I saw the words, "My Fatherland—right or wrong". The Scharführer re-counted the rows of men. Our column paused behind the gate, the order was given, "Labour column dismiss!" and off I went to the place where our Block had assembled for roll-call that morning.

This time, too, the roll-call took more than an hour to conclude. For some reason, the names and numbers of certain prisoners were announced through the loudspeakers. At the stock, men were being beaten in turn.

This time I was standing in such a way that I could see up to the gate. I could see the microphone and the Camp Commander, S.S. Obersturmbannführer Rödl, a stout man with a puffy face and clumsy, bearlike movements.

An S.S. man strode up to the microphone. This was the Sergeant Major of the Camp, S.S. Hauptscharführer Strippel, a man in his thirties, with a not unpleasant face, somewhat corpulent, but still athletic in his movements. He bellowed some instructions over the loudspeaker system.

I could not see the stock, but I could hear the sounds of the beating and the cries of the victims. I was terribly hungry and all my limbs were aching. I only wished the roll-call would come to an end.

Now Rödl himself delivered a speech through the loud-speaker, although I could not understand a word he said, nor, it seemed, could anyone else, for most of them were obviously not listening to him. Only a few paid close attention to his words, and suddenly they made a sign which indicated that he was finished. In fact, at this moment Rödl walked away from the microphone. All this was inexplicable to me.

Rödl had only walked a few paces before he again returned to the microphone to utter one word, which I could not understand, either.

The band began to play the melody, "Castle in the Wood", paused, and, at a second attempt, the tens of thousands joined in half-heartedly as a mass choir. However, a start had to be made three or four times before the song caught on, but after this the voices roared across the square like a hurricane, through the whole camp, filling the woods around and the valley beyond with a thunderous choral song which would probably have sounded like the trumpets of the last judgement in the imagination of a religious person.

When the final note had faded away, Rödl beckoned to Strippel, who stepped to the microphone to dismiss us, and we prisoners moved off to the barracks one after another, according to the number of our Blocks.

* * *

It was the job of newcomers to collect the food buckets from the kitchen, but when Franz, our senior, saw what a bad state we were in, he instructed other men to carry out this job, and this they willingly did.

Several men who had been detailed for certain jobs were missing. Their food was kept for them, but as my table was not fully occupied, I was able to have a seat there. Normally, I would have eaten my food while standing.

The rest did me good. There was cabbage soup to revive me, although it was watery, and being without meat, was not sufficient to appease my hunger. I ate half my bread ration with it. I wanted to eat the lot, but I had to think of to-morrow.

I walked over to the washroom for a wash. The cold water refreshed me. Then I went in search of Franz, to gather more details about life in the camp. Hans Schulenburg had not yet returned, although he was expected, and I could not find Franz, so I decided to walk around the camp and look about on my own accord, for it was now possible for us prisoners to do as we liked, within the framework of camp discipline.

I was seeing things far more clearly today. I could differenti-ate between the camp elite and the mass. I nearly always dis-tinguished the political prisoner from the anti-social, and again and again I noticed lamentable figures, particularly among the prisoners wearing black triangles.

The Jehovah's Witnesses, with their violet triangles, were almost all clean and tidy and of good bearing. The Greens, too, seemed to be sturdy men, likely to cope with camp con-ditions. Different were the Jews of various categories. Most of them wore the red triangle, but among them were far more broken down, worn-out, starved and sick figures than among the political "Aryans".

The latrines were less hygienic and even more dreadful than I had observed at dusk the previous evening. An irresistible nausea prevented me from using them.

At present it was forbidden to enter the wood beyond the bottom end of the barracks; I therefore turned towards the upper end of the camp.

I was now able to inspect one of the Black Barracks in more detail than I had the day before. The men were still more closely penned up in their stuffy day-room than we were in our room in the stone barracks.

The dormitory consisted only of benches with plain sacks of straw, at the foot of each being a rolled-up woollen blanket. Three or four men had to lie on two sacks, although in our political block we each still had our own bed.

I noticed that here, too, the social life was far less disciplined than in our place. I saw two Blacks pick a quarrel with each other and in no time their abuse developed into a fight. Yet none of the other men took any notice of them. Not until the senior of the Block came on the scene did the combatants let go of each other and quickly disappeared into the crowds of prisoners.

I came to the Administration Barracks at the top end of the camp. Standing in front of the post office was a long line of prisoners, waiting to receive registered letters and the like. Here, too, was the camp library, but relatively little use was made of it.

A great activity was carried on outside the rooms of the camp seniors, a constant coming and going, but the square where the roll-calls were held was itself now deserted, the small barred windows of the detention building on the right of the gate covered with wooden hatches.

I walked down to Barracks IA to VA. This was the special camp for Jews, who wore civilian clothes which were torn, creased, dirty and unbelievably neglected. I saw that the men's hair had also been shaved off.

They were forbidden to leave the barracks towards the side where the main camp was situated, just as we were forbidden to approach the wire fence. Between the barracks I could see evidence of plenty of gloom and misery.

I noticed how notes were wrapped round stones and passed between the occupants of our camp and these Jews. Both sides observed the greatest caution in doing this, unwilling to alarm the guard who overlooked the camp from the tower behind the electrically charged wire fence. The paper-covered stones flew from camp to camp in high arcs.

When I returned to my own barracks, I found Hans Schulenburg waiting for me. During my conversation with him, I learned that Richard Elsner was also in the camp. I had known the latter very well for many years. He had served three years' penal servitude for attempted high treason, and after only a few days of freedom after his release from prison he was again taken into protective custody, without any legal justification, just as I had been. I knew him for a genuine person and felt I must see him at once.

Hans Schulenburg took me along to the Block of Richard Elsner, and on our way he told me about other prisoners in the camp who came from our town. I knew almost all of them, although the majority were not here for political reasons. Still, they were acquaintances from my home town and I did not feel quite so forsaken and alone, in the knowledge that I could see them.

We could not find Richard Elsner, so after waiting for him in vain, we returned to our Block, knowing it would soon be locking-up time, after which no prisoner could leave his barracks. From the watch-towers the searchlight would then play on the camp roads, and if anybody showed himself the fat squirters would rattle and the offender liquidated.

The "no-smoking" order which had been imposed on the camp three weeks before had not yet been lifted, but by paying attention to certain precautionary measures we could still smoke, if secretly.

There was a lovely blue cloud of smoke in our washing-room. "Isn't this free and easy smoking a bit risky here?" I asked Schulenburg.

"Of course," he answered; "and naturally everybody does it at his own risk. But the chances of being caught here are a hundred to one. First of all, the Scharführer have left the camp. Secondly, we are pretty clear of informers in this Block; or I should say, the informers don't worry much about such things. Thirdly, we operate a system which always warns us in good time if danger is imminent."

"Well, then, we can puff away in peace," I returned, and we both smiled.

"You know," Schulenburg went on, "on the whole, we must risk all sorts of things, both for ourselves and for others in the camp. You will learn that soon enough. There is nothing to it really, because it is all the same whether we are ruined one way or the other. One man risks his head and neck and nothing happens to him, the other keeps completely in the background and dies. That's how it is here. We must see how we get along best. It is easier with mutual assistance."

"Is it at all possible to help one another effectively?"

"Yes, certainly. I cannot yet explain it to you properly. The position in the camp is that everyone must gain experience for himself. There have been many bitter experiences and more than one person has perished because he was not careful enough. To begin with, nobody trusts anyone else. Confidence must grow laboriously, slowly."

"Does any political organisation exist in the camp?"

"I do not know. If I did know, I would not tell you," he returned. "You must learn not to ask dangerous questions."

"I am only asking because during the first twenty-four hours I have noticed several times that the political prisoners receive preferential treatment and apparently hold well together."

"That is only natural. We have unwritten laws."

"Even if they are unwritten, someone must have formulated them."

"I don't think anyone did. They are not personal. They originated from a common distress. Nobody will tell you that you should or must follow them. Everyone must rely on himself."

"Hännes, you have known me for some time. Fundamentally, I have not changed. Surely you can tell me. No second person can hear what we are saying," I urged.

"You must say, no third person. Sometimes perhaps the second is already too much."

"If that is so, then I ask you, why did you interest yourself in me? Why do you assist me in finding my way about the camp?"

"I don't do any more than others do. What I do is a matter of course. You will also do it in your turn, and if you are unlucky, you'll go under in doing so."

"I understand. We have just got to risk a lot of things."

"Well, obviously!"

"But tell me, what justification do the politicals have for treating one another preferentially? Aren't the others also human beings, just as badly off, and perhaps in need of help more than we who know how to look after ourselves?"

"I have already told you once—you must get out of the habit of asking dangerous questions. For my part, I have no doubt that your experience will give the answers to your questions, perhaps even sooner than you care for."

"You will see! You will find out! Again and again I come up against the same sentences. Is there nobody here at all who will answer the burning questions which burden every newcomer?"

"Yes, there is. You will find them too, not today, not tomorrow. It all takes time. I can only tell you to keep your mouth shut and your eyes open, and if you do find out anything, then keep that quiet too!"

I must confess that this evening I was not fully satisfied with my comrade; but I did him a great injustice. It was really tremendously difficult to place confidence in anyone in the camp, for by doing so one placed one's fate in his hands; even with the noblest of intentions and with the most faithful of hearts, many a man thereby finished as a corpse.

In this perhaps may be found the key to the psychological puzzle as to why the German people, this race of poets and thinkers in whom the strongest impulse of man's freedom was once a vivid force, did not find the strength to fight the crime of National Socialism. I really did not need the object lesson of a National Socialist Concentration Camp to realise the consequences which, because of its nature, inevitably followed the "Law to remove distress from the People of the Reich" which was dated 24th March, 1933; but I do believe that the German people will be in need of such an object lesson for years to come.

7. The Work Goes On

THE sands of time run slowly but constantly. The next morning the tens of thousands were again standing on the square for roll-call. It was not yet daybreak, and the severe cold of the night numbed our limbs and the sharp wind blew through our clothes.

Snow had fallen. Nature had laid its shroud, its kind, white linen, over everything. But here in the camp even nature was in revolt against itself, for everything was infinitely desolate, bare and empty, miserably wretched, totally devoid of all kindness and love.

We were made to stand for over half an hour, before the loudspeaker crackled, "Room orderlies, into the wood!"

I heard the order pass from Block to Block, relayed by the prisoners with a curious howling. About forty to fifty men gathered at the lower end of the square before moving off into the wood in a loose group.

A strange movement ran through the rows of prisoners, as if a sudden gust of wind had disturbed a peaceful forest. I failed to understand what this meant. The men beside me did not know or did not wish to know, but one of them informed us that roll-call would not come for some time.

We stamped our feet, clapped our hands, rubbed our noses, cheeks and ears. Suddenly, I heard someone behind me call my name quietly. I turned round. Doubled up, a prisoner squeezed himself past the others, and showed himself to be Richard Elsner. He had taken the opportunity to crawl to me from Block to Block under cover of darkness, despite the danger of his being caught and receiving severe punishment. He had been informed by his room orderly the evening before that I was in the camp and could no longer wait to find me.

We rushed towards each other. He could only say, "Walter".

I could only manage the single word, "Richard".

Then we shook hands, both so moved by our meeting that we were actually embarrassed. We were not normally emotional, and perhaps by now should have learned not to be, but we could not evade a momentary overcoming of our feelings.

We had been companions in arms, as well as comrades, in the years before the German people set out on this road to darkness. Not that we had been actual friends; but we had known each other well, just as any two people would who share similar opinions and strive for the same political aims.

Within our own province, and to the best of our ability, we had both continued to fight, illegally, against the onset of the disaster we knew National Socialism was bound to bring upon Germany and the whole world. He, too, had been caught by the merciless and criminal machine of Nazi destruction.

He had still been a young man in his middle twenties when he had sat in the dock of the so-called "People's Court". The Senate had sentenced him to three years' penal servitude for attempted high treason, and this he had served to the last day, despite the fact that his health had suffered severely from the hard work he did in the mines. Then the unscrupulous machine of destruction had transferred him to Buchenwald.

After we had quietened down a little, he said, "I must return to my Block. I will come along to you this afternoon after lunch. We are only working until twelve o'clock. I knew you would be coming here in the next few days. I have already spoken about it with my friends."

"What's the matter here with these room orderlies?" I asked him.

He answered casually, as if the matter were a trivial one. "Probably someone has put an end to it. Now they are fetching him from the wood. After all, the roll-call must be correct."

Then, with a friendly and encouraging smile, he nodded, "Well, until this afternoon," ducked again between the rows of men, and disappeared among the prisoners. I saw him leaping over to another Block of prisoners, until he finally vanished among them.

"I have already spoken about it with my friends!" Today, as I write these lines, that sentence rings in my ears like a bugle call. At the time I took no notice of what this meant to me; at the moment it seemed to me to be an ordinary remark of no special meaning. And yet this was the key to that which did nothing less than save my life.

I still suspected nothing even months later, after I had missed death by a hair's-breadth. Not until I was a seasoned inmate did the importance of that lapidary sentence dawn upon me, when I knew of a thousand things which at the time I did not imagine existed even in my wildest dreams; when, in fact, I myself became a modest part of a machinery which saved hundreds, even thousands, of human lives, thus fighting the battle against National Socialist crime in the very camp itself.*

The first light of dawn had by now appeared over the camp. My feet felt dead, the cold creeping up my legs inch by inch. A howling sound came from the wood, a sound taken up by the lower Blocks, and from there travelled like a wave from Block to Block up to the gate itself. I could not make it out; but after a few minutes, over the loudspeakers the usual commands of roll-call became audible.

I spread the news among the labour detachment that we were only working until twelve o'clock. Most of the men did not believe me. Some asked me how I knew this. I was about to give the source of my information when I suddenly remembered that it might be as well not to give it. I answered with the very words I had cursed the day before: "You will see!"

In fact, it was just as well I had said nothing more, for if that thread of Ariadne's had been followed through the labyrinth of the camp, it would have led to an S.S. man who was well-disposed towards us prisoners. Once this fact became known, the S.S. man would no doubt have himself become a prisoner.

* * *

* After the English had entered Belsen, a hundred London medical students went voluntarily to the horror camp in order to see what could be saved through their medical fight against hunger and disease. Their unselfish work, their boundless humanity, is beyond all doubt. Many of them gave their lives in carrying out this work. In many cases they could only watch helplessly as thousands died under the hands which tried to save them, but other victims of National Socialism were won back to life and brought them a thousandfold reward for their endless efforts. These London medical students are men who have inscribed their names in the book of history. What such men were in the light of world opinion, so also were those men in Buchenwald to whom my comrade, Richard Elsner, referred as "my friends". None of them laid claim to any mention or reward, but I know of nothing better as an example of unselfishness to help restore to the German people their belief in themselves and in mankind.

Our Kapo detailed us for snow clearance. With brooms, shovels and snow-shifters, we had to clear the wide roads which led from the camp to the S.S. Barracks. The work was not particularly heavy, and did warm us, and we worked pretty well without supervision. The assistant Kapos now in command were real comrades, working with us and never driving us.

Whenever an S.S. man crossed the road we were expected to step aside, pull off our caps and stand to attention. At one time we were so busy working that we did not notice one coming up from behind us. As he reached a prisoner working in his path, he kicked him with such force that the man was hurled aside. The S.S. man walked on as if nothing had happened. We were a little staggered, although we were now so inured to brutality that we hardly regarded this action in the same category.

"My word, you were lucky," said a fellow to the victim. He smiled and seemed to be of the same opinion, for the incident could certainly have been far worse in its results.

We drew our lesson from what had happened and arranged our column in such a way that we could observe both ends of the road, so that if an S.S. man showed up in the distance, a whispered warning would run speedily through our column.

Our next job was to clear the road which led to Weimar. In that direction I saw for the first time a chain of guards, standing at a distance from each other of about thirty feet, on the left side of the wood. Because of the cold, they were wrapped in fur coats and had ear protectors and Balaclavas. In their hands were machine-pistols at the ready. Some of them seemed to be colder than we were, for they had a fire at which they could warm themselves.

The guards did not appear to worry about us, so that although at first we eagerly swept, brushed and pushed the snow away, conscious of their supervision, we later worked more sensibly and at an easier pace.

A guard suddenly addressed a prisoner, who went near the ditch within reasonable distance of him, and, taking off his cap, stood to attention. The guard asked how long he had been in the camp and where he came from. Having been answered, the guard sent him back to work.

Our assistant Kapo gradually moved up to the prisoner and asked what had happened, working all the time. He explained that conversation between prisoners and guards was forbidden. The main point was never to approach a guard too closely, for one could not foresee his tricks.

We had swept a good stretch of the road when we noticed the road block. "The death belt begins there," explained our assistant Kapo. "Miles wide, this runs right round the camp. We are forbidden to enter the area, and we are warned that we will be fired on without challenge. There are signboards everywhere and the wood is constantly patrolled. So we are hermetically sealed here twice over. A stranger or an unauthorised person can never approach the camp."

One of the newcomers, a Black, was so impressed by this report that he forgot to work for a moment as he looked thoughtfully at the road block.

"Here, you there!" The guard suddenly frightened him from his thoughts. "Come here!" The startled man ran to him.

"Carry on, and don't look round," our assistant Kapo whispered. We went on working towards the road block. When we were about thirty feet further on, he said, "Hurry up! We must free that Black." We had no idea what we had to do, but we redoubled our efforts.

After we had cleared the road almost up to the road block, our assistant Kapo ordered us to fall in and led us back, en bloc.

The Black stood with bent knees near the ditch in front of the S.S. guard, the snow-shovel in both his outstretched hands, maintaining his position with great difficulty. The guard's machine-pistol was aimed at him.

As we marched by, our assistant Kapo commanded in a gruff voice such as we would never have credited him with, "Come along!"

The Black promptly carried out the order and the guard—did nothing! We newcomers were speechless with amazement.

After we had marched on a few yards, the assistant Kapo asked the Black, "Did he make a note of your number?"

"No," replied the other.

"Well, then, it will probably be all right," the assistant Kapo assured him.

To fill in the time until twelve o'clock break, we moved a pile of snow into the ditch. Meanwhile, our assistant Kapo replied, in answer to our eager questions, "Of course it could have come wrong, and still can, but mostly it works out all right. If the guard does not make a report, and we can assume he won't, then the Black will not be put through the stock. If he reports me, then I might get away with it through the fact that I am responsible for keeping the column together. If not, then I am just unlucky."

We profited by this experience, an important one; but I soon profited by a second.

"You must dirty your coat a little," said the assistant Kapo to the Black. "Anyone can see you're a newcomer a thousand yards away. The guards usually play the fool with newcomers, as he did with you. It's not so easy for them with seasoned inmates. Do you think he would have done that with me? I would have vanished immediately, not paying any attention to his call. That gangster there must not leave his picket. He can only make a report for punishment and to do that he must first have my number. That is why you have got to get out of sight as quickly as possible."

Have a number? This ran through my mind. Have a number? What number had the Black? A five-figure number? Hang it, that indicated he was a newcomer. But I had number 996, a number which had become available through the death or discharge of a seasoned concentrationer. Why yes, I remembered, the other politicals in our column also had low numbers. Good gracious! I had found how I had been helped even from the beginning!

Truly, it had been my lucky day. First, the meeting with Richard Elsner, then this light work, to do only until twelve o'clock; then the new experience with a new type of Kapo; and now this revelation, worth more than gold to me, for it strengthened my belief in the good of mankind.

Although my bones still ached from yesterday's work, I marched back through the gate quite differently today.

*   *   *

I spent several hours of the afternoon with Richard Elsner. He was still the same man I had always known him to be, only more mature, more cautious and serious. His physical condition gave him trouble. He had been in the camp for almost a year and, because of his health and with the help of political friends, had succeeded in finding a position in the sock-darning section. Apart from this, he made himself useful in his Block in connection with canteen purchases.

He was open-hearted, gave me many a good tip, and cared for me with touching affection. He himself was a non-smoker, but he had obtained a few cigarettes for me because he knew I smoked. He had also got a piece of fruit bread—heaven knows from where—and, dividing this, he forced me to take the larger part for myself.

8. *The Medical*

THERE was no work outside the camp during the two Christmas holidays, for the majority of the S.S. men were on leave and no chain of guards could be mounted.

After the roll-call on Christmas Day, my number was called over the loudspeakers, with those of other prisoners. We were ordered to assemble at signpost 2. I had been previously informed that this signpost marked the assembly point for those about to see the camp doctor, and so I ran to the gate without special concern.

We were taken into a barracks which had been cleared, and ordered to undress completely and to keep absolutely still, so as not to interfere with the medical examination.

Two prisoners dealt with the writing, one taking notes of our personal data, the other writing what the doctor dictated about our state of health.

The doctor himself was a lean, elderly man, with furrowed, severe features, a prominent hook nose, narrow lips and a sullen mouth. He wore a smock and, like us, was also close-cropped.

He seemed to know his job. Choosing his words slowly and with dignity, he asked precise questions about past illnesses, now and again testing hearts and lungs with the stethoscope, dictated diagnosis, changed necessary information from the prisoner's into the expert's language, and closely examined sores, skin rashes, wounds and scars.

He thundered at those who behaved clumsily or gave obscure information, and showed by his bearing that he knew how to preserve absolute authority. He represented, indeed, the whole dignity of a stern Medizinalrat.*

I informed him that I had had malaria, and he returned, "Malaria Tropica?" as if he perceived in me an understanding of medical differentiation of terms.

That afternoon I asked Hans Schulenburg if this man was the camp doctor.

"No," he told me; "he is a prisoner who is employed in the ward and is actually supposed to have been a former Medizinalrat. The camp doctor does not trouble about examining newcomers and leaves it to this man. No one knows why he is here, but he wears green, so perhaps it is because of an abortion or such like. Still, it's a good thing for us prisoners that he carries out the examination of newcomers. The former camp doctor, Dr. Kirchert, used to carry out such examinations personally, and that was always a hot business."

Later, I frequently noticed that this man was addressed by others as "Herr Doktor" or "Herr Medizinalrat", and he raised no objections to either title.

But actually, he was neither. The "Herr Medizinalrat" was Hans Rösler, a criminal repeatedly convicted for embezzlement and swindling. He had gained his medical knowledge in the camp and used his astounding talent for swindling in order to appear as a former Medizinalrat among the other prisoners.

In the end he lost his job in the ward because we caught him at some dirty machinations with medicines and some no less dirty money transactions and fraud, carried out by taking advantage of the general misery.

I would admit, however, that he helped many a person

* A title given to distinguished German doctors.

74

and, as far as I could observe, was never brutal towards his fellow-prisoners. And that was worth something at Buchenwald.

9. The Procession of the Dead

ON the morning of Boxing Day I was standing on the stone steps of my Block, looking at the coming and going of the prisoners on the paths between the barracks. It was a cold but calm and sunny winter day, with a cloudless sky.

Somehow, the sun did not seem suited to this activity, with the worn-out figures which loitered outside the political Blocks in the hope of "inheriting" from a political prisoner a piece of bread, a drop of cold soup left over from the previous evening or a discarded cigarette end. The sunny morning did not accord with the dirty and torn clothes I saw, and the slow, sluggish gait of those who passed me by.

The senior of the Block occasionally chased away the loitering Blacks, for it was forbidden, under threat of severe punishment, to give food to other prisoners. He himself would walk the stocks if any of his own men were caught offending against the order. In spite of these facts, however, as soon as he turned his back, they returned like vultures.

I gazed up the path and saw the same picture of loitering Blacks outside all the political Blocks. The road was as lively as the shopping centre of a small town at its busiest shopping time. Only the general pace of the passers-by was slowed down, as if a cameraman had reduced the speed of his handle for the purpose of taking pictures in slow motion. Yet perhaps it was not the picture of a German provincial town, but far more like one of those roads between the shacks which suddenly sprang up overnight on the Klondike at the time of the gold rush.

Along the path strode a man wearing an armlet inscribed with the words "Camp Police". Long before I saw him coming from my vantage point, I was warned of his approach because the Blacks suddenly disappeared as if by magic. They were afraid of the punishment on the spot which this prisoner could exact, and feared still more the report he was supposed to make to the camp management, although he did not always do so.

A strange procession suddenly appeared on the main path which ran through the whole camp and across the barrack path at right-angles. Four prisoners were carrying a bier on their shoulders, and on it, judging by the contours, a man lay, covered by a woollen blanket. The procession crossed the barrack path, to disappear behind the higher-lying barracks in the direction of the gate.

Was that a corpse? I wondered. The first procession had hardly disappeared before a second one came into view.

I asked a nearby prisoner what this meant. He answered quite calmly, and without a trace of emotion, "They are last night's dead from the ward. They are now being taken to the mortuary."

A third, fourth, fifth and sixth caravan appeared in turn, a gruesome procession which touched my heart, all the more because I saw that hardly anybody else was troubled by the sight, so hardened had they become to it.

Richard Elsner had confirmed the day before that the death-rate in the camp was very high and that the cynical conversation I had overhead between the two S.S. men in the passage of the political department had probably not been exaggerated. Yet I was so shaken by the sight of these processions that I could not help asking my companion, "Do so many really die here in the camp every day?"

He answered as calmly as before. "The column of the corpse-bearers has already passed a few times today. You only have to wait half an hour and you see the next batch of six."

It was indeed so, just as the man said.

*　　　*　　　*

I was shown round the camp that afternoon by Richard Elsner, who showed me the big prisoners' kitchen, the technically ideal laundry and the extensive kitchen gardens. We entered the wood along the path which led past the sick ward which was later to be of such importance to me. I saw the prisoners' ward for the first time. We wandered through the wood towards the big stables and thus came to the north-west end of the camp.

A broad strip of the wood had been cleared here and we could see for some great distance across the valley, beyond the electric wire and past the watch-towers.

Elsner pointed out the heights of the Thuringian Woods, the Gickelhahn and, far away to the north-west, the Harz with the Kyffhäuser. Again and again I gazed over to the Gickelhahn, so near and yet so infinitely far away.

My thoughts returned to those weeks, almost twenty years before, when, after a Weimar Youth Assembly, I had wandered through the Thuringian forest to ascend the Gickelhahn —a young, free, light-hearted man without any worries.

Everything I had then felt and desired, all my faith and rapture, all my ideals, my happiness of heart and my cheerful mind, all these rose before me.

And now . . . everything, everything was shattered to pieces. What were those verses by Goethe?

> *Ach, ich bin des Treibens müde,*
> *was soll all die Qual und Lust?*
> *Süsser Friede,*
> *komm, ach komm in meine Brust.* *

"No! no! no!" I thought within myself. "Don't resign! Don't tire! No, not here! Especially not here! Because the shattered pieces of today must be the last, hard, most painful tribute to the foolishness for which humanity must pay. No! no! no!"

> *Und würfen sie zehnmal uns nieder,*
> *aufsprängen wir wieder und griffen sie an*
> *und wieder! und wieder! und wieder!†*

* Oh, I'm tired of the struggle;
    What is the use of all this joy and pain?
    Sweet peace,
    come, oh come to my heart.
† And were we thrown down ten times over
    We'd rise and attack them
    Again and again and again.

10. The Dreadful Days

THE man in charge of the labour detachment detailed me to the prisoners waiting to do stone quarry work. I knew nothing of such work, yet felt fresh and healthy and equal to any physical labour, even the hardest.

After entering on his list the names of all newcomers detailed to his detachment, the Kapo allocated me to the column of prisoners who were to carry broken stones up the slope from the bottom of the quarry.

The quarry was surrounded by S.S. men.

I found the slope fairly steep, with two narrow footpaths already trodden out. The path downwards was as straight as a die, while the path along which we were to drag the stone to the top had a few winding bends, which often skirted the chain of guards placed there.

As I slid down the slope for the first time, I found myself running over the rubble. Once I had started, my speed grew ever quicker. I tried vainly to brake, and then it took all my time to save myself from falling on my face. When I finally reached the bottom I was completely out of breath; yet I joined in the laughter of my comrades, realising as I did what a funny figure I must have seemed coming down over the stones and boulders at an ever-increasing speed, like a mad jumping jack.

I shouldered a stone like the other prisoners and joined the long row of men ascending the path. It was tough going, for one had to be careful not to stumble over the rubble or other obstacles in the way. I had to hold the heavy stone on my shoulder with both hands, which made it difficult to keep my balance. Several times I nearly lost the stone, but always succeeded in catching it before it could roll down the slope again, and thus managed at last to bring it to the top.

I had first to accustom myself to this primitive work, and on my second trek the whole process went better.

I arrived safely at the bottom, and this time chose a stone I could hold with one hand, using the other to keep my balance and steady myself should the rubble give way under my feet.

78

I was still a little out of breath as I threw the stone into the tip-up waggon at the top, perhaps even more so than I had previously been, but I knew that no man is born a master of his craft and I had no reason to suspect that I would not see this work through.

Toward midday my toes began to ache and I felt a burning, stinging pain, particularly when going downhill. I had continuously braked my speed with my foot and in doing so had pressed my toes against the toecaps of my boots. As a result they were skinned, and I had a blister on my right heel. My hands were also grazed through my having fallen so often, and my knees were sore.

When I now went downhill, I could only brake my speed with my heels. The pain in my hands and knees was more bearable in this way. Still, the work was hard, and it was obvious that I had to pay for my experience, my leg muscles would have to get accustomed to the continuous climbing.

Then the first incident happened. A prisoner suddenly swayed, after he had climbed about twenty yards up the slope with a stone. At the time I thought he was one of the older men, not knowing how quickly the general conditions of life and work in Buchenwald aged a prisoner. He staggered off the path like a drunken man, then fell to the ground like a felled tree, rolling head over heels down the slope.

I made an involuntary movement to assist him. But the man behind me pushed me forward in an officious way, growling, "Are you mad? Carry on!" Before I could get what was happening quite clear in my mind, he whispered, "What do you think the S.S. would do with you if you went to that man's aid!"

As we reached the top, the signal for the midday break was given, so we had to descend again, there to join the others, already lying or sitting down, despite the cold.

The man who had fallen down the slope was stretched on the ground in a strange position. His haversack had been put under his head and he was covered by a second coat. His exceptionally haggard and furrowed face was as white as chalk.

His skin was grazed on the left cheek, on the temple and on the left side of his nose. Blood trickled from a cut under his left cheekbone; strangely blue-red, unhealthy and thin, it trickled in a small stream down his cheek, to lose itself under the upturned collar of his coat.

His eyes closed, one could well believe him to be dead, had it not been for the evidence of his sunken chest rising and falling. His hands were no more than skin and bone, strangely waxen and unusually long.

The man who had been behind me in the labour column came to sit beside me. Only now did I notice that he was a Black. He took out his bread, and chewed vigorously.

I pulled my boots off to examine my feet, and found my toes were bleeding.

The cold air was comforting, but the Black warned me, "Don't cool them too long. That is dangerous. You must wrap up your toes tightly; otherwise you will be of no use tomorrow."

When he saw me wrapping one foot with my handkerchief, having nothing for the other, he rummaged in his haversack and gave me a dirty strip of linen. "But you must give it back to me tomorrow," he warned.

"Is there no first-aid man?" I asked, nodding towards the injured person.

"Sure," he answered; "but of what use could one be to him? If it were permitted to take him to the camp now, he would only last another few weeks. After all, that's nothing. We'll take him along with us this evening, and if he isn't dead then, he will certainly be dead tomorrow morning."

"One can't just let the man die like that!"

"You have no idea! You will be amazed at what you will experience here. Take care that you yourself are not lying there some time. And above all, don't play about. Do you remember a short time ago you wanted to assist that fellow? It wasn't only for your sake that I pushed you in the back. When they up there get wild"—he nodded his head to the chain of guards encircling the edge of the quarry—"then we all have to dance like puppets.

"First they play about with you, and then, when they have tasted blood, they get mad and turn us all topsy-turvy. The main thing is that we last out this week. Then it's the others' turn and we can break stones. In doing that, we can snatch an odd rest without being noticed. Dragging stones always means constant movement without interrupting the work under any circumstances. You may fall over, but only on the slope. If you fall over anywhere else, those beasts will think you are shamming, and then they will make you jump about."

"Why only on the slope?"

"Look here," he retorted disdainfully, as if unable to comprehend my lack of understanding; "you just fall over on the slope! Do you believe that you will remain lying on the same spot? No, you won't, my friend. You know perfectly well that if you do fall you're bound to roll to the bottom, and nobody wants to do that."

Work recommenced. My knees were stiff and lame. The blister on my right heel hurt, particularly during the first few steps, while the stone on my shoulder pressed painfully against me. I tried to drag it along under my arm, but this way soon proved to be still more toilsome.

I made a pad from my empty haversack, and placed this on my shoulder between my coat and jacket. This produced good results. The bandages around my toes also turned out to be an aid to me. However, the hard work taxed my general physical strength, each tour leaving my knees more shaky than before.

I was not the only one in this perilous condition. My comrades were also slowing down, the column closing up more and more. Each man could only keep the pace of the man in front of him because of the narrow paths. While the column formed a closed circle at the beginning, it now took the form of a snake which moved in a circle. The head of the snake grew shorter and shorter as the tail increased in length.

Soon there were only four or five men in front of me. At one of the bends, as the first prisoner neared a guard, he suddenly changed his slow walk, and the man behind him tried to follow his example.

The head of the snake drew apart. I realised in time what was happening and also made an effort to pass the guard as quickly as possible, so that I could join the end of the column. It was a great struggle, but I succeeded without being driven on or being otherwise molested by the guard. The speed relaxed again.

There was still about half an hour to go before work finished.

I felt worn out, my knees shaking, all my limbs aching, lips dry. As soon as I reached the top of the slope, where the cold wind blew through my clothes, I began to shiver, a stinging pain coming near my groin. My heart hammered and I was out of breath.

Suddenly, one of the guards took it into his head to "turn the heat on". Nearly every prisoner who hurried past him was kicked. He kicked me on the calf. I stumbled but managed to balance the stone and moved quickly away from him.

The whole labour column was startled. For a moment it was as if we were again entering the Karacho Way. I had to pass the guard once more, before the prisoners at the bottom ceased work.

We fell in, and the Kapo counted his men. Oh, sweet rest! Even though the journey to the camp would be hard, toilsome and painful, in my physical condition, even though my feet burned with every step I took and my limbs were as heavy as lead, there would be no more walking up and down hill.

I marched in the middle of the column, where I felt reasonably safe from the maltreatment of the S.S. men who brought us back to within the general chain of guards near the camp gate.

*   *   *

I was still in bad shape the next morning when I shouldered my first stone; but I had bandaged my toes tightly and made myself a shoulder pad from an old woollen scarf. The experience I had bought yesterday paid dividends too. I conserved my strength and took care not to miss a single trick or any of the dodges I had wrested so painfully from yesterday's hard work.

Yet I found it difficult to get going. I was like a machine which first needs warming up, like a new and not exactly well-made millstone which must first be ground down. However, after a few rounds of uphill and downhill toil, my bones and joints grew more flexible, the slight dread which had come over me when starting work giving way to a confident mood.

I noticed some new guards, nineteen to twenty-year-old

youngsters of the type occasionally pictured in the Nazi illustrated periodicals, although not with the physiognomy shown in the magazines. These were farmers' lads, violent and immature, and it was plain to see that their mental horizon was limited, with few intellectual interests; obviously frivolous, they were certainly no good for any other trade or profession than a soldier's one.

The first few hours of labour passed without trouble. Two rounds at the double to which the guards forced us with threats and ill-treatment died down again, for the Kapo collected the largest number of us in order to move a huge boulder. After this, again uphill, downhill, without pause, in toilsome, strength-sapping work.

At the top of the quarry someone could no longer hold his stone and allowed it to drop. It rolled and jumped in mad leaps down the slope, bringing other stones down with it, straight towards the row of men acting as carriers at the bottom of the slope.

A shout warned them of their danger, and most of them managed to jump aside. One of them, however, was caught by the falling object. I could not see where it hit him, but I saw him literally hurled aside by the impact. He spun half round, collapsed, slipped and rolled somersaulting down the hill, until he came to rest in a snowdrift.

Those who had been in the ascent stopped immediately. The man who had lost the stone stood where he was, terrified, looking down at the man in the snowdrift with wide and frightened eyes. But as soon as the latter got up of his own accord and crawled down the hill on his hands and knees, the column of men started to move again.

I saw the unlucky man at the top still standing helplessly on the spot. He did not seem to know what to do. He tried to take a few steps down the path, but found this impossible because of the ascending men in his way. He was thus obliged to walk up the path directly towards the guard nearest to him, whether or not he wanted to do so.

"Come here!" the guard yelled at him.

At first the man hesitated, but seeing he could not avoid his fate, he reluctantly complied with the order.

"Where is your stone, you dirty dog?"

The prisoner made a helpless movement, as if not knowing what to answer. He pointed mutely down the hill.

"Oh yes?" bawled the S.S. man. "You want to stone your comrades, ha? You've gone crackers, ha? You were dropped on your head as a kid, ha? Just a minute, pal. I'll give you one on the head so that your brains will fly about! Lie down! Get up! Lie down! Get up! Lie down! Get up!"

While the rest of us continued our toilsome rounds up and down the path, this monotonous "Lie down! Get up! Lie down! Get up!" went on for about a quarter of an hour.

Soon, the prisoner was completely exhausted. He could only rise slowly from the ground, before dropping down and collapsing—forward, sideways, backwards, whichever way he fell, with no attempt to protect himself with his hands, the intervals between the order becoming longer and longer.

"Go on; let him pirouette" called out the neighbouring guard, standing some twenty paces from his comrade.

"Pirouette!" the guard promptly ordered the prisoner, even now barely staggering on his feet.

The victim stretched his arms sideways and began to turn himself around where he stood. He found strength to turn himself three, perhaps four times, before falling like a drunken man. He rolled down a short steep slope, where he remained lying a few seconds, as if dead. Then he struggled to his hands and knees, collapsed, rolled about ten yards down the slope, and finally lay there as if lifeless.

After an interval of half an hour, the first-aid man climbed up to him. The prisoner did not move under his ministrations.

"Send someone up with a rope," the first-aid man at last called to the Kapo. The latter instructed someone to climb up the slope with a thick rope. The two men fixed this round their comrade's body and brought him laboriously down the slope.

Meanwhile, two of the guards had moved away and had taken up positions where we were throwing the stones into the tip-waggons. They amused themselves each time we passed them by kicking us and beating us with their sidearms.

I felt myself gradually losing strength. My knees shook, my throat was parched, my lips dry and chapped, and I had hardly any feeling in my stiffening hands. My neck ached dreadfully.

and there was a feeling of iron clamps pressing against my temples and the back of my head.

I was overcome by a yearning to fall, just once, if only for a few seconds, so that I could somehow rest myself. Opposed to this was the knowledge that to do so would bring me the inevitable, painful end.

But what is the end? I argued. The end?—If I now walked beyond the chain of guards, what then? Would I not die painfully? If I took this stone and beat it against the heads of those two torturers there?—that would also mean a certain end!

But what would be gained by these actions? Certainly I would die, and with me, perhaps, one of those tormentors who deserved death a thousand times. But if I did this, would not the machine-pistols rattle, to cruelly mow down those who were with me? Would not the whole camp suffer for my deed? Had not Richard Elsner told me that our comrade Förster, who used violence in trying to escape from this hell, was hanged in front of the prisoners? Had not the whole camp suffered terribly at the time. Had not many prisoners, having nothing to do with Förster's action, died cruelly? No; if I had to die, I had to do so alone, without bringing suffering on others.

Still my knees grew weaker, my whole body worn out, my condition far worse than it had been after the interrogations I had endured at the hands of the Gestapo. The world around me seemed unreal. I could barely make out the man in front of me.

I grabbed my stone mechanically. Toiling, step by step, I stumbled up the slope. I no longer felt the guard beating me.

I was about to shoulder another stone, when someone near me, yet sounding far away, said "Don't be silly; it's the mid-day break."

Midday?—Midday?—I lifted my head. There the prisoners were, all lying and sitting about. Only now did I truly see them again.

Midday?—Break?—Oh yes, break! And I fell over like a sack. I breathed deeply, happy that I could rest on the cold and stony ground.

Rest, oh precious, sweet rest! And still more rest! More and more! What did I care about the afternoon? What did I care about the next minute? This second, in which my heart was thumping so madly, in which I draw breath, was mine, all mine! Nobody tortured me; above me was the sky, around me the clear fresh air.

As with every living being, with everything on this earth, this universe, I realised I needed to complete the cycle of my existence in accordance with the laws under which I had begun. But had the die been cast? Was I to perish under the yoke? Would the wheel of fate crush me?

Giordano Bruno, Savonarola, Ferrer, Uriel Acosta and thousands of others—they also had been crushed because they had remained true to themselves. What more could I do in this hour of decision than follow their example, I, a small cog, a grain of sand on the world's beach?

A free community of all human beings had always been my heart's desire, and because I had aimed for that goal, I was here on this Hill of Calvary. I knew, moreover, that no matter what the end would be, I would be true to myself.

Work began again. I had gathered my strength during the short interval of rest, but I was still only able to complete the first two rounds with clear senses. Then everything began to swim before my eyes. My knees shook, my limbs ached, and I was once more in a condition of complete indifference and apathy. I only knew I had to carry on and on, up the path, down the path. My thoughts were obsessed with the one idea. I was unaware of what went on around me. I could see only the man in front of me, nothing else.

I did not wake from this trance until I found myself marching into the camp at the end of my column, with a comrade at my arm, helping me along. I was indifferent to everything, for everything seemed unreal, as distant as a dream, removed from all actuality. I was on the other side of time and space. I did not realise that I was on the threshold of death. I did not even wish for that end.

* * *

I have little recollection of what happened after that. Only a few impressions remain in my mind. It seemed as if all torture and cruelty had exhausted itself in me, as if the veil of eternal night had been mercifully lowered over me, and as if a condition of complete numbness had proved itself stronger than all the physical and spiritual pain I had endured.

I troubled about nothing more, and I do not know if anybody worried about me. I only remember that I went to bed and must have fallen asleep immediately, and that I did not wake up again until most of the prisoners were in the day-room.

I still remember that I then stood again on the square for roll-call, with the haversack round my neck, unspeakably tired, without any powers of resistance and totally, disinterestedly, resigned to my unavoidable fate.

I know that a prisoner said to me, "You! 996! Go to the gate, to sign 2." I remember that I stood with other prisoners at the sign, that the various labour column marched through the gate, that it was then remarkably quiet around me, the square suddenly empty, and that our small group was led down the camp by a Kapo. I remember also that I stood outside the sick ward and that some prisoner told me, "You remain in the camp today"; but I do not recall how I spent most of the rest of that day.

During the later afternoon, my brain cleared and memory functioned once more. I found myself in the day-room of my Block.

Franz and another man were engaged in cutting up portions of blood-and-liver sausage. Franz asked me where I had been and I answered that I had been sent to the doctor, who had not, however, seen me.

I felt very refreshed as I washed myself thoroughly in the washroom. Music sounded over the loudspeakers, the signal for the return of the labour columns. I went up to the square.

After roll-call, I spent a short time in the day-room of my Block. Feeling tired and weak again, I asked Franz if I might be allowed to go to bed before the normal time. He gave his permission, and again I slept without interruption until the general waking time.

11. Doctor's Clerk

THE next morning, when again my name was called over the loudspeakers to report to sign 2, I ran up there under the impression that I would have to see the doctor that day.

Again a prisoner outside the sick barracks told me, "You stay in the camp today. Go over to the woodshed and busy yourself. If anybody should come, say that you are keeping yourself ready for the doctor and show them this paper." He handed me a small duplicated form on which were entered my name and prisoner's number and the date.

I found brushwood, a hatchet and a chopping block in the woodshed. A Kapo came along to me and said, "You need not do much here. Just keep your eyes open. If anybody comes, whether a prisoner or a Scharführer, you must busy yourself chopping twigs. Above all, you must not fall asleep."

I spent the whole day in the woodshed. Now and again the Kapo came along to talk to me. He questioned me a great deal, but I was cautious in answering him.

Once, a prisoner came and asked me if I could do office work. I replied "Yes", but when I asked him if there was such work available for me, he only returned, "Perhaps for one day. We shall see."

Shortly before the day's work was ended, he returned, to give me a small form. "Tomorrow morning you will report at sign 2 again," he said. "Show this paper if you are questioned."

The next day I was again taken to the sick ward. On this occasion I was obliged to stand in front of the barracks for about an hour before a prisoner came and took me inside.

The work I was given to do was to transcribe entries of the medical treatment of prisoners from small dirty cards on to clean ones for record purposes. After finishing each card, I submitted it to Hans Rösler, who, with dignity and great exactness, corrected every little misplaced letter and punctuation mark.

I found this rather petty; but what did it matter to me! At least, there was no more "up the path, down the path", and a little misplaced letter was easily rectified if one took time over it; while the "Medizinalrat" did not seem to concern himself with how many cards were completed in a given time.

By the evening, standing among the ten thousands on the square for roll-call, I felt fresh and bright again, and of as good cheer as I could possibly be in the circumstances.

Not until many, many weeks later was I to realise what had happened to me and around me in those days. No one ever explained that by risking his own life, he strove to snatch mine from death's portals and National Socialist revenge.

I had first to grow into the unseen organisation, the silent unassuming heroism which arises from the taciturn sense of duty possessed by the camp elite, before I could understand the whole matter. To comprehend how my tireless friends had saved me from the jaws of death I had first to become that prisoner who filled in the application forms to see the doctor and drew up the list of attendants, to be forwarded almost daily to the camp management.

I had already learned that somehow every political prisoner was given preferential treatment by other politicals, but I did not yet know that it was an unwritten, cast-iron law in the camp that special prisoners were to be protected.

Richard Elsner had drawn the attention of his friends to me. They did not as yet know for themselves whether I was worthy of their protection, but they helped me because a friend whom they knew took responsibility for me.

They said nothing to me for two main reasons. First of all, what they did for me was a risky matter. If anything had gone wrong, and they had been found helping me, they themselves would have died a cruel death. Thus, their caution can perhaps only be understood by someone who himself had been similarly active in the camp. Secondly, their actions were based on motives which find their origin in the deepest and most secret of human impulses and beyond all superficiality, without the need of outward fame, outward honour or flattery of any kind.

For these two reasons my friends have remained silent to this day, and perhaps will be for ever. This does not alter the fact that a prisoner observed that I was within a hair's-breadth of the brink of death, and through some channel of organisation my name was arranged for the purpose of going to the sick ward where, without the doctor's knowledge, it was placed on the attendants' list for him.

Three days of rest were procured for me in this manner, and this won me back to life. When this period had passed, I did not have to report back to the detachment for the quarry but was placed on other labour. The work now was difficult and hard, too, but did not exceed my physical capabilities.

After a few weeks even of this, Hans Schulenburg informed me that I would be employed as a writer on night duty in the sick ward.

This last activity was at first unofficial. The camp management and the man in charge of the detachment had only allowed a certain number of prisoners to help out in this work, but the number proved too small.

Medical cards were piled high, waiting to be transferred to the record cards which were compiled in the sick ward file for every new prisoner. Even many of these record cards had not yet been made out because of the increasing number of newcomers.

With the silent approval of the camp doctor, therefore, a few writers on night duty were organised, and between them endeavoured to reduce the pile of work which had accumulated.

Night duty was from seven p.m. until morning roll-call, but there was so much work to do that we were soon compelled to work a few additional hours per day, and even on Sundays.

As I knew how to type I was gradually given all sorts of urgent jobs to do. The prisoner who sat in the doctor's room and acted as his clerk, dealing with all the writing for the doctor, found no time to do everything.

I got to know Dr. Ding, the camp doctor, and I was soon employed in the sick ward more often by day than by night. In time, it was found more practicable to have me claimed officially from the labour detachment as writer for the sick ward.

This procedure was easier to conceive than to execute. I had not been long enough in the camp to warrant such a "cushy" job, and the man in charge of our labour detachment refused on principle any such assignment for a comparative newcomer to the camp. But the difficulties were smoothed over, with some risks on the parts of doctor and prisoners, and I obtained my official appointment—"temporarily in place of a writer who had suddenly fallen ill."

In this way I became a writer in the sick ward and the thread on which my life hung was knotted twice for the time being.

The reader may now ask why prisoners who had the power and the opportunity to save me from the arms of death had allowed things to go so far in the first place before doing anything to help me.

In actual fact, their powers and opportunities were very limited. As a rule in the great majority of cases they were obliged to watch helplessly as thousands of wretched men grew languid and died or were murdered. They could only intervene in a few exceptional cases, and then only at the risk of their own lives. A thousand times and more they were confronted with the dreadful decision of choosing from a thousand men one single prisoner whom they could keep alive.

Imagine a doctor who comes to a barracks where there are a hundred people perilously ill with typhus, and yet possesses only enough medicine to win five of these lives from otherwise certain death. He must decide on which five to give the medicine.

The greater his sense of responsibility and knowledge, the more difficult will he find the task of making his decision. Should he give life to a human wreck who is a burden to himself and the world, only to allow that patient to die who is lying alongside him, who could perhaps in the future perform most valuable work for humanity?

We political prisoners found ourselves in a similar situation. We helped each other in the first place only because we hoped to do better work in days to come. But this fact certainly did not mean that prisoners of other categories were neglected. Many a time the decision to save him was made in favour of a Black or a Green, instead of a Red who had proved to be a scoundrel.

Our second unwritten law was that those political prisoners were to be protected who had especially exposed themselves in their struggle against Nazism, although even this fact gave them no special privileges.

Our main protection consisted in endeavouring to transfer chosen prisoners to less strenuous labour detachments than they had and where they were also removed from the immediate attention of the camp management. This did not always succeed.

In view of the unscrupulous hatred of the Nazis for us, we met success more often than one might imagine. Even if thousands of our best men did die painfully under torturous treatment, many others are alive today to co-operate in a better and more dignified human development because they owe their lives solely to that solidarity between human beings which did not perish, proving itself worthy even in the hell of the concentration camp.

*   *   *

I soon grew accustomed to the internal working of the sick ward. I had often looked behind the scenes and had seen many things which horrified me again and again. I had noted with what self-sacrifice the prisoners operated here. They had taken a great deal upon themselves, carrying out works which almost compared with that of the Danaids in the underworld. I had associated myself with them, and was always deeply touched by my good fortune when able to do my comrades a good turn in any way.

Later, I often wondered how I could have been so completely unsuspecting of the things which meanwhile were going on around me—in the room next door, in the doctor's room, which I had often entered to find in the best order, and in the rooms of the sick ward. It was as if an impenetrable wall had surrounded me, as if I had been blind. And then fate removed the merciful wall which had obscured my vision.

The doctor's clerk, Herbert, was suddenly discharged. The prisoner Paul Grünewald, who had already been trained as his successor, was dangerously ill with severe rheumatism and very severe heart neurosis. There was no one available who could take over the duties of doctor's clerk, who had to know something of the clerical work involved in the sick ward and could type perfectly.

I was the most junior of the writers, but there was nobody else suitable for the job. Herbert proposed me as his successor to S.S. Untersturmführer Dr. Ding, who first asked me if I felt equal to the job and then persuaded me to take it on, appointing me his clerk.

In the short hour left to him before he reported for his discharge, Herbert instructed me in the details of my work. My head buzzed with all the new and strange information I received, while in a thick pile the prints and forms were piling up. A hearty handshake with Herbert, "Best of luck, pal!" and then I was left to fend for myself.

The Scharführer attached to the camp doctor had not the faintest idea of the clerical work they had to do and which was carried out by the doctor's clerk; nor was Dr. Ding informed on all the details. Paul Grünewald was too ill to be disturbed. Klangwarth, the first nurse, was a printer who had gained an astonishing medical knowledge in the sick ward, and even carried out operations and amputations in a masterly manner. But even he did not know everything I had to do, although he assisted me as best he could, leaving me to ferret out everything else for myself.

*　　　*　　　*

I cannot describe here in detail what my approach was, especially as I only wish to write what seems necessary to me in order to create the atmosphere of the camp. I will only say this, that from this moment on I was introduced step by step to all the horrors of Nazism. The incapability and laziness of the S.S. men on the one side and, on the other, my cold-blooded determination to disguise my true feelings no matter what the situation, paved my way to an almost unbelievable reality which opened my eyes to the unmasked face of National Socialism.

In the following pages of the Second Part of my record, I will endeavour to give a picture of this face of National Socialism. I can only touch upon certain happenings, but I hope these will speak for themselves, for each single one of them represents a general and typical event and is not a particular exception in itself.

PART TWO

1. The Hell of Buchenwald

THERE was no sensible person in Germany who did not know that life in the concentration camp was hard, although it must be said that the extent of the Nazi atrocities was either not known or simply not believed, because the real facts were so incredible.

It might be as well to remember in this connection that we concentrationers ourselves sometimes said, "No one will accept our story if we tell about it all, outside. No one will believe us. No one can believe us. What can we do then to make them believe the truth?"

We camp prisoners had none of those means at our disposal with which modern information services are conducted—no camera, no sound film, no dictaphone, no possibility of producing a convincing document in proof of what we endured. We knew exactly with what care the S.S. men destroyed everything which might at some time serve as proof against them, and saw them daily doing this.

We knew how they sealed the camps hermetically. We knew how cleverly they understood the art of covering themselves in their criminal activities. We also knew how particularly careful these monsters were to arrange documents, through forgeries, so that these could prove their unimpeachable conduct and make refutation difficult.

There remained, and still remains, only one hope, one proving the truth, the unbelievable truth, only one possibility of showing the true face of Nazism to decent Germans.

And that is: all concentrationers still living must be interrogated independently of one another and their statements taken under oath. What they personally saw, experienced and suffered must be exactly established. For the future information of those who will be responsible for the welfare of the German people, the State can put down as evidence everything which

97

can be proved by corroboration in a book which will bear the only true insignia of the "party".

Every person of sense in Germany at this time knew that the threat of the "concert camp" was enough in itself to suppress any independent movement and crush any opposition. The people said "concert camp", not "camp for protective custody", as the National Socialists described it officially. Why did nobody else in Germany speak in terms of protective custody? Because everybody knew that it was not protective at all! Why did nobody talk of education camp, penal camp, forced labour camp? Because they knew that the concentration camp was something far worse than any of these!

Despite the camp being termed one for protective custody, no one in Germany or in the world called it by that name. This is typical and—revealing. In connection with that most hideous crime of all times, which camouflaged itself with the words National Socialism, there is not a single aspect which does not prove there were always two sides to the business, a fine outward appearance and an unworthy, inhuman, rotten inner core!

The true description of what the Nazis called so innocently a "camp for protective custody" was known by a few, suspected by some and feared by all. Everyone should know the whole terrible truth, that without exception everything in connection with National Socialism bore a horrible double face.

Many people in Germany will be surprised to hear that, in accordance with legal regulations, protective custody could only be decreed for three months, or a period of six months at the most—that is, in accordance with the regulations laid down in writing by the Nazis themselves.

Yet it is well known that these opponents of Nazism who were caught in its clutches were not only kept two, three and four years in the concentration camps, but that some victims had to live there five, six, seven, even twelve years, and would, without doubt, still be there today had not the Reich, which was to last a thousand years, died in the meantime.

I would like to include a passage here which actually does not belong to this book but which I consider so important that I cannot repeat it often enough.

There are people who, referring to the fact that people lived as prisoners in the concentration camps for twelve years and still did not die, point out that life there could not have been as bad as it has been described.

People who endured twelve years in a concentration camp are the very few exceptions which prove the rule. The hundreds of thousands who perished miserably are the rule!

Moreover, it is not due to the Nazis that the few remained alive. Credit for that fact is due only to the intelligence, to the tremendous will to live, to the great human qualities and to the good fortune of those few exceptions.

The simpletons could say that the Nazis were not obliged to limit the time of protective custody to six months, and therefore it was inconceivable that they did so!

Oh, sancta simplicitas! The simpletons have already forgotten by what abject means the Nazis came to power and retained it. I must write still more of the concentration camp of Buchenwald, even though my pen is unwilling to continue.

2. The Camp Doctor Murders

I HAD been acting as a doctor's clerk in the prisoner's sick ward for a short time only, and if questioned as to whether Dr. med. Erwin Ding was capable of murdering a prisoner, I would have sworn on oath that such a deed was impossible for him to do. But I would have been mistaken.

Dr. Ding was a highly intelligent man, who was well-mannered, of an agreeable disposition, friendly and sometimes actually genial. His features were rather pleasant than stern, his eyes lively and observant. Above all, he was exceptionally self-assured, and I was repeatedly surprised at the ease with which he always found a way out of the most complicated situations.

Many a time he sat before me at his writing desk, reading the papers I had prepared, and my eyes would rest on his high, nobly formed forehead, on the fine line of his nose, on the handsome, regular features so full of character, and often I pondered the puzzle such a man set me, his high qualifications and abilities contrasting with his abominable crimes.

It is not my task to write the story of this man, however tempting and enlightening such a work would be for the understanding of the spiritual side of Nazism. I can only indicate through sketches what Ding was, leaving the reader to reflect upon the psychological depths which, despite great talent, made a charlatan and murderer of this man.

Ding was the son of the doctor and African explorer, von Schuler, who lived in a loose concubinage with an office girl from Dessau who had three sons by him. No doubt von Schuler intended to adopt the three boys, but his relatives put so many difficulties in his way that he died while legal proceedings were still going on. The mother fought for the rights of her children, but at last succumbed to the narrow-mindedness and social supremacy of the so-called gentry around her.

The proceedings for the adoption of the eldest of the three sons were completed before the father's death, the second son took the mother's name, and the third was adopted by the merchant Ding, from Leipzig, whose own marriage was childless.

Ding was on excellent terms with his adoptive father, although his relations with his adoptive mother were less cordial. When old Ding died, he left a small allowance to the adopted son and transferred the administration and profits of his property to his wife. Young Ding soon quarrelled with his adoptive mother.

At the University to which he had proceeded, he fell in with those circles which, with their Master-Race Ideology, were to become the perfect breeding ground of Nazi criminality.

There is no doubt that Ding possessed all the qualities necessary for making his way honourably and with dignity as a doctor. But how much easier it was to succeed with the aid of the Party, which did not inquire into one's degree of knowledge and ability but only as to one's conviction in its political aims. What others can only achieve through years of effort and privation, the Party dropped overnight into the laps of those who had such a conviction or even merely pretended to it.

Dr. Ding was pushed for time. He lacked sufficient financial assistance from home, and as soon as possible he wanted to reach an income which would enable him to marry. He chose the short and comfortable method of succeeding through the Party! He obtained his doctor's degree with a composition of "Pavor nocturnus" and was first a junior medico and then made doctor in the concentration camp of Buchenwald.

Nobody who knew Dr. Ding could avoid the impression that he was a man of undoubted talent and even of fine character. The expert who held a short conversation with him was surprised at the extraordinaril[!] manifold and precise knowledge this man seemed to retain behind his high, intelligent forehead.

Yet all this was mere façade! The splendid head, intended by nature to carry out valuable work for suffering humanity, had been hollowed and refilled with the stench of Nazi doctrine.

I cannot possibly tell here all the facts which prove that everything about him was pretence; but a few should suffice.

In his desk I found records, medical histories and photographs of prisoners and their relations who suffered from diabetes. Ding told me that he intended writing a treatise on "Diabetes mellitus", and suggested I should examine the records and, if possible, complete them.

I learned that these records had been compiled by a Jewish doctor named Perth who came from Vienna. Despite the definite prohibition against the employment of doctors as prisoners' nurses in the sick ward, Ding allowed this man and two other Jewish doctors to practise there in order to improve his own very negligible knowledge. In masterly fashion the three doctors contrived to pretend to be ignorant scholars while at the same time instructing their "teacher"!

After the Jewish pogrom of 1938, among the mass internments appeared an unusual number of coma cases. This turned Ding's interest to the study of diabetes, and Perth called his attention to the fact that the camp offered excellent material for examination and research in connection with the hereditary problems of this disease.

Firstly, as the camp was supplied with prisoners from all parts of Germany, material for examination from wide stretches of the country was now concentrated in a very small area; secondly, normal research work was confined almost entirely to hospital findings, whereas every prisoner could be included in the examination in whose family or relations diabetes mellitus had been diagnosed; thirdly, it was known how unreliable the scientific results of research were sometimes rendered because the examining doctor had no means of applying pressure which could cause the patient to state the most important factors of his case, a different matter in the camp!

These three reasons were evident to Ding and he got Perth and other Jewish doctors to collect the initial material he wanted. A mountain of documents soon accumulated, particularly in view of the fact that a short letter from the camp doctor to the prisoners' relatives was sufficient in itself to bring him all the necessary photographs, statements and documents needed; for those outside the camp erroneously believed that in this way they could help their imprisoned relatives.

Genealogical trees were marked in order to clear up disputes of dominant or recessive trends of heredity factors, photographs were affixed, statements of all kinds were recorded.

I worked through the material and soon mastered it. Ding provided all the literature on the subject of diabetes mellitus he could obtain from Jena and Leipzig. I dealt with this also, recording the most important results I could find, drawing up a literary reference, and thus constantly bringing more order into the material and taking pains to complete it all round.

I must say that I took my work seriously. It was not my worry that to me personally all this meant very little.

One day, a prisoner, cited in a case regarding a dispute of parentage, was examined minutely by an expert who came from the Biological Institute of the University of Jena. This man brought with him measuring and examining instruments which interested me immediately. I noted how he measured physical characteristics most exactly, and from photographs and sketches I learned about the analogy diagnosis. From this new perspective I viewed the material on diabetes mellitus.

After studying family and individual photographs of sick parents and their sick and healthy descendants, I thought I discovered a surprising likeness between the various carriers of the illness, with hardly any likeness at all among the healthy descendants.

The next day I submitted my discovery to Ding. He was immediately filled with enthusiasm, and at once began to add to this material all possible records of particularly noticeable characteristic similarities which he alleged he had himself ascertained in detailed physical examinations. When I witnessed these manifest forgeries, any illusions I may have had about Dr. Ding were quickly dissipated.

It was my intention to use the literary references I had recorded as a means of enabling a scientifically correct work on the subject of diabetes mellitus to be prepared.

Shortly after the outbreak of war, Ding was about to take the material we had collected to the Kaiser Wilhelm Institute, there to be submitted to the leading expert in this field of research. He instructed me to include a literary reference in the file, although this, with its forgeries, had no further scientific value to me.

To my question as to whether I should record only the work actually dealt with, he answered, "No, everything we came across. That is half way to victory, for do you think this expert has read everything about this disease? And if he sees everything I have read, he won't start asking questions, for he will assume that he may make himself ridiculous. Do you believe that I swotted through all the literature I quoted in my 'Pavor nocturnus'?"

The reader may be shocked by this report of the irresponsibility of a man who later received a chair at a scientific institute in Graz; but to me this revelation was by then nothing new. The fact that he dictated a completely untruthful report concerning the results of a dysentery experiment; that he related some stories to his colleagues from Oranienburg about a highly interesting series of scientific experiments he had made in connection with the combating of inflammation of the lungs by using Salvarsan injections, experiments about which he had read a short time before but had never actually carried out in the camp; that he submitted entirely untruthful or partly true reports to the medical journals in order to be accepted on the staff of contributors; that he forged death certificates or case histories of illnesses; that he killed his patients either through negligence or deliberately: all these facts had for a long time caused me no alarm or horror. After all, Dr. Ding was an

S.S. Sturmführer as well as an S.S. doctor of the typical type, made, nurtured and furthered by the S.S.

Yet what a long hard way was my progress from the day I began as doctor's clerk to Dr. Ding to that day when nothing about him could any longer surprise me. With how many brutal blows was my faith to be destroyed merely because I would not believe that a man with such great gifts could represent nothing but a criminal façade.

I received the first blow to my confidence in him in this way:

For the first time, since I had become better acquainted with him, one sunny morning I found Ding less good-tempered than usual, and slightly nervous. The change in him was hardly perceptible, and would not have been noticed by a superficial observer; but this struck me because experience had taught me the importance of noting the smallest details in my superiors, in order to safeguard myself.

The doctor was erratic and jumpy and dealt with a second matter without having settled the first. He was usually surprisingly quick and extraordinarily calm in changing from one subject to another, and understood how to finish off within a few minutes sometimes three, four and five totally diverse matters.

While he usually reacted to the slightest remark and seemed to miss nothing, he now took no notice of what I said. He gave the impression of a man entirely absorbed in some other matter or, to use a popular expression, of a man who is absent-minded.

I learnt to regard this change of character as an indication that he contemplated crime or murder.

I left the surgery for a short while, and when I returned Ding had gone. In the pen tray on the table, however, I noticed a 20-cubic centimetre hypodermic syringe, completely filled with a clear, brownish fluid. I still did not suspect what this meant, but the quantity of fluid did surprise me somewhat, for until now I had only seen Ding inject one, two or at the most, three cubic centimetres to patients when necessary.

It was not clear to me afterwards whether the doctor carried out these manipulations on purpose, either to note how I reacted or cautiously to get me acquainted with matter to which he knew I might object and would despise.

It could quite well have been that Ding did not think of me at all when he put the filled hypodermic syringe into the tray for me to see, but only put it down while he went to make some further arrangements in the operating theatre situated in the centre of the sick quarters, which were parallel to our barracks, separated from it only by an alley.

From the top end of the camp, along the path to the sick quarters, came S.S. Scharführer Sommer, the brutal man in charge of the detention barracks. Our signal service informed me of this fact and, being alone in the surgery, I went to the window to watch him.

Sommer came along with quick, sloppy steps. A very thin, pale prisoner hobbled behind him with great effort. At first I did not recognise who this was. I watched him, seeing him find it difficult not to lose his boots, which were far too large for him, without laces to keep them in place. He kept up his trousers with his left hand, his braces having been taken away from him, as from every prisoner under detention; at every other step, he made a peculiar rowing movement with his right arm, as if this assisted his pace. Now I recognised in this skeleton the man Mohr.

Mohr was a political prisoner, an official from Frankfurt on Main who was once the senior of the camp. He was dismissed from this position by the camp commandant, S.S. Standartenführer Koch. Had he been favoured by some lucky chance, he could have "lost" himself, as we called it; that is, he could have vanished from the immediate attention of the camp management and disappeared into the mass.

He was generally advised to be extremely cautious in the future and avoid doing anything which would draw the camp management's attention to him, for it was known that he only narrowly missed death. His frivolity, followed by the turbulent happenings in connection with the arrival of more than 12,000 Jews after the Jewish pogrom of 1938, had caused Mohr to forget his need for caution. He was again placed in detention for some alcoholic excesses.

Now he hobbled along behind the Scharführer Sommer like a wounded rabbit, a walking skeleton. As he passed my window, I could see how he turned slightly towards a prisoner whom I could not see, and, with his right hand, indicated the unmistakable sign of hanging. Sommer disappeared with him into the operating theatre.

Dr. Ding soon afterwards came quickly into the surgery, took the hypodermic, and left instantly. I remained without suspicion of his intentions.

He returned after an interval of about a quarter of an hour. He washed his hands, before demanding from me the file with the papers for signature I had to give him.

He was now calm and collected, passing joking remarks, and telling me of the latest political developments in the outside world, knowing I was interested in such matters.

Through the window I saw Mohr on a stretcher being carried back to the detention barracks. He was sleeping peacefully. Sommer walked beside him.

After Dr. Ding had finished his work and had left the camp, I went to the operating theatre, to find what was the matter with Mohr.

In answer to my question, the nurse who worked here returned, "Nothing."

I: "How do you mean, nothing?"

He: "Well, nothing."

I: "Something must have been wrong with him."

He: "Look here; don't you know?"

I: "Know what?"

I had a sudden foreboding, for there was a particular note in the nurse's answers. A horrible suspicion came to me. My mind balked at the monstrous idea conjured in my mind, and yet I felt, I knew, that what I now suspected was true. My throat went dry, my head reeled.

As if from a distance I heard the nurse speaking in a calm and indifferent way:

"Well, if you don't know, you will soon find out."

I did find out. Early in the afternoon I was ordered to make out a certificate of death for the prisoner Mohr, who had died in the detention barracks.

The next morning Ding dictated a false death report about him, and with that, my last doubts of what had happened were removed.

3. The Barracks for Corpses

OUTSIDE the camp, between the wire fence loaded with high-tension current and the outlying grounds of the Buchenwald Zoo which had been built with extorted Jewish money, was the mortuary, a small, wretched, broken-down, wooden barracks, the size and standard of a miserable building shed.

Yet even a building shed which had been erected for workers by an inconsiderate builder intent on exploitation and only barely meeting official regulations as to its being wind and water tight, would still have been a decent habitation in comparison with this place.

Before the camp's own incinerator was erected, here all prisoners made a short rest before completing the bumpy journey to the Crematorium in Weimar, Gotha or Eisenach, after death had relieved them from the tortures of the camp.

It is not of course customary to establish mortuaries in busy centres. Yet this one seemed to have crept out of the way as if it were frightened of the public or indeed of any attention, even of those in the zone of death which ran all round the camp.

I need not emphasise the fact that this barracks was deliberately built in a part to which hardly anybody came. Even the S.S. men, visiting the zoo and seeing the barracks from a distance, probably did not suspect the circumstances connected with this wooden shed, looking as it did so like a primitive store-house.

The mortuary was so completely isolated that when I stepped into it for the first time, I had a strong feeling that to reach it I had passed through an area forbidden to all but a few living beings. As often as I went there—and that was many times—I always had the same feeling. Perhaps the secluded position of the barracks, together with the fact that nobody came near it, contributed to this feeling, or perhaps the source of it was to be found in those irrational sensations which, in a double sense, had more effect here in this desolate place than anywhere else in the world.

The barracks was divided into two rooms. In one were the

107

corpses of the prisoners, in the other stood a primitive oblong table which was used for the purpose of dissection. The dead men were immediately placed in coffins, as far as these were available. This deed was carried out by the bearers, for which duty Jews were exclusively detailed, and these Jews were often actually envied by many of us for their "cushy", if sad, job! If sufficient coffins were not available, which was often the case owing to the wholesale activity in death, the corpses were simply piled on top of each other.

The dissecting room was so small that the dissector could hardly move. His assistant, carrying out the opening of the head while he himself did the post-mortem examination of the chest and abdomen, frequently bumped against the walls.

Dissection was practised on all bodies where death certificates showed as the cause of death "suicide by hanging", or "suicide by electrocution", or "shot while escaping".

For a long time the post-mortem reports were kept from me. The first ones I saw consisted of ten to twelve typewritten lines, full of typing errors, and often containing half-finished sentences. They were made out by the S.D.G. (Medical Orderly), S.S. Oberscharführer Seehausen, who was attached to the sick ward.

He was a typical S.S. man, with no manners, an inferior education and of an animal-like disposition. Seehausen had little knowledge of typing and could not cope with the numerous Latin descriptions common to such reports. This meant that the dissector had to spell nearly every Latin word for him.

That fact may have led to the dissector demanding a better typist, particularly as corpses for post-mortems constantly increased in number. The dissector himself came from the Pathological Institute of the University of Jena and was, of course, an S.S. man.

In accordance with regulations, all writing had to be done by medical orderlies. For this, however, most of them were both lazy and incapable. Were another S.S. man to be requested for this purpose from the camp's administration centre, the camp commandant, Koch, would have to be asked. By so doing, the inefficiency of the medical orderlies would thereby be disclosed to him, a fact which would have led to unwelcome complications, considering his brutality towards even his own men.

In the end, a way was found by instructing me to make the necessary reports. Because of their negligence, or laziness, or through circumstances beyond the control of the medical orderlies, I had by now become familiar with all possible internal details, so that it did not matter to them or to the camp doctor if I became acquainted with yet another plague-spot.

So far, the experiments made with me had been satisfactory. Perhaps it was thought I would not understand what would be happening, for so far I had kept to myself all the shady matters I had seen. I could always be silenced, if necessary.

What mattered most to them was for the second camp commandant not to discover my activities. That exceptionally stupid and extremely rude Bavarian, Rödl, mattered less, although second in command to the camp doctor. It was thought that he could easily be deceived by our little tricks.

Nevertheless, we were once noticed. I do not know how Rödl's attention was drawn to my strictly prohibited activity in the mortuary. It may have been that he himself had watched me. It may also have been that some good S.S. comrade reported the matter to him; for those members of the S.S. who were not welded together by common interests through crime so that they had to keep their mouths shut against unwelcome revelations, were almost invariably hostile towards one another. Anyway, one day Rödl forbade me to attend the dissections.

Now, in the case of Rödl one could help oneself. I had to carry my typewriter and papers past Rödl's office window to the dissection room. We got round this by packing everything on a bier, which was covered with a woollen blanket, and, in charge of a medical orderly, all were carried as a corpse by bearers, another orderly bringing me to the mortuary by a long detour.

With the excuse of taking up the least possible space, I placed the typewriter on a shaky box in a corner near the door in such a manner that I could follow the dissection exactly.

The bearers had already placed the body on the dissecting table. They had to leave before the post-mortem began or, if several bodies were to be dissected, were ordered to remain in the second room with the other corpses.

No sooner had the dissector entered the barracks than he began to dictate, "Male corpse, about five feet seven inches in height, in a satisfactory state of nutrition. No outward recognisable injuries. Semi-round, evenly opened pupils . . ."

Again and again I found that the dissecting records were falsified and forged if necessary, as were almost all the other documents used in the camp. What the dissector was not to see, to find, to ascertain, he did not see, find or ascertain, or the other way round. The obvious facts did not trouble him, for he understood how to cleverly cover them up.

For example, shots in the abdomen were Buchenwald specialities in connection with shooting while escaping. The dissector brought variety to the otherwise monotonous records of post-mortems of this kind by constantly introducing new variations into his statements.

I do not know whether he ever noticed what peculiar "shooting-while-escaping" it was, when he had to carry out the post-mortem on twenty-one Jewish bodies, for in these cases the S.S. men had proved themselves to be master marksmen, all twenty-one bodies showing shots in the back of the neck at close range.

Now, I do not know whether a dissector has to worry about such peculiarities, but in any case, from the medical point of view, an examination of the head sufficed to ascertain the cause of death. Whatever there was beyond that, he probably considered the exclusive affair of the camp management. However, from his behaviour, I often concluded that he formed his own private opinions on these matters.

Neither the camp management nor the camp doctor appeared completely to trust their S.S. comrade. Regularly at night, previous to the new post-mortems, all available bodies were sent to the crematorium, while none of the prisoners who had died during the night were taken to the mortuary until the afternoon.

One day I attended the autopsy on the body of a work-shy prisoner—one of those rotten creatures who endeavoured to gain some advantage for themselves by acting as informers for the camp management. For some time past his fellow-prisoners had suspected this man of being an informer, and one evening this suspicion was confirmed. The result was that he received a thorough hiding.

The next morning, still incensed, some of the men set about him again while at work on a building site near the camp, and knocked him down with the shafts of their shovels. Others kicked the unconscious man, before throwing him in a pool.

The records of this case stated that the dead man had been found on the edge of the pool.

Before the post-mortem began, I had an opportunity to examine the body in detail. The head showed several gaping wounds, the bone above the temple being completely smashed, the right eye totally drained. The whole body showed innumerable contusions which had undoubtedly been caused by injuries from kicks and blows.

It was obvious that the man had been beaten to death by his fellow-prisoners.

I wondered how the camp commandant would deal with this disagreeable case. Clearly, the fact that the prisoner was dead could not be altered. As death had occurred outside the camp, some formal verdict had to be given.

Yet could the camp management admit that they could not avoid such an occurrence?—that anything like this could happen in the camp at all?

To charge the two prisoners mainly responsible for the murder would have led to a trial, which might have revealed many foul facts about the camp management. After all, one could not blame two murderers, fighting for their lives, for producing some evidence in their defence resulting in a charge against the camp authorities.

Yet the camp management not only had to cover themselves in all circumstances, but had also to assert their authority over the prisoners, seeing that the dead man had been an informer. The two prisoners were interrogated and placed under arrest, and an autopsy ordered.

I had to type the records. Before the post-mortem began, Dr. Ding had a short informative talk with the dissector, whom he informed that the management were interested in a speedy settlement of the matter without any complications.

The record began with a description of the external injuries to be seen on the body. It was by now already clear to me that the cause of death would not be attributed to the severe head injuries, nor to those other injuries to the chest and abdomen. When the chest was opened, I noticed that all the ribs on the right side were fractured. This evidence was not put on record. After the lungs had been examined, the record merely stated, "Alveoli filled with a whitish-yellow liquid. Nothing to report on other internal organs."

Upon opening the stomach, the dissector discovered something which he examined minutely, a small, slimy, tight lump which he carefully disentangled with little glass rods and then held against the light.

A piece of parchment? He looked at the paper through a magnifying glass and, spreading it out, held it again to the light.

I had to smile despite everything, seeing how much effort, with what a learned face, and how much university wisdom wasted itself on this piece of paper, obviously the paper skin of that small piece of floury, rubber-like sausage we prisoners had received the evening before. It was no wonder that the prisoner had swallowed the paper skin as well as the sausage, considering the degree of hunger which existed in the camp.

The dissector probably suspected a murder by poison, for, although making no note of his discovery in the record, he packed the paper carefully, no doubt to take home and examine microscopically and chemically.

No attempt was made to open the head, and "Death by sinking" was at last stated as the cause of death.

Death by sinking! That was something of which even Dr. Ding had not yet heard! But it was the ultima ratio of this case, for the two prisoners who had been arrested could now no longer be considered as murderers. The administration had done everything to clear up the matter carefully and in a far-seeing manner, so that no objection could be taken by anyone.

The examining magistrate could "justly" decide, upon viewing the records, whether or not the prisoners could be released from arrest, the public prosecutor had only to study the files to realise that it was not even necessary to open proceedings against anyone.

Everything, in fact, was clear: all, the camp management,

the political department, the criminal investigation police, the magistrates and the public prosecutor, would in turn "thoroughly" investigate the matter "independently of each other", without prejudice and with great care.

The prisoner was dead, the tragedy had passed, and the case had come to a happy end. On that day, the evidence which might possibly have caused some trouble was devoured by the flames of the Weimar crematorium.

4. The Suicide

TIME and again, after the many thousands of prisoners had assembled in the morning on the square and roll-call took a particularly long time to come, the loudspeakers would blare, "Room orderlies into the wood!"

We knew then that again someone had found the courage of despair and had voluntarily ended his camp torture. The block seniors would accompany the room orderlies as they went into the Buchenwald (Beech Wood), which was at the foot of the camp.

Often the search would last ten or twenty minutes, sometimes far longer, until a calling and howling would spread like a wave up to the camp and indicate that the "rotter" had been found. A Scharführer would assure himself of the identity of the body before roll-call was taken.

The incident made an impression on newcomers alone. The seasoned inmates remained completely unmoved, while the camp management certainly considered the affair in a most indifferent manner.

Cases of suicide by hanging were particularly numerous in the detention barracks. The reason for this fact was only too plain to us prisoners, for we knew Scharführer Sommer was in charge of the detention building, and he was always one of the party when a prisoner was tortured in a particularly cruel way, or even put to death.

We knew that, as a rule, detention for those prisoners who

113

had been noticed—that is, who had committed something against what the camp management called camp discipline—usually meant the last short halt before the long journey from which nobody has yet returned.

Of course, post-mortems were carried out even on these bodies, for post-mortem records were the best and most determinate conclusion to a camp file.

It was not until I had attended many suicide post-mortems that I noticed how the dissector sometimes took special interest in the strangulation implements. While he usually cut through any rope with which the poor devils had ended their lives and carelessly threw it away, he sometimes picked up any other thing they used—pants, stockings, a rag of a towel, or whatever had been used for hanging themselves. He would look at the knot, and then leave it on the dissecting table.

At one post-mortem this behaviour was so noticeable that I made up my mind to have a good look at the tattered shirt the suicide had used. But after the completion of the post-mortem, the shirt had gone.

Still, my attention had been aroused, and from then on I looked for, and invariably found, an opportunity to inspect the strangulation implement more closely and unobtrusively. I never found anything peculiar—always a noose knotted sometimes to the right, sometimes to the left; sometimes quite simply, sometimes very carefully knotted.

But one day the body of a prisoner was on the dissecting table with no noose around his neck—just a knot, a double one, the so-called sailor's knot. It did not require the trained eye of a detective to discern what this peculiar type of suicide meant. It did not require the acute logic of a C.I.D. inspector to come to the correct conclusion about the matter. No eyewitness was needed to state that this man had not hanged himself at all but was hanged by someone else!

Again the dissector closely inspected the knot, again he threw it carelessly on the table, and, after the internal organs had been replaced, the strangulation had disappeared as usual. The assistant sewed up the incisions, and a short time later the flames of the crematorium in Weimar, Gotha or Eisenach finally destroyed the last shred of circumstantial evidence there might have been against any criminal involved.

5. The Fate of a Prisoner

ONE exceptionally sunny morning I was sitting alone in the surgery and rattling off more or less stereotyped death certificates on my typewriter. I had a great deal to do and was in a hurry.

The loudspeaker suddenly crackled, calling the prisoners' clothing store. As this had nothing to do with me, I hardly listened, and continued to pound the keys of my typewriter. Vaguely, I knew that there was some talk of a clothing bag.

My typewriter rattled on. What did it matter? My own number, 996, was not mentioned, and my reports were more important to get through. Probably some prisoner was to be discharged, or perhaps it was something to do with the clothing bag of a prisoner who had died and whose private articles were to be dispatched or handed over to someone else.

My work was urgent—the sad, monotonous work, to which I had now become so accustomed that all the untruths I typed appeared like the endlessly long, unimportant figures of a ledger clerk, who might register them without knowing where they came from or where they went, lifeless figures because he would not know what they implied or what values they actually represented.

An excited comrade entered the room.

"There, Walter!" he exclaimed. "Did you hear? That was Opitz's number!"

Opitz? I interrupted my work. Opitz?—the Kapo from the photography department? What did this mean? Surely he had protection enough, for which of the S.S. men, Scharführer and Sturmführer, had he not obliged with a small private favour?

"It won't be so bad," I returned, casually.

"Do you think so?" he said, and, seeing I had a great deal to do, left me alone.

I rattled off the sentence I had started, before continuing the imaginary sick reports with their constant new variations, until I reached the words "despite the most careful attention the unavoidable could not be prevented".

Opitz? Well, I knew him, a charming fellow, a pleasant

115

comrade. Perhaps he had been lucky and had been discharged. He already had several years of concentration camp life behind him and, who knew, with his photography perhaps he had managed to get round some influential Sturmführer. Best of luck, comrade!

I put another sheet of paper into the typewriter, ready to deal with the next death certificate according to files. Although I was not unaware of the causes of the prisoner's death, I had the record card at hand which we prisoners made out on arrival and on which all past illnesses had been noted.

"Had already been under treatment for enlargement of the liver," I read. That could therefore have been the cause of his death. There were books with case histories, and instructions for treatment were also noted.

This would be a classical case with classical treatment. Indeed, the mode of treatment could not have been better even at the best of clinics. Any expert who would have to read the report would admire the camp doctor for his masterly diagnosis of the sick man's illness. There was no hint of a mistake.

That the patient had died in the end—well, we human beings must all die once; for apparently all that was humanly possible had been done in this case. Thus it was stated, in black and white, logically and expertly, without any lies or inventions!

I put a fresh sheet of paper in the typewriter.

Midday came at last. The prisoners engaged in front of the administrative barracks entered the camp for an hour. The photographic detachment was missing and the rumours ran like wildfire through the camp—Opitz was under arrest, the other prisoners were isolated and were being individually interrogated. Nobody really knew precisely what had happened.

Opitz was no ordinary prisoner. Many knew him because each prisoner was photographed in his department upon arrival at the camp.

All those political prisoners knew him without exception who were in the camp because of their membership or activity in anti-Nazi movements. He was one of those men who stood above political trends. He was like a sad heritage of former times, which spread its influence in the camp but would sometimes unfortunately arouse opposition of the most regrettable nature. Quiet, frank, sincere, interested in all that was good and fine, always helpful, of an active mind, always on top of a situation, he was a steadying power even here in the turbulent life of the camp.

I had often spoken to him about political matters, economic problems, cultural affairs, questions on art, and had philosophised with him about God and the world. Fundamentally he was a kind man, a decent character through and through.

Never had we inquired of each other in which movement we had formerly been active. All personal, private matters were as much of a secondary nature to him as they were to me, and never did we allow the flow of our ideas to slip into the usual, understandable, yet comparatively unimportant sphere of personal fate.

We were both fully aware of the necessity, beyond all former political and worldly differences, of a united movement with the noblest and highest ideals of humanity, in order to clear up the wreckage which National Socialism was bound to bring about in time. He believed, as I did, in the final victory of the best in man, and, with me, was prepared one day to give his best to exterminate Nazism and to rebuild a dignified, just and comfortable world.

He belonged to those few of the camp elite who were willing and determined to fight to the last if—as all knowing and politically trained minds expected—the S.S. henchmen, in final desperation, should resort to liquidating the prisoners in the camp so that they could draw a final line under all its horrors and terrors. He was one of those men of action who do not suggest the stereotyped fanatic, but are the only, the real, the true and the most noble of all fanatics.

It was hard to credit Opitz as being under arrest. Still, although this fact was bad enough, it was not quite hopeless; for Opitz was one of those personalities who spread an atmosphere around them even in their silence. His physical bearing, his expression, his clear, frank, noble eyes, his high, intelligent forehead, all united to produce an immediate impression upon one. In addition, Opitz was a man of initiative. In how many critical situations had I found myself defenceless and at the mercy of the Nazi criminals, and yet I got through! Should luck not also be on his side? I thought.

Later in the afternoon, the first prisoners from the photographic department returned. We then learnt that his arrest concerned a photograph which had been found in Opitz's clothing bag. A photograph? I did not know what kind of photograph it could be, but I did now realise that he was condemned.

After roll-call, Opitz was brought from detention. He was tied to the stock and whipped. Not one cry of pain crossed his lips. Twenty-five terrible bows with a steel whip rained down on him. Yet he remained conscious. He rose from the stock without assistance, walked up to the Obersturmbannführer Rödl, and made his report of the duly executed punishment. Yet he was not freed, as we had hoped for a moment. He was put back under arrest; and this was the last time I saw Rudolf Opitz alive.

That evening I learnt more. On the black 6th of December, 1937, two political prisoners, Johannes Bremer from Harburg and Oskar Fischer from Berlin, were called out during a roll-call and were taken through the gate by two armed S.S. men. A short time afterwards shots rang out.

Nobody could explain why the two men had been shot. I knew, however, that Bremer was a friend of Opitz.

For some reason, the two bodies were then photographed. It may be that S.S. Standartenführer Koch, the camp commander, wanted a spicy addition to his Buchenwald Museum.

Opitz had to develop the photographs and at the same time procured one of his friend for himself. Then he got a trusted prisoner from the clothing store to let him have a family photograph from his clothing bag, pasted it carefully on the reverse side and had it returned to his bag.

The photograph had been discovered, obviously through some deplorable treachery. We tried naturally to discover the traitor, but our inquiries were in vain. Those S.S. men with whom we prisoners had contact and would have given us the traitor's name knew nothing, while the rogues who probably did would give nothing away.

About eight days later, the detention barracks ordered us to make out a death certificate for our comrade Rudolf Opitz . . . Suicide by hanging . . . Post-mortem ordered for the day after tomorrow.

His body had already been laid out when I entered the mortuary. There he was now, my good comrade, my friend in spirit and in deed, cold and rigid. The pallor of death kindly concealed the traces of the bestial maltreatment which he had been compelled to suffer during the last days of his ordeal. His eyes were closed, and on the peaceful face and the high, clean forehead was imprinted the inexpressible, majestic spirit of a great and noble man.

The cord round his neck did not show a noose, but was merely knotted.

6. The Stock

THERE are certainly many people who would have been shocked could they have seen one of those forms which the Nazis used in connection with the reintroduction of corporal punishment. Some people will even be shocked to learn that the Nazis really carried out on grown up men an aspect of mediaeval punishment.

Perhaps there are still people who consider that such punishment was in order. If so, I dedicate this chapter to them, with the heartfelt wish that they could themselves have felt on their own bodies the full effect of such a punishment.

I recapitulate from memory. The sheet of paper which was used in connection with the punishment by flogging was a yellow foolscap form, printed on both sides and divided into several columns. It was most carefully prepared. Dashes were printed where entries were to be made or information to be given, and dotted lines provided where signatures had to be appended.

First came the prisoner's personal data, including the reason for and length of his imprisonment, then the act which had been perpetrated, with the signature of the S.S. man who could give evidence of the case; further came the proposed amount of punishment—5, 10, 15, 20 or 25 strokes with a stick, perhaps —and information requested as to how many times and with how many strokes the prisoner had been previously flogged, together with the result of a medical examination as to whether the culprit's state of health would permit the execution of the new punishment.

The authorisation of the Reichsführer S.S. (Himmler) or his deputy to carry out the punishment was to be given, in connection with which it was emphasised that this was not to be carried out without approval in writing.

There was a column for confirmation that the punishment had been carried out, with two dotted lines for the signatures of both the S.S. man who carried out the punishment and the person who supervised it.

Detailed instructions were given on how the punishment was to be executed. It was forbidden to tie the prisoner down when carrying out this task, or to hold him down, or to strip him, or to apply more strokes than were authorised. It was expressly stated that the culprit had to lie freely over the stock.

The size of the canes for the birching were exactly prescribed, as were the parts of the body allowed to be struck. Immediately before and after the punishment had been inflicted, the camp doctor had to state the results of his examination in two columns given for this purpose, and to sign that he had been present at its execution.

Altogether, it was a well prepared form, and I wish with all my heart that those who support corporal punishment could be given merely five strokes of the birch under strict observance of such printed regulations. Although I know that five strokes à la Buchenwald would be far more applicable to such people, I would not wish them that, for these were in a special class of their own.

The stock used in Buchenwald stood at the top end of the camp, at the gate alongside the detention barracks, and was only placed behind the barracks to be out of sight of any unauthorised witness.

It was a big tub, the height of a table, on a rough wooden frame. A mechanism tightly fastened the legs of the prisoner below the bend of the knee to the support of the frame, a second mechanism fastened his body to the tub by a broad strap across the back. If at some time the fastening arrangement for the legs broke, or the Scharführer were too lazy to shackle the legs, the prisoner had to place his feet behind a wooden crossbar which was connected with the supports of the frame, and lie across the stock in this awkward position.

When the day after my arrival in Buchenwald I had walked through the gate with my labour detachment, I had seen the execution of corporal punishment for the first time. Later, I saw innumerable and even more cruel floggings. Again and again the sight of them caused a choking in my throat; but none stirred me more than had the first one.

We had still been some distance from the gate, with the camp's band droning on, an unceasing beating of time, magnified by the loudspeakers. Yet in spite of the din we newcomers could hear the terrible screams of pain. Frightened, we looked for the cause, not dreaming of connecting such terrible cries with the stock and corporal punishment.

As we marched closer to the gate, we had seen the execution of the punishment. We were magnetised by the terrible scene and hardly needed our Kapo to call out to us, in a loud, brutal voice, "Newcomers! Eyes right! Look at this! That is how you will be flogged if you do not work enough. That fellow on the stock there was lazy at his work."

I did not notice the fact until it came to my mind later at my work, while I was still inwardly upset as I thought about the scene I had witnessed; but strangely enough, the Kapo himself did not look at the flogging. It had not been long, however, before I had learned that there was nothing strange in this fact. Corporal punishment was so often carried out in Buchenwald that one soon became indifferent to its sight. One had to have a close interest in the flogged man, or some personal reason, to force one to look more closely at the proceedings.

We had come still nearer to the stock. With horror, we had soon seen the worn figure strapped to it. His terrible screams of pain resounded in our ears. We saw the twisted pain-stricken features of the prisoner, distorted by the fear of death. He was strapped down in such a manner that he could only move his head.

We saw an S.S. Scharführer wielding a thick, flexible stick with wide-reaching actions as he swung it with all the force of which he was capable, letting it crack down on the fettered man. Again and again we heard the stick whistling through the air, to land with a loud smack on the prisoner's buttocks, and he howled like an animal.

Meanwhile, the camp band had gone on blowing, thumping its march into our feet. Our Kapo warned us that we must go on marching. As we emerged by the gate along the Karacho Way to our place of work, we had felt lumps in our throats, as for a long time we still envisioned the horror before us.

On our return that evening, marching through the gate again, worn out, exhausted, at the end of my strength, in large letters above the entrance to the camp I saw, "Right or Wrong, My Fatherland!"

I was then too exhausted to meditate on the fact that the very people who claimed exclusively the copyrights of everything German should make such doubtful alien words their watch-word. Yet when I later passed the stock which stood lonely, forlorn and inexpressibly silent, I realised for the first time in my life that Cicero's "Ubi bene, ibi patria" had an intrinsic justification. My Fatherland is Germany and always will be, but henceforth I cannot be angry with any German who, having once gone through the stock in Buchenwald, chooses as a result the words, "Where I am happy, that is my Fatherland."

During my time as a prisoner in Buchenwald, not one of the many thousands of whippings was carried out in accordance with the regulations stipulated on the forms. Hardly one of a hundred whippings was dealt with by filling in a form for the files. I know this to be so, because such forms had to be submitted to the camp doctor for signature, and I myself had to pass on each document for that purpose. The S.S. men were far too lazy to deal with each case of flogging even formally.

When the regulations were carried out, however, it was because the Supreme S.S. Security Office in Berlin had to be shown that such matters were dealt with in the camp, and that Office could thus prove this point with documentary evidence. Clearly, to everybody concerned form-filling in connection with flogging was just so much camouflage.

Cases which were actually written down on forms proved to be still more unpleasant for those involved, leading as they did to a second whipping for the same infringement.

The regulation that an authorisation to carry out a punishment was first to be obtained from Berlin was a paper one; for all the whippings were carried out immediately after the punishable act had been established or discovered.

As long as I was the doctor's clerk there was no single case in which a prisoner had first been examined by a doctor to see whether his state of health would permit punishment being given him. In no case was a medical examination performed immediately before the punishment was carried out.

And after the whipping? If the camp doctor happened to pass by after a mass-whipping, and knew that a certain type of homosexual Scharführer and S.S. officer stood at the gate, he arranged a little special entertainment for them, which he called a medical examination.

In no case was medical examination applied if the corporal punishment resulted in injuries; in fact, the nurses were specifically forbidden to treat the victims, and if they did so, it was at their own risk.

In almost all cases the prisoner was strapped to the stock. Twenty-five strokes were the maximum allowed according to written instructions, but in reality thirty, forty, fifty and more strokes were given, depending on the toughness of the prisoner concerned, and whether the intention was to whip him into unconsciousness.

According to regulations, the number of strokes had to be counted aloud by the Scharführer. In practice the prisoner did this, and if, due to the pain, he forgot to do so, the original five strokes which may have been ordered were often increased to thirty or more, depending upon the Scharführer's mood.

When a mass punishment took place in the camp—that is, hundreds of totally innocent men were picked out to be whipped—the Scharführer sometimes satisfied themselves with two or three strokes on each person instead of the five ordered, simply because they had become tired after hours of flogging and had lost interest in the whole business.

The type of whips to be used were laid down by regulations, but were seldom as stated. Instead, there were flexible sticks soaked in water, or leather dog whips, or horse whips, or hard cudgels or even steel whips. The Scharführer wore flogging gloves to prevent injury to themselves and to keep their hands from becoming sore.

It did occasionally happen that a punishment was not as brutal as usual. This was sometimes the case when S.S. Standartenführer Koch or S.S. Obersturmbannführer Rödl had ordered a whipping which was quite exceptionally unjustified and S.S. Hauptscharführer Strippel or S.S. Oberscharführer Bergmann were ordered to carry out the punishment.

Then it happened that the prisoners suffered only very little, for these two S.S. men had developed the fine art of appearing to beat a man more cruelly than they actually did.

Unfortunately, Strippel and Bergmann carried out comparatively few whippings, while the other gangsters in "Adolf Hitler's black uniform of honour" did not trouble about such mere details as to whether or not a punishment was justified.

At various times during the carrying out of a punishment, I watched Obersturmbannführer Rödl, who was actually mad on flogging.

When he was at the gate, after a flogging each prisoner had to report to him on these lines: "Work-shy prisoner No. 13714 punished with ten strokes because of laziness at work", or "Political prisoner No. 7063 punished with five strokes because I could not keep step in the marching column", or "Criminal prisoner No. 11689 punished with five strokes because I spat on the square during roll-call."

When a fairly long line of delinquents stood against the wall of the detention barracks for punishment, I often watched Rödl walk up and down the line to muster them critically, obviously choosing some special victim. When they were lying on the stock, he patted their faces with his hands during the execution of the punishment, and pressed the lower part of his body against the structure.

On the same level was the tasteful idea of allowing the camp band to play a merry tune while a number of prisoners were being whipped; once I even knew of Rödl having a violin solo played at the same time.

I have already indicated the types of offences which were punished by whipping. On one occasion a prisoner did not know why he had received his punishment of five strokes of the whip. Rödl immediately ordered another five strokes to be given him. Even after this the victim had no notion of the reason for his punishment.

Actually, Rödl had a slip of paper on which an S.S. man had reported Prisoner No. so-and-so for smoking at his place of work. The number belonged to the man who had been whipped.

But when Rödl told him, "Because, you swine, you nearly blew up the barrels of petrol in the garage with your damned smoking," the prisoner returned, "Herr Obersturmbannführer, I beg to report that I have never been in the garage. I work in the camp laundry."

"What? What?" Rödl stuttered with surprise, and after a short pause said, "Call the Kapo from the laundry."

The laundry Kapo was summoned through the loudspeaker and confirmed that the man who had been punished had worked for a long time in the camp laundry. Obviously the guard had made a mistake in the number he had reported.

Rödl settled by the matter by saying, "Well, that's all right. You have now ten in advance. When you are to receive twenty-five again, report to me, then you will only get fifteen."

The blood trickled through the prisoner's trousers, and a few days later he had to enter the sick ward for a long time, for owing to the maltreatment he had developed a serious illness.

I remember another case. In the immediate neighbourhood of the camp, masses of soil were being removed in a very primitive way. Narrow gauge rails had been laid down a steep slope. One column of prisoners carried the hods filled with earth to the tip-up waggons, while another had the task of guiding the full waggons down the slope to the dumping ground.

The speed of the waggons was regulated by wedging a strong beam between the wheels. Despite this, they sometimes still got out of control, so ropes were attached on the left and right sides so that six prisoners on each side could control the speed. Because of this, the downward journey proved mostly satisfactory.

Once, nevertheless, a tip-up waggon gathered speed of its own accord and most of the men let go the ropes. Having unwisely fixed the loop round his shoulder, one man could not free himself and had to accompany the vehicle on its furious journey down the slope, being dragged along on the last few yards of its ride.

Although he had nothing whatever to do with this labour column, a second prisoner hurried to assist his comrade. Unfortunately for him, at that moment S.S. Standartenführer Koch came on the scene. Without a word, he took down the numbers of the two prisoners and then went on his way.

In the evening the two men each received a punishment of ten strokes of the whip.

7. Sterilisation and Castration

DURING my time at Buchenwald about two hundred prepared files in connection with cases of castration and sterilisation were lying in the drawer of the camp doctor's table, having been drawn up by the former doctor, Kirchert. These had not yet been settled, nor did Dr. Ding show any special interest in them.

These files consisted of a cover, with the name of the prisoner who had been considered for castration or sterilisation, and two sheets of paper. One sheet contained the personal data of the prisoner and a register of previous convictions of sexual misbehaviour, as stated by him; and the other showed a printed declaration, according to which the prisoner himself voluntarily applied for the operation. Although a number of these had already been signed, on many a dotted line merely indicated the place for the prisoner's signature.

An order requested the political department to report to the camp doctor the name of every prisoner whose file showed him to be afflicted with schizophrenia, epilepsy, innate imbecility, insanity or dipsomania, or had been previously convicted for indecent assault.

In view of the carelessness and stupidity with which these files were compiled, few reports were actually made, and invariably it required a hint from the camp doctor to secure names from the political department.

The card index kept in the sick ward by prisoners were seldom produced by them. Only in the cases of homosexual prisoners was an exception made, for the camp doctor had ordered a special card index system to be used for certain groups of prisoners, among them the homosexuals, in order to make them easily distinguishable from the others. It was regarded as a matter of course that homosexual prisoners were to be castrated.

It is quite plain that there was no legal basis for such a compulsory castration or sterilisation, the regulation being carried out only if voluntary application was made, with the recommendation of at least two doctors. But this was a formal means to satisfy an inhuman attitude of mind or some sadistic and animal-like desires of those who carried out the operations.

It goes without saying that no prisoner really voluntarily applied for his own castration or sterilisation, but in each case was summoned by the doctor and forced to make the application.

In many cases the doctor had only to utter a few energetic words to him to make the prisoner sign without hesitation, the atmosphere of the camp having forced him into a state of inopposition.

After he had been instructed by fellow-prisoners as to how he should make his report, the prisoner was taken into the surgery to give his signature.

The doctor sat behind the writing desk, an ominous file in front of him, the orderlies in the background. The prisoner entered the surgery in stockinged feet, adopted a smart bearing before the writing desk and reported, "Work-shy prisoner No. —— reports!"

The doctor would then pretend to study the file, without giving the prisoner as much as a look. The ensuing silence made the man still more uncertain of himself than he was before.

After the lapse of two or three minutes, the doctor would look up slowly and say, at first leisurely and quietly but ending in a roar, "Well, you swine. You are quite a special type. What all isn't there against you? But still, now we have got

you. We don't dally here! It certainly would be better for you
if you were not here at all, you dirty dog! But at least we will
prevent any more pigs like you running about! You'll be
sterilised now, understand?"

Then he would add quickly, quietly and in a businesslike
tone which expected compliance, "Here, make it short. Sign!"

In most cases the prisoners obeyed without even reading the
application. If the victim made the slightest attempt to question or to object, a few blows or kicks from the orderlies helped
to settle him, and he signed the form with a shaking hand.
Only in a very few cases did the voluntary signing cause any
greater difficulties than these.

8. *The Case of the Protesting Jew*

AFTER serving a term of imprisonment for an offence against
the Nuremberg Racial Laws, Julius Meier, a Jew of about
twenty years of age, was sent to the Buchenwald concentration
camp. He was a tall, strong, very healthy lad, intelligent,
educated, modest and not to be recognised as a Jew had he not
described himself as one.

For the initiated, it was clear from the beginning that his
was a comparatively harmless case of racial disgrace by intercourse between a Jew and an "Aryan". At that time a term of
imprisonment was only passed by the courts if all relevant
circumstances proved that such an intercourse took place with
the consent of the acquainted partner, without the Jew having
taken advantage of a condition of dependence, or making a
promise, or offering various inducements as a means of exert-
ing pressure on his partner.

The files which the camp doctor had demanded after Meier
had been reported to him by the political department, showed
the following facts: For some time Meier had had intercourse
with his parents' housemaid, whose reputation in matters of
sex was not very good. Neighbours observed incidents one day
from which they concluded that there was intimacy between

A dreadful piece of equipment: the infamous whipping-block.

Inmates massed for roll call: a long, exhausting procedure which for the weak became an ordeal of endurance.

One of the rare pictures of the camp hospital. The doctor's room was to the right, not visible in this photograph.

Memento mori, Nazi style: human skin makes a lamp shade and other carefully tattooed items for the discerning connoisseur.

Shot, impaled on the wire, bodies such as this would sometimes remain for days as a grim warning to those still alive.

A typical group, not in the final stages of emaciation but certainly men for whom hunger had taken on a new meaning.

New inmates, packed into their bunks and still, as yet, reasonably clothed. How many would survive the first year?

EXTRACT FROM CAMP ORDERS:

Every prisoner has the right to send and receive two letters or postcards
per month. The writing must be well spaced and legible. Mail which does
not comply with this regulation will not be accepted, i.e. forwarded. No
parcels of any description may be received. Money may be received but in
the form of money-orders. Money must not be enclosed in the letter. Information must not be sent on the counterfoils. Any infringement of this
rule means confiscation. Everything is on sale in the camp. National Socialist
newspapers are allowed but must be bought by the prisoner from the camp
post office. Illegible and obscure letters will be destroyed. The dispatch of
pictures and photographs is forbidden.

THE CAMP COMMANDANT

*This was the heading to inmates' letter-forms. The pictures which follow add
a postscript more eloquent than any words.*

The quarry, scene of nightmares for many a survivor.

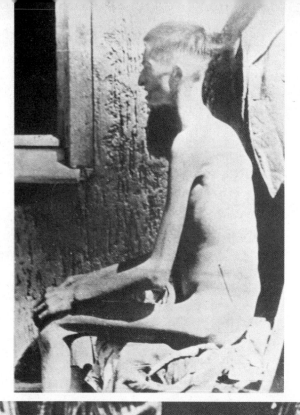

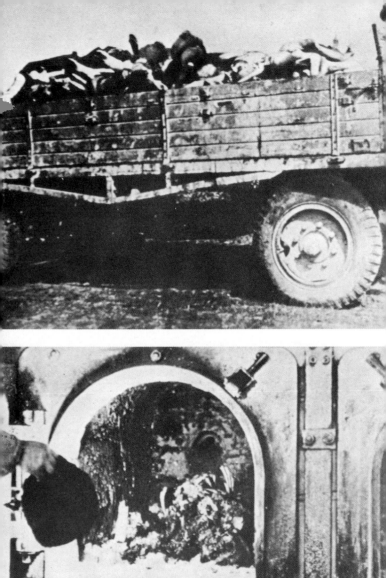

Meier and the girl. One informed against the pair. Both parties were arrested and admitted "racial disgrace", in connection with which the contradictory statements of the housemaid herself, naturally wanting to make it appear that she had been raped, were not believed even by the court. Meier would without doubt have received a far heavier sentence of imprisonment had the maid lied a little more intelligently.

It was never clear to me why the doctor wanted to carry out castration on this particular Jew, for other cases of racial disgrace existed where castration could have been effected with far more pretence of legality.

Perhaps the doctor himself had decided on this operation, perhaps it was suggested by Rödl, whose speciality it was to pick out one case from a thousand others which he entirely ignored; perhaps the suggestion came from the camp commandant, S.S. Standartenführer Koch, who was supposed to read through the records of all newcomers, but only occasionally did so when his attention was drawn to a particular file.

I do not know the truth, but to me it seemed extremely unlikely that the doctor himself first thought of the idea, as he had plenty of other files in his desk from which he could have conveniently picked a case.

The danger in which Meier found himself was quite clear to him, for, like all offenders against the racial laws, he too had been detailed to a penal detachment, and the frivolity and want of consideration with which prisoners were castrated or earmarked for this was no secret to them. The degenerate Nazi beasts considered that sexual intercourse between Jews and "Aryans" constituted a major sexual crime.

Meier knew, however, that his relations were doing their utmost to get his emigration papers put in order. In those days, Jews who possessed valid emigration papers, and had nothing against them politically, were released from the camp on the understanding that they would leave Germany within forty-eight hours.

Several times in my experience the files in connection with castration or sterilisation had been temporarily put aside if a prisoner withstood the pressure applied to him and refused to sign the necessary paper. Of course I did what I could to remove these files from the immediate view of the doctor whenever I could, and therefore knew that if Meier refused to give his signature, he still had a chance to escape.

The doctor usually arrived between nine and ten o'clock and prisoners ordered to see him were taken to the surgery immediately after the morning roll-call, there to take up their position alongside the barracks until his arrival. This gave me the opportunity of talking to Meier in advance and to find that he was determined not to sign.

Meier's manner and bearing were perfect when he stood before the doctor. He allowed the barrage of the doctor's words to descend upon him, without moving. Not a quiver, not an involuntary movement of his body, not a flash of his eyes, betrayed what was going on within him.

When ordered to sign, he walked quietly up to the desk, took up the pen, and read the typed application. Then he replaced the pen on the desk, looked firmly at Dr. Ding, and said, in a clear, quiet voice which showed no emotion, "I cannot sign that."

This statement sounded so definite and so modest, so natural and matter of fact, so quiet and yet so disarming, so superior and yet so unassuming, that one was transported out of the office to another and saner world. Such a situation was fascinating because it was so out of keeping with what usually happened in the camp, and it was no wonder that Dr. Ding, whom I had never seen lost for words, had nothing to say for three, four, five seconds. Even the two orderlies. Oberscharführer Seehausen and Scharführer Hofmann, remained in the background without remembering that, according to programme, they were to beat the prisoner into submission.

Then Dr. Ding broke the silence. "Why not?" he shouted, sharply and domineeringly.

Without any hesitation, Meier answered quietly and modestly, "I have been sentenced for an offence under the racial laws and have undergone my term of imprisonment. I have bound myself in writing to leave Germany immediately. The greater part of my emigration papers are already in order. As soon as they are all complete, I will leave Germany at once."

Ding composed himself. "Oh? Leave Germany at once?" he interrupted Meier, as if highly amused. "And you believe, you swine, that we will let you loose on humanity, just like that? That's what you thought, eh? So that you can exhaust yourself in your perverted obscenities, ha? No, cesspool! Here! Sign!"

Meier stood motionless and repeated once again, "Herr Sturmführer, I cannot sign that."

"You cannot? What?—cannot? We will see about that."

In the meantime Seehausen had advanced from the background. He kicked Meier brutally, hitting him with his fist two or three times with full force in the face so that blood immediately poured from his nose and mouth. Meier staggered backwards a little, but again got hold of himself, adopted the prescribed smart bearing, and steadfastly looked Dr. Ding in the eyes, taking no notice of Seehausen.

"You can be made to do anything here, my lad!" said Dr. Ding, leaning back in his chair and placing his hands on his hips. His voice sounded so superior, so self-assured, so merciless and brutal, it would have frightened the devil himself. "We will teach you that, you swine, whether you believe it or not! You are not in a sanatorium here, you flatfoot! You think you can put on your airs and graces here, eh! Either you sign or we will finish you off!"

Meier still remained completely unmoved. One could distinctly see that he heard every word, but he gave no sign to show whether this attempt to intimidate him had any effect on him.

Blood trickled from his nose and mouth; it dropped on his chest and from there to the floor.

When Seehausen saw this, he set himself in front of Meier and, imitating the sound of his lord and master's voice, bellowed at the stricken Jew, "What? Making a mess on our floor here? You pig! You son of a whore! You cesspool!" At each sentence the S.S. Oberscharführer hit him with full force in the face with his fist.

Yet Meier stood there, although he staggered at each blow, making no movement in defence. The stoicism with which he patiently bore this ill-treatment was unbelievable.

One could feel that all this show was leading nowhere. This Jew, who had only been a short time in the camp and was therefore still in possession of his physical and spiritual powers, would rather let himself be killed than sign.

But Seehausen, that dull hireling, could only think slowly. "What do you actually imagine, you nitwit, you!" Again the blows rained down on his victim. "Can't you see that, you lump of muck?" and he pointed with his sausage-like finger to the blobs of blood spreading on the floor.

Without a word, Meier pulled out his handkerchief, stooped and wiped up the splashes of blood. Seehausen kicked him. Meier fell with every kick, but got up again each time, and continued to wipe the floor. He made no single movement to defend or to protect himself. Dr. Ding gave Seehausen a sign to stop.

When Meier had finished his task, he again stood upright, and, unwavering, almost like a statue, stared at the doctor. I saw him straighten himself, expanding his chest and throwing his head slightly backwards, as if he carried not only his own pride, but also, by way of an order ages old, his part of the pride of a people who, as long as man has striven for happiness and peace, have again and again been crucified.

"I'll tell you something," Dr. Ding said, at the same time narrowing his eyes, talking through his teeth, and giving his voice a satanic intonation: "I will give you twenty-four hours for reflection. You will be here again tomorrow morning. Then the little dance will start afresh if, in the meantime, you have not thought it over. Don't think it will be as simple then as today. We still have a whole bagful of nice things for you. Then you will experience something!" He suddenly roared like a bull, "Get out!"

Meier calmly turned about in the prescribed smart manner and walked to the door. On his way he received another terrible kick, this time from Hofmann. After Meier had closed the door behind him, Ding laughed artificially, his two henchmen joining in the laughter.

In cynical tones, Seehausen said, slowly and drawlingly, "What a cesspool!" But I could clearly see that the three torturers did not feel happy after this experience of defiance.

Shortly after midday, and after the doctor had finished his two or three hours' duty, Seehausen came to me before the orderlies could disappear, and said, "You needn't make out a chit for Meier."

So-called Surgery Report Chits were made out for prisoners

who were to be treated in the surgery during the day, or had the previous evening been recommended for treatment by nurses, after having been reported sick, or because the doctor demanded to see them for examination.

Such chits had to be signed by the doctor or by an orderly, but it had become a custom that they could be signed by the senior nurse or the doctor's clerk, just as we could sign the first death reports required for the roll-call report, if neither doctor nor orderlies were in the camp, mostly the case in twenty out of twenty-four hours. The chit had to be submitted by the prisoner to his Kapo, and it authorised him to remain in the camp for that day.

We had made a list of the names and numbers of prisoners to whom we were unable to hand out such chits. This list was given to the controller of the roll-call, who then read the numbers out through the loudspeakers at the morning roll-call. The prisoners called in this way had to report to Sign No. 2, from where they were all taken together to the surgery. Anyone round still in the camp without such an authorisation, or who could not prove that he was engaged on necessary work there, was cruelly punished, so that hardly anybody dared to shirk his daily task.

It was instantly clear to me what Seehausen's order meant. I therefore called on the senior of the penal detachment and informed him what had happened. We found the following way out: Meier was detailed to that part of the penal detachment which worked within the camp, and the Kapo was instructed to let Meier work near the surgery, in order to be within easy reach of me.

On the following morning, naturally, Meier was not among those waiting alongside the barracks to report to the surgery, but I saw part of the penal detachment working close by. When Dr. Ding ordered me to call in Meier, I went outside the barracks as usual and called out his name in a loud voice.

I saw that Seehausen was completely taken aback by surprise as I re-entered the surgery with Meier. By his first question I perceived that Ding was also a party to the vile game they had intended to play on the Jew.

"From where do you come?" he demanded.

133

His face swollen and bruised, Meier answered, "From work, Herr Sturmführer."

"What do you mean, from work?"

"I work along the road out here, Herr Sturmführer."

Now once more Julius Meier refused to sign the form "in order to rid myself of my perverted sexual instincts I herewith voluntarily apply for my castration", and again the terrible torture began.

I could see that Meier was softening, yet as soon as he was told to sign the application, he shook his head. Again and again and again! And then he fainted.

Seehausen poured water on his face until he slowly revived and was pushed to his feet. He could only keep upright with difficulty.

Seehausen pressed the pen into his hand. But Meier still did not sign. Suddenly his body quivered and shook, his eyes flickered, and in a voice which would have melted a heart of stone, he said, "But I am engaged, Sturmführer. My fiancee is waiting for me. When my papers are in order, I will leave Germany at once."

"Sign!" Ding demanded. "And you can leave Germany alive!"

Meier shook his head.

"I'll give you half an hour to think it over," Ding said.

Seehausen took Meier out of the surgery and let him stand in the lavatory with his arms raised above his head.

After the lapse of half an hour, Meier was brought back, but still refused, shaking his head silently.

Ding gave up, even Seehausen and Hofmann allowing the poor devil to leave the room unmolested.

The next day Julius Meier was taken to the detention barracks. When, after twelve days, he was again brought before the camp doctor, he was a pitiful sight. Though there were no more traces of severe ill-treatment on his face, he looked as if he came from the grave.

He was painfully thin, his cheeks hollow, his eyes looked out from deep, black-rimmed sockets, the skin of his face, fresh and healthy a fortnight before, was withered and of a terrible yellow pallor, his body bent and shrivelled.

If I had not seen the evidence with my own eyes, I could

never have believed that the body of a healthy, strapping man of athletic build could change so greatly in twelve days.

"You probably did not know what goes on here?" Ding said to him, and his voice was quiet and matter of fact.

"No, Herr Sturmführer," Meier answered weakly.

"Do you want to leave the detention barracks again?"

"I would like to, Sturmführer."

Ding's voice was now quiet and persuasive. If anyone had heard his words with no knowledge of the previous happenings, they would have convinced themselves that the doctor was a fatherly friend of the poor fellow who stood before him, so broken and so dangerously ill.

"Well, then, be sensible and sign."

A pause, only lasting seconds, and yet seeming to be endlessly long. It was as if a lead cupola had been placed over the surgery; as if the room existed out of this world.

Julius Meier stood motionless in the centre of the surgery, staring before him and breathing quickly and heavily. He was obviously struggling with himself. Would he sign? Would he now take the pen, ready there for him?

Ding pushed the typewritten sheet towards him, dipped the pen into the ink, and put it on the edge of the table.

Meier looked at the pen, then lifted both arms slightly in a hopeless gesture, saying sadly, quietly and in complete despair, "I cannot, Sturmführer. I will rather die."

Ding made a disparaging gesture with his right hand, as if he wanted to say, "Now I give up the whole business!"

Meier was sent from the surgery, and I put the file among the others lying on the table.

I met Meier in the camp about a fortnight later. He had been released from the detention barracks and, although still looking rather haggard, he had nevertheless recovered from the worst of his punishment.

I gave him words of encouragement. For the time being, I told him, he need not worry about again falling into the hands of the camp doctor, and meanwhile his emigration papers would be put in order, his release from camp following automatically.

"At first I did not trust you," he returned. "I would like to apologise for that."

"Don't mention it, comrade," I replied. "I know how difficult it is to trust anyone in this camp."

All would have ended well had the people outside only known what went on in this concentration camp. But how could they know?

Some released prisoner had informed Meier's parents of the danger which threatened their son. They had gone to great lengths to get the emigration papers in order, and succeeded in doing so. Then they got in touch with the S.S. Chief Security Office and succeeded in gaining contact with an important officer, who knows how, the love of parents being capable of anything!

They knew that the castration of their son was imminent, and managed to get a wire dispatched from the Chief Security Office to the camp, saying, "Postpone castration of Julius Meier. Reichsführer S.S. fears atrocities propaganda."

S.S. Scharführer Hofmann, the orderly, brought the wire to the surgery from the political department, and put it in the file for the doctor's signature, and I saw it there.

Postpone castration? Why did the wire not read, "Release of Julius Meier is authorised"? the thought flashed through my mind. Such a request would not have come directly into the hands of the camp doctor, and Meier would have been released without much ado. The few situations in which Meier might still have been noticed, pending his release, could have been avoided by us prisoners. We had secured the power to do this and were hourly prepared to risk our own uncertain existence in order to return a comrade to life.

Postpone castration? Oh, you misguided parents, what have you done! I thought. You could not know, although love should intuitively have found the right way to save your son! Why did you have to fail?

Not an hour later, Julius Meier's number was called through the loudspeaker. "To the gate at once! To the gate at once!"

Meier was again taken to the detention barracks, and the next morning Dr. Ding dictated a death report to me concerning a certain prisoner named Julius Meier who had died in the night, despite careful and devoted nursing.

The wire from the Chief Security Office was no longer in the file for signature when I put this report away.

136

9. Cases of Castration

STERILISATION is a rendering of sexual unproductiveness by way of a surgical operation. In the male one understands by this the severing of the spermatic cord, in the female the discontinuation of the ovary functions. The capability to continue sexual intercourse as well as essential characteristic and physical signs are mainly unchanged, only fertilisation being thus prevented.

For some years sterilisation has been introduced in several countries in order to eliminate hereditary disabilities such as mental disorders, hereditary blindness and the like.

Castration is the removal of the male's germinating glands and results in far-reaching characteristic and physical changes. It was demanded by many scientists and biologists as a safeguard against dangerous criminals sentenced for sex crimes, but its commitment was also very much in dispute. As a safeguard, provisions were made for it in the German Penal Code.

The law dated 14th July, 1935, to prevent hereditary disease was intended to "prevent serious dangers to the healthy heritage of the German people". Those persons were considered to be afflicted with hereditary disease who suffered from inherited imbecility, recurring mental disorder, inherited epilepsy, inherited blindness or deafness or severe physical deformity.

By a decision of the Erbgesundheitsgericht (Court for Health and Heritage), such people, as well as chronic alcoholics, could be sterilised even against their will.

Through the observance of certain defined provisions of this law, castration could also be carried out on a criminal sentenced for sex crimes, or an abnormal person, if a voluntary application, recommended by two doctors, was submitted.

Sterilisation and castration played a great part in Buchenwald life. The first operation did not lead to very great tragedies, especially as, during my time, it was carried out by specialists in the Weimar Hospital. For obvious reasons, however, castrations took place without exception in the camp itself.

In the previous chapter I have described how and with what methods the conditions for operations were created. I would like to emphasise that the case mentioned does not by any means represent an exceptional one, but was rather the general rule.

Now who was sterilised and castrated in this camp? Naturally, there were cases of sterilisation where, according to human judgement, all those conditions were present which were provided for in the law concerning health heritage, particularly those cases properly submitted to the Erbgesundheitsgericht for their decision. On account of my experiences, I am not, however, fully convinced that decisions of the court were not influenced by the shadow which spread from Buchenwald itself.

There were only rare cases of recurring mental disorder, inherited epilepsy, inherited blindness or deafness, but alcoholism and innate imbecility—i.e., those cases which were difficult to define within fixed limits—were more frequent. Nazism found its domain in these things, enabling the fundamental frivolous and criminal attitude of National Socialism to revel in uncontrolled violence.

The basic principle of "in dubio pro reo" (the benefit of the doubt), which once caused German judges to be held in the greatest esteem in the world, did not exist for the Nazi despots. On the contrary, they were like the devil after a soul, breaking all laws in order to follow their inhuman instincts and their criminal dispositions.

It was considered to be a case of alcoholism if someone had at one time been in the workhouse or had been in police custody in order to sober up from a drunken session. All illiterates—and nearly all gypsies in the camp could be classed as such—and so-called work-shy prisoners, were considered to be of innate imbecility. A person who had at some time been sentenced for an offence or an indecent assault, was considered to be a dangerous criminal.

Not one of the many castrations carried out in Buchenwald during my time were subject to the conditions laid down by law. I witnessed some cases in which the court had even refused the application for castration.

Not only were criminals castrated who had been sentenced

for sex crimes, but so were homosexual prisoners, men who had sinned against the "racial laws" and men who at some time, however many years back, had violated the "law" in a comparatively minor way, or had committed any so-called offence.

The decision of the Erbgesundheitsgericht was not obtained for a single castration. The "voluntary" application of the prisoner, together with the formal signatures of two S.S. "doctors" (could they really be called doctors?), were sufficient for carrying out the operation without further consideration, and, from a surgical point of view, sometimes not even properly.

In order to illustrate such Buchenwald castrations, I will choose three average cases, typical of all.

A prisoner of Königsberg was sent to the camp as work-shy at the age of nineteen, and was soon after castrated by the former camp doctor, Kirchert. I did not personally get to know Kirchert and decline to relate hearsay stories concerning this man, although through the files he left I could ascertain that, apart from other cruelties, sterilisation and castration were his specialities.

I became better acquainted with the case of the prisoner because, after his release, inquiries were made by the State Police Office of Königsberg concerning the castration made on him.

He was released from the camp in connection with the action which was no doubt part of those preliminary negotiations in the spring of 1939 which were aimed at the conclusion of a treaty of friendship and non-aggression with Russia.

At that time, a number of prisoners were freed in order to create a necessary atmosphere of normality in the country for the negotiations. Any actual proof of a norm according to which such releases were effected was not visible to us prisoners. In fact, we had the impression that a budgerigar indiscriminately picked out the cards from the files of the Chief Security Office in Berlin, from where the release notices were forwarded to the camp.

Any person could be freed, among all categories of prisoners —seasoned concentrationers and people who had arrived only the day before, convicted and non-convicted men, comrades

139

who had never been noticed in the camp and those who had a whole string of camp punishments behind them; important political officials of parties opposed to the Nazis and men with no political record at all; healthy men and men who were dangerously ill; comrades who were simply numbers and those who held important positions; prisoners who, as old Nazis, enjoyed a certain favouritism from the camp management, and those who would eventually have died in the camp.

There was no possible doubt that the Nazis did not intend to grant an amnesty with this action but only to provide a figure which would make an impression on the Russians for two reasons: "See, we are so stabilised that we can afford to be lenient!" and, "See, we can be so obliging towards you because you have always demanded the opening of German concentration camps!"

So it was that during this period this prisoner had been released. He began to change in certain characteristics. When he arrived at his Nazi parents' home in Königsberg, the dear people were very much taken aback by what they perceived. Indignant because they were Nazis and not mere ordinary nobodies, they used their influence as far up as the State Police Office to have the matter investigated.

The Königsberg State Police Office requested an explanation from the camp management. And the camp management sent this request to the camp doctor, for his comments. And the camp doctor ordered his clerk to find the required files. That clerk, the last of this long and more or less official chain of authorities, was myself.

The information in his files read that the prisoner from Königsberg had been in the camp because he was supposed to have shown himself to be work-shy. At the age of seventeen he had undergone a sentence of six months' imprisonment for indecent behaviour with fourteen-year-old girls. He was eighteen when he left the prison. Is it not conceivable that, when he had to live again among free people, this young fellow felt ashamed of his past conduct? Is it difficult to guess that he avoided work because he assumed that everybody must see in his face what an evildoer he had been?

The answers to these questions were given on another sheet of paper, which read: "In order to rid myself of my perverted sexual instincts I herewith voluntarily apply for my castration."

I believe the prisoner did not even know what the expression "perverted sexual instincts" meant, but he signed the application, whether under torture or not I do not know, and Dr. Kirchert was the surgeon who carried out the operation.

Dr. Ding rid himself of this awkward case by passing it for action to Dr. Kirchert, who had meanwhile been posted elsewhere. I did not hear the final outcome of the case.

A prisoner from Troppau was also a Black. He was such an unimportant, harmless man that he would certainly never have been noticed in Buchenwald at all, had he not written on his political questionnaire and in his own awkward handwriting, that he had had about fifty previous convictions, although he had now forgotten the details connected with them.

"What? Fifty previous convictions? That must be quite a special bird!" the official in the political department must have thought, when he looked through the questionnaire, and demanded from Troppau an extract from the list of convictions.

When this arrived, he read it through and neatly underlined in red all those passages which referred to convictions for causing public annoyance or indecent behaviour. This was then submitted to the camp commandant, who in turn wrote "Castrate!" and forwarded the file to the camp doctor.

Now the poor devil stood before the doctor like a figure which only needed a bottle of alcohol to exhibit the last insignia of a homeless tramp. The situation was so comical that Dr. Ding omitted the usual theatricals. The prisoner signed without hesitation and without reading the declaration.

Filling in the red form for castration presented some difficulties, for on this all questions were set out in detail, and from the court files which had meanwhile arrived, it was learned that the longest sentence this prisoner had ever received was one of a term of three months' imprisonment. All his other sentences consisted of six days, three days, ten days, twelve days, three weeks, two days, one day, etc., etc. The cause of the public annoyance of which he was guilty consisted of his having relieved himself in the street. And the indecent act? He once lay completely drunk and practically naked in a ditch by a path along which school children had passed.

A somewhat longer report was made in an endeavour to make the case look more convincing. This required a little sweating over, but it rendered the need for castration less difficult. The unmanned from Troppau did not live for long after this "improvement". As it is well known, those who have been castrated are inclined to stoutness under normal living conditions. The food in the camp produced exactly the opposite effect on him, and during the severe winter of 1939–40 he froze to death.

A third prisoner came from the Ruhr area, the land of foundries and mines, on which, so the Nazis boasted, the enemy could not drop a single bomb. He had homosexual tendencies and had undergone imprisonment before being brought to the camp.

He was far too intelligent not to realise the inevitability of his fate, and was too soft to dare resisting the usual means of pressure. He signed the application for castration and readily gave any information required of him in order to complete the red form for this operation. The camp doctor arranged his release from the punitive detachment in order to impress other candidates there accordingly. He was still alive when I left the camp.

10. The Fate of Ernst Heilmann

IN the evening of the second day after my arrival in the camp, I had gone to see Ernst Heilmann, hoping in conversation with him to find out something of the conditions in the camp and of the political situation there.

During my political activity in the time of the Republic, I had often met Heilmann without, however, making any close personal contact with him. There were two main reasons for this. Firstly, Heilmann was chairman of the Social-democratic faction of the Landtag (Provincial Parliament) so that, because of this fact and several other political functions, he was so overburdened with work that my discussions with him were always of short duration. Secondly, his attitude to numerous political and personal problems did not coincide with mine, so that the main incentive for friendship with him was lacking on my part.

Yet I was strongly impressed by his great knowledge, and the energy and consistency of his way of thinking. Heilmann was in any case a highly intelligent man, respected even by his opponents.

I found him in a barracks for Jews which was crammed to bursting point. The prisoners were forbidden to enter other barracks, those disobeying this order being usually punished with five or ten strokes of the birch, with the barracks senior receiving the same punishment, the camp management having made him responsible for the observation of camp rules. As it was only very seldom that those who offended against this particular rule were caught, nobody worried about it.

I have described some of my impressions before, but would like to do so again as a background to my story of Ernst Heilmann.

The conditions in this Jews' barracks were far worse than those in Block 36, itself six times overfilled, with far more men standing in the day-room than could sit.

The Jewish prisoners stood crowded together as if in an overcrowded tram. I had literally to squeeze myself through the crowds before I could reach the table of the senior of the room.

The place was unbelievably stuffy, with stale air so thick that the electric light bulbs were enveloped in a light fog.

Some Jews had retired from the crowd and had settled down on the rafters beneath the ceiling of the barracks. There, they sat like chickens on a roost, eating their bread, reading old, torn books, or chattering to one another.

One of them had crawled into a dark corner of the ceiling and swung his legs in rhythm. As I passed him, I noticed that he was playing a mouth organ; yet despite the fact that I was not three yards away from him, I could not hear him playing above the noise of the four to five hundred prisoners who lived in a room normally accommodating sixty prisoners.

Obviously recognising in me a newcomer who saw this for the first time, a prisoner cried to me from his balcony seat, in

143

a sarcastically humorous kind of market voice, "My friend, here you see the chosen people! Just as they are, in joy and in sorrow. The veritable images of God. Come up here and get a bird's-eye view of the mob. You will kill yourself with laughter; then you won't have to carry on, and that is certainly the best for you!"

"If it is the best, why have you not yet killed yourself with laughter?" I called out to him.

"Ah," he said, and raised his right index finger like a wise rabbi, "I am not a goy like you. I belong to the Mischpoche. I may only laugh at myself and others like me. That sort of laughter is not enough, and death through crying is forbidden here."

A few steps further on I saw two or three prisoners assisting a comrade who had apparently fainted or was seriously ill. None of the other men, however, took the slightest notice of them. At that time I did not realise that, within a few weeks, I would be just as stoically silent when a comrade at my side met his fate.

At last I reached the room senior. Aided by others, he was distributing the food rations which, of course, were still smaller for the Jews than they were for other prisoners.

I had to shout to make myself understood as I asked for Heilmann. He looked at me for a second, and then banged a wooden ladle against a suspended iron bar, producing a loud bell-like tone.

The noise and shuffling in the room immediately died down. He called out, "Heilmann!" and at once returned to his work, taking no more notice of me, the others resuming their conversation.

There I stood amidst a confusion of talking, shouting, singing and noise, in the thick, stuffy air, being pushed and shoved, with no one to trouble about me.

Then I saw Heilmann squeezing himself through the crowd to the table. Although his head had been shaven and he had no moustache, I recognised him by the bushy, gingery eyebrows, the characteristically formed nose and the typical look of him.

There were traces of sorrow and of pain endured during five-and-a-half years in the concentration camp deeply engraved on the wrinkled face. His tattered clothing was dirty and patched. He walked slowly, with sagging shoulders. His hands were chapped and showed signs of heavy work. He was no longer the human being Heilmann; he was merely a pitiable wreck.

He did not recognise me, and only when I mentioned my name did he remember me.

"Let us chat a little," he said, and took me over to a bench near the large stove.

Those who were sitting there willingly made room for us when we told them that we had something to talk about.

Heilmann could only sit with difficulty. Slowly, he folded his arms across his chest in his customary manner, rubbing his stubbly chin with the same characteristic gesture he had once used as he would run his hand through his beard.

Then, as if he were laboriously digging out memories from a deep hollow in his brain, he recapitulated quietly. "Yes, you were in Westphalia. You belonged to that young element which caused us anxiety. Your father in Kiel, the deputy town councillor, whom we helped to succeed in Prussia during the Kaiser's time, is he still alive?"

When I answered in the negative, he continued meditatively, "I knew him well, very well. Karl Legien was his member of the Reichstag. Was he seventy? Seventy-five? Well, well, a good age. Did they collect him, too? No? Reduced pension? Yes, yes, as usual. But he was able to die unmolested. At least his last hour passed in the manner to which his life entitled him. And you? Four years' penal servitude? Following that, here?"

We talked about people we both knew, of political matters, of the reasons which, in our opinion, led to the downfall of democracy and the establishment of the gangsterism of National Socialism.

Heilmann confirmed that, from Oranienburg, he had been taken to the notorious camp of Esterwegen near Papenburg, where he was illtreated and tortured again and again. He confirmed that several times he was locked in a dog's kennel and had to bark at people who passed him.

He went on to tell me that one day he had reached the end of his powers of endurance and had decided to get himself shot. He passed the usual chain of guards and ignored their challenge. But he had only been shot in the right leg.

When I asked him how he envisaged further developments in the country, he declared, "There will be war. You will still have a chance because they will need you, but they will probably kill all of us Jews."

I met Heilmann several times during my time in the camp, without, however, having any longer discussions with him than the first one.

While it was generally in the powers of the Kapos to keep a prisoner from the immediate attention of the camp management, and give him work of a more tolerable kind than he might otherwise get, this was not possible in Heilmann's case. He was one of the prominent men there, and was a particular victim of both S.S. Obersturmbannführer Rödl and the camp commandant S.S. Standartenführer Koch. Rödl always gave him particularly hard work to do, being constantly ready with little tricks to play on him, as a result of which Heilmann had to suffer more than any other prisoner.

On the other hand, the deputy of the Obersturmbannführer, whom we prisoners only knew by his nickname of Jonny (his other name was Hackmann) was always prepared to counteract the orders of his superior.

Jonny looked like a film star. He was smart, had wavy hair, a good figure, and was always well dressed. Though he was a gay spark, he was feared by the prisoners because of his brutal beatings; but he always enjoyed a certain amount of popularity.

Many stories were told of his love affairs and drinking escapades. For instance, it was known that he was a constant visitor to a Weimar establishment which was officially out of bounds to the S.S. because, on account of its fairly openly conducted brothel, it was notorious.

Jonny, who had no financial background whatever, always had money and appeared as a man of the world. He freely bragged of his adventures to the prisoners whom he kept as batmen. If he succeeded in getting some S.S. comrade to visit the prohibited establishment, or met any of the S.S. there, he would relate the story with particular amusement, although he knew that they had to keep quiet about what he told them.

146

Jonny had previously been a guard in Esterwegen, where he had got to know Heilmann. Because of some mood, perhaps also in order to do something to help him raise the money which subsidised his style of living, he made decisions and passed instructions which resulted in certain reliefs for us prisoners. As he was intellectually far superior to the Obersturmbannführer, he often knew how to tie him mentally in knots, and Jonny several times gave Heilmann less strenuous work to do than ordered.

One day during spring, Heilmann was engaged in rooting out tree stumps in the wood within the camp. Work in the camp was esteemed a favour because no guards were present to try to relieve their boredom by tormenting the prisoners, while the speed of labour, too, had to be increased only if an S.S. man were nearby to watch.

The wood contained the dog kennels in which ferocious dogs were kept by S.S. Standartenführer Koch and other S.S. officers. Heilmann worked nearby with other prisoners.

Our own signal service warned us . . . "Rödl in the camp with strange S.S. men, apparently visitors who are to be shown the camp." We arranged ourselves so as to attract as little attention as possible.

From the window of the surgery I saw Rödl come down the path with the strangers. When he passed the labour column in which Heilmann worked, the Kapo of the group ran up to him, according to regulations, pulled his cap from his head and reported, "Four prisoners and one Kapo engaged in rooting tree stumps."

Rödl liked to behave like a strutting peacock, especially in the presence of strangers, and now he walked up to the labour column and gave instructions on the correct method of rooting. He thus discovered Heilmann and, pointing him out to his companions, said, "That's that dirty dog Heilmann, you know, that swine from the Prussian Parliament. We've trained him. You watch." To the amusement of the others, Heilmann was made to perform the barking dog routine forced on him in Esterwegen.

Then Rödl and his company continued on their way to the stables, where pigs were being fattened. From the stables they went to the dog kennels. The kennel attendant was ordered to bring the dogs out for inspection. This man was an evil type of prisoner who, some years previously, had committed an indecent assault. For a long time, however, he had kept out of trouble, so that there were no valid reasons for keeping him in preventive custody, but was in the camp as a habitual and dangerous criminal.

During the inspection Rödl thought he would demonstrate that the dogs were trained to attack humans, the object being Ernst Heilmann.

Heilmann had to stand against a stout tree, while Rödl, his visitors, and the attendant with two large ferocious dogs on the lead, stood at a distance from him of about eight to ten paces.

The attendant set the beasts on the defenceless Heilmann. The latter stood there, anticipating the attack with outstretched arms and a pitifully frightened expression, his eyes glazed and his mouth open with terror. Just as the dogs were about to seize him, the attendant called them back to him, and they instantly obeyed his command.

The process was repeated three, four, five times, without Heilmann being bitten; the dogs seized him at the sixth time. They tore his hands and arms, and the attendant had trouble making them hear his command of recall.

The latter looked questioningly at Rödl. Should he continue?

"Carry on!" Rödl ordered.

The dogs seized the old man, pulled him to the ground and held grimly on to him.

While Heilmann was still struggling with the dogs, without showing any feeling and laughing sardonically, Rödl signalled his guests to walk on. The attendant subdued the bloodthirsty dogs, Heilmann lying almost unconscious on the ground, and the S.S. officers walked away without once looking back.

A few weeks before his death, I spoke to Heilmann for the last time.

As already stated, according to the camp rules, a prisoner was allowed to hold ten Marks in cash, an amount he could draw from his account per month for purchases in the canteen. The Jews, however, were not permitted to draw any money, unless they required some to pay for a doctor's certificate in connection with their intended emigration or for buying new spectacles, a truss or the like.

It was part of my duties to procure spectacles for the men. Those who needed new ones reported to me; I sent for the optician from Weimar, and claimed the money for payment from the cashier's office.

As my work was not checked, I began to claim twenty-five Marks for spectacles which, for instance, cost fifteen Marks. I did this especially after the outbreak of war, when the so-called concentration camp reinforcements arrived to augment the old guards and were not familiar with the organisation of the camp.

Sometimes, I submitted claims for money even without an order for spectacles. In this manner I could let the Jewish prisoners obtain money.

It was obvious that such manipulations could only be carried out with confidential prisoners, for I risked my neck at the same time, although such risks were customary and an un-written law among the prisoners.

One day Ernst Heilmann came to me to order spectacles. He looked tired and dispirited, but he still held himself up-right and was calm and collected. We spoke about the new war. "Germany cannot win this war," he said.

Some time later Heilmann was ordered to go to the doctor. He was one of the few prisoners who, at lengthy intervals, received visits from relatives. Though it was possible for the relatives of every prisoner to obtain permission for visits through the Chief Security Office in Berlin, advantage of this was only taken to a very limited extent. Most of the prisoners knew nothing of this concession, or if they did, were not per-mitted to write home about it.

Moreover, the camp conditions were such that the prisoners themselves had no desire to receive visitors. The Chief Security Office inquired of the political department by telegram whether any doubts existed against granting permission for visiting. The various departments were asked to give their opinions on this matter and the camp doctor examined the prisoner to be visited to ascertain whether he was fit to be seen. The camp commandant gave his final decision.

Heilmann's relatives had applied for permission to visit him, and for this reason he was ordered to see the doctor. It was the last time I saw him alive.

Shortly afterwards, Heilmann was taken to the detention building. There was no obvious reason for his isolation, but it was clear to the experienced men that Heilmann had reached the end of his sufferings. The attention of the camp management had again been focused on him because of the projected visit, and he was to die because of it.

Only a few days elapsed before I was instructed to make out his death certificate. I had to give a fictitious cause of death. When I saw the corpse in the mortuary I noticed a fresh cut near the right elbow. Heilmann had no longer been under medical treatment.

11. Song and Music

ALL inmates of the camp had to report twice a day for roll-call on the huge square—in the morning before work, and in the evening, after the labour columns had returned to the camp. The roll-call seldom proceeded smoothly, for there was almost always some inaccuracy which made it usually last an hour or more.

It was the whim of the Senior Camp Officer, Rödl, to walk up to the microphone after he had received the report, and stutter a short speech. We prisoners seldom understood him, for Rödl was a Bavarian and mumbled a completely incoherent German dialect. Even the S.S. Unterführer who stood directly next to him at the microphone often could not make out what he wanted to say. Only the end of these speeches was always clear to us, for the last word invariably used was "Arseful".

Rödl tried to show his appreciation of music by two innovations, which at the same time served to deceive visitors from whom the true face of the camp had to remain hidden.

Firstly, there was the camp band, whose main task was to play marches when the prisoners entered or left the camp, so that the endlessly long columns marched in time through the gate.

150

Secondly, it apparently gave him great pleasure to be serenaded by tens of thousands of prisoners. The repertoire of the serenaders consisted of two songs, the "Castle in the Wood" and the "Buchenwald Song", both of which had to be sung so often that the prisoners soon got sick of them. It was surprising, indeed, that Rödl himself did not get enough of this monotonous fare.

The prisoners frequently had to start ten or fifteen times before a song was rendered by the masses with some degree of proficiency.

As, during these initial trials, Rödl invariably lost his temper and ordered some nonsensical mass or individual punishment, we organised things in such a way that those in the blocks nearest to him sang with double vehemence, while those in the most distant ones, receiving the sound seconds later, merely moved their lips in mime.

Despite this, the mass choir still sounded like a roaring gale. Yet I believe that the inhabitants of the villages down in the valley, who lived miles away from the camp and could hear the muffled roar of the mass choir every day, neither understood the lyric of the main song, nor had any idea of what was going on in the camp.

How, for instance, could a stranger form even an approximate idea of camp life from the Buchenwald song?—the first verse of which was:

> *Wenn der Tag erwacht,*
> *eh die Sonne lacht,*
> *die Kolonnen ziehn*
> *zu des Tages Mühn*
> *hinein in den grauenden Morgen.*
> *Und der Wald ist schwarz*
> *und der Himmel rot,*
> *und wir tragen im Brotsack ein Stückchen Brot*
> *und im Herzen, im Herzen die Sorgen.*
> *Buchenwald, ich kann dicht nicht vergessen,*
> *weil du mein Schicksal bist;*
> *wer dich verliss, der kann es erst ermessen,*
> *wie wundervoll die Freiheit ist.*
> *Doch Buchenwald, wir jammern nicht und klagen,*

und was auch unser Schicksal sei;
wir wollen trotzdem ja zum Leben sagen,
denn einmal kommt der Tag, dann sind wir frei.*

The camp management's mentality made it difficult for them to comprehend the double sense intended by the words.

Needless to say, an endeavour by Rödl to create new camp songs through the introduction of a competition met with no success.

12. Roll-call Experiences

ROLL-CALL always proceeded smoothly on those days on which the S.S. men had some arrangements of their own. It was then quite obvious that they were interested in getting their time off as soon as possible. I suspected for a long time that they sometimes simply "cooked" the roll-call, until I finally had proof of this for myself.

I quote this case here in order to show with what irresponsibility these dissolute mercenaries fulfilled their duties when their private interests were affected in any way.

> * Before the break of day,
> The columns make their way
> Back to the toil and strain,
> Back to their work again,
> In the dawn's gladness.
> And the forest is black
> And the sky is red,
> In our satchels we carry a little bread,
> In our hearts, in our hearts a deep sadness.
> Buchenwald, I never shall forget you.
> This is my lot but still I see
> How I shall treasure when I leave you
> The privileges of the free.
> Yet Buchenwald, we shall not weep and sorrow,
> No matter what our fate may be;
> We'll take what comes. The bright tomorrow
> Soon may dawn, and we'll be free.

A very infectious and dangerous eye-disease had been brought into the camp by gypsies who had been sent there in great numbers, particularly from Burgenland. Three of the affected prisoners were taken to the university clinic in Jena. Two of them returned to the camp after about a fortnight. Owing to a mistake at the camp gate, it transpired that the three prisoners had not been marked off the camp establishment during the whole time of their absence. Though the matter was eventually straightened out with the aid of a few fictitious reports, the fact is more than puzzling that the roll-call remained ostensibly correct during the time they had been away.

One very cold winter's day roll-call had once again lasted for a particularly long time. Again and again the Scharführer had recounted their Blocks, again and again the single reports had been added together. The number of absent prisoners and of those in the sick ward were checked. There was an error, but it could not be verified. The fact was that one prisoner was missing. The seniors of the Blacks called out the names of their comrades, with negative results. The man in charge of the sick-ward roll-call again checked his figures, without success.

The previous evening some forty to fifty dead and dying prisoners had been taken to the sick ward. They were recorded as having been sent there in order to speed up the roll-call. Not until the next morning were they actually entered in the report as having died or as having been brought in during the night.

In the centre of the Sick Barracks II was a toilet with a stone floor. The dead and dying men were put in this room because it was easier to clean the stone floor of any messes made by them.

The man who took the roll-call had made a mistake when checking. This was not surprising in view of the fact that the room was approximately nine by twelve feet in size, so that when about forty to fifty dead and dying men had to be accommodated in it, one could not avoid piling them on top of one another. It was certainly no pleasure to ascertain from this terrible heap of humanity how many bodies there were and what numbers were stitched on their clothing.

The man who took the roll-call was now in considerable personal danger, for Rödl was present at the main roll-call. Owing to his sudden sadistic impulses, it was quite possible that he would have our comrade beaten, dismiss him from his position and send him to the punitive labour detachment.

It seemed impossible to hush his mistake up in any way. At first we were helpless; then we decided to stake everything on one card.

The sick ward had a telephone connection with the gate. I rang S.S. Hauptscharführer Strippel, whom we had previously assisted in hushing up the discrepancy in the roll-call when the three gypsies had been sent to Jena. I told him the whole truth and begged him to see that the matter was put right. He promised to do so.

We now lived through some minutes of high tension, not knowing as yet whether all would proceed smoothly. At last the loudspeakers crackled. Would our man be called to the gate? The seconds became small eternities. The man responsible for the mistake stood with a face as white as chalk.

Again the loudspeakers crackled. Then, "Attention! Eyes right!" Good heavens! This was the normal command of roll-call. There was a weight lifted off our minds. The culprit, thus relieved of his anxiety, smacked his thighs like a madman, repeating over and over again, "Boy, oh boy! Boy, oh boy!"

On another occasion at roll-call, the prisoners had already been standing on the square for over an hour, waiting for the last labour column to move in. For some reason, it stood in front of the gate without being admitted.

Suddenly we heard, "One is missing!"

As the men of this column had worked on the new garage, they were commanded to search there for the missing prisoner, who was shortly found.

He was a half-starved work-shy prisoner who had crept under some timber and had been found asleep there. He was completely apathetic and answered none of the questions put to him as to whether he had tried to escape, whether he had fallen asleep, why he had crawled under the timber, etc. Even blows and digs in the ribs could not stir him from his apathy.

The roll-call was taken as soon as this man was back in

camp. Rödl put a few questions to him, but receiving no reply, he settled the case, as far as he was concerned, with the short order, "Twenty-five!"

The man was tied to the stock and received twenty-five lashes with a horse-whip. During all this he still remained wholly apathetic. Although, in accordance with regulations, he himself counted the strokes in a painfully subdued voice, he gave up counting after the sixth blow, and was unconscious when released from the stock. Then he was thrown aside like an empty sack by another prisoner, who took his turn to receive the punishment prescribed for him.

An hour later, the warders from the sick ward had to collect the work-shy prisoner, and found him dead. It was then too late to ascertain whether he had actually died on the stock.

His death certificate stated that he had died of a weak heart shortly after his entry into the camp, despite the immediate administration of a sufficient dose of cardiazol.

13. Mass Retaliation

ON the morning of the 9th November, 1939, after roll-call, we were very surprised not to hear the usual order over the loud-speakers, "Labour columns, fall in!" Instead, we heard, "Move into the barracks in blocks. No prisoner may leave the barracks."

We had no idea of the reason for this command until the prisoners who performed orderly duties in the administrative barracks returned to camp with sensational news. "Yesterday, an attempt was made to assassinate Hitler in the Bürgerbräu-keller. Hitler not injured. Instigators unknown."

Despite the ban, the news spread through the whole camp like wildfire, and it was not long before the most absurd rumours flew about, nourished by the fact that Rödl was supposed to be in Munich and was a recipient of the so-called Blood Order.

Two Scharführer came along the empty camp roads at

about nine o'clock. One of them was the notorious Scharführer Sommer, the hangman from the detention barracks, the other being an Oberscharführer known to the prisoners by the nickname of "Anna", because of his undisguised homosexuality.

They entered one of the Jewish barracks, and there indiscriminately chose five Jews and brought them outside. From a second barracks they brought out eight more. From a third they selected a further seven.

The Viennese dentist, Kende, was an orderly in the third barracks. As the senior of the Block did not happen to be at the door to make the official report to the Scharführer, Kende himself reported the number of prisoners there, and unsuspectingly asked, "What do you wish, Herr Scharführer?"

When the twenty Jews were standing before the barracks in rank and file, about to march off under Anna's orders, Sommer turned to Kende at the last moment and said, "You there, come along too!"

Among the twenty-one Jews was an eighteen-year-old lad, whose father was also in the camp. This young Jew was a modest, talented fellow with a wonderful disposition, who had just been discharged from the sick ward, where S.S. Obersturmführer Zahel, the camp surgeon, had successfully carried out a difficult operation on his ribs.

The news service which we prisoners had established among ourselves soon told us of the incident, although we attached no special importance to it, merely assuming that some kind of work was to be carried out outside the camp.

Some time later we heard a burst of firing from the direction of the stone quarry. It was now clear to us that the earthly existence of our twenty-one Jewish comrades had ended.

Shortly after ten o'clock Hauptscharführer Strippel phoned through to me. His voice sounded rough and drunken. "Well, do you know where those twenty-one swine are?" he demanded.

I did not quite know how to answer him. Of course I did not doubt the fate of the Jews, while I knew that one did not have to weigh every word spoken to the Hauptscharführer; yet his voice was so dreadful that I quickly decided to appear ignorant of the event.

"No idea, Herr Hauptscharführer," I replied.

Whereupon Strippel roared into the telephone like a mad animal. "They've gone to blazes! Understand?"

"Yes, Herr Hauptscharführer."

"Well, then, write the reports." Then more quietly, he added: "Do you need the numbers?"

"Yes, Herr Hauptscharführer."

He then dictated to me twenty-one prisoners' numbers. Upon receiving this information, I went to the files, pulled out twenty-one cards, wrote twenty-one death certificates, and twenty-one times wrote as the cause of death, "Shot while escaping."*

I saw the bodies in the mortuary the next day. They all had wounds in the back of their heads, obviously from close range. The injuries were horrible, but at least had caused instant death.

I was still in the process of writing the death certificates when I heard the next alarming message, "Withdrawal of food for the whole camp. Detention in barracks in complete darkness for all Jews."

The first two days passed fairly easily, but hunger became evident on the third day. The kitchen scraps from the S.S. barracks, brought into camp in troughs for feeding the pigs, were searched for food. Increasing numbers of gypsies and work-shy prisoners greedily seized any scraps they could find. Potato peelings were cooked and eaten. Bruised turnips were stolen from the cellar of the prisoners' cookhouse.

On the following day the political prisoners, having until now shown the best powers of endurance, were also seized by the wave of hunger. The raid on everything eatable was organised by individuals in the most adventurous and risky manner. Despite the ban, a lively traffic proceeded during the night.

Single Jews succeeded in breaking out of their closed and darkened barracks. What they related about conditions there

* Walter Abusch, Herbert Wolfgang Adam, Wilhelm Martin Cohn, Herbert Deutsch, Otto Frischmann, Josef Godel, Artur Gross, Leo Jablonski, Erich Jacob, Stefan Kende, Theodor Kritzhaber, Julius Levite, Emil Levy, Artur Maschke, Ernst Meyer, Hermann Rautenberg, Alfred Schlaefrack, Franz Erich Schneider, Leo Unger, Kurt Wolffberg.

was horrible, but they were successful in their attempts to get some bread and turnips and, above all, fresh water into the barricaded buildings.

I myself received a little bread from S.S. Scharführer Rose, and shared it with my friends. But our hunger grew ever more intense.

While the greater number of prisoners sank into complete apathy, the eyes of others began to flick, as the courage of despair gradually formed.

My political friends came to see me during the night. We discussed the position, and slowly derived a clear and unequivocal decision from our inner determination to live and from our political convictions. We would not allow ourselves to be murdered without defence. We had to do something, if only as a last desperate step into nothingness, a step to justify ourselves in our own eyes, and which in time to come would perhaps serve as an example to further our cause, the cause of mankind's triumph over treachery.

Until then the strongest force within us, enabling us to withstand Buchenwald, had been the vague possibility of once more working for the establishment and construction of a just, dignified society; but now we believed we must give our lives for one short struggle for freedom.

Just as desperation threatened to reach its culminating point and we expected an outbreak of the last revolt we had planned, the food ban for "Aryan" prisoners was lifted.

The Jew comrades, however, remained in darkness under detention, although this measure, too, was repealed after four or five days. The camp management obviously noticed the absence of the final consequences which they hoped from their brutal orders. During the day the S.S. myrmidons could guard the Jewish barracks, but during the night none ventured into the camp. Even though it was forbidden to leave the barracks at night time, even though the searchlights from the watchtowers continuously flashed their beams across the camp, we again and again succeeded in getting at least some food and fresh water into the Jewish barracks.

At last these were opened on the morning of the twelfth or thirteenth day, which was sunny and almost warm. Never in my life will I forget that scene. When, as a child, I had seen rather than heard Beethoven's opera, "Fidelio", for the first time, I could remember how immensely touched I was by the prisoners in the story being brought from their dungeons into the sun. What was then impressed on my mind only by the power of art, became a frightful experience at Buchenwald, an almost incomprehensible reality.

There they came, out of their barracks into the light, dazzled, pale, wretched, weak and staggering. There they brought their sick, out into the sun—the dying, the dead, a horrible train of human suffering and pitiful misery. Around their barracks was silence, incredible silence, and yet, far, far away in the distance, I thought I heard those immortal melodies with which the greatest musical genius of mankind had expressed exactly their misery one hundred and twenty-five years before.

We later learned that it had not even been a Jew whom the Nazis accused of the attempted assassination in the Bürgerbräukeller, but a quite respectable "Aryan" of the Otto-Strasser Group.

14. Dragged to Death

THE May sun is shining, warm and kindly, as I write these lines this morning. The cloudless sky is a deep, mild blue. The trees in their dark fresh green are motionless before my window, and a deep, promising, blissful peace has descended upon all nature. The sparrows are chirping, a tit is rendering its happy tune without intermission, and a missel-thrush is piping its love song. . . .

I had only been a short time in the concentration camp and already all the terrible details of existence there had impressed themselves upon my brain with such dreadful force, that I had the feeling I had been dreaming for years, the most horrible dream a poor human mind can imagine.

I was beginning to get apathetic. I felt it distinctly. I did not want to, but I was. I could tell this by the fact that the flogging scenes which had at first so agitated me were now beginning to be uninteresting. My ears were oblivious to the cries of pain of the tortured men, and only laughed with the others when someone gave particularly loud cries of pain during his flogging.

I then had an experience which pulled me back from drifting into this general apathy. When I now look back at my time in the concentration camp, I can state that the S.S. myrmidons themselves, with their practically inexhaustible inventions of new methods of torture, saw to it that not a single human emotion within me was killed, in however temporary a measure.

On a bitter cold day in January we had fallen in on the square for the morning roll-call. The wind whistled through our thin clothes, and the roll-call simply would not come to an end.

Then, over the loudspeakers, came the command, "Room orderlies into the wood."

Aha! Someone had again put an end to his life! Yet what had this fact got to do with us?

To keep the blood circulating, we began to stamp our feet, at first imperceptibly, then more and more energetically as we saw that the camp management paid no attention to us.

Our block stood at the far end of the square, the furthest away from the gate. In the light of dawn, we could even risk running about a little, especially as our Scharführer was also out in the wood.

Suddenly we heard a howling coming from the wood. The missing prisoner had been found and the other searchers were being called together.

Soon we saw a group of prisoners returning from the wood, down the main road of the camp. Then they stopped, we could not see why. Our ever-ready quick interest flagged as soon as the group moved on again. Once more they stopped, as they reached the square.

Now we could see that they had a prisoner with them who was resisting all their efforts to bring him to the gate, digging his feet in the ground in a desperate effort to free himself from their grip.

One of the men had got hold of him by the back of his collar and the seat of his trousers, and pushed him forward in this undignified manner. But after a few paces, the prisoner threw himself to the ground.

At this moment two Scharführer joined them and the rest of the prisoners stepped aside for them.

Now the situation was clear to us. At the last moment of his attempted suicide the poor wretch had not had the courage to put the rope around his neck; yet now that he was brought to the gate and knew what to expect, he resisted as desperately as an animal about to be slaughtered.

Although the Scharführer beat him, he refused to get up. They grabbed him by the arms, but he lashed out with his legs. In doing so, he kicked one of the Scharführer, and was thereupon beaten furiously until he whined and crumpled up on the ground.

The Scharführer grabbed a leg each, dragging him along over the hard-frozen marly soil and over the sharp stones. He was face downwards, and now raised himself, pressing his hands against the ground and trying to protect his face by walking on them as he was dragged along pitilessly.

As children we had played at barrows with our playmates just like that, with the difference that we had pushed our friends forward, and now a new variation was being given to the old game. It looked so comical, the prisoners nearby began to laugh; the longer they looked the louder they laughed.

The Scharführer themselves seemed amused, and stalked across the square with exaggerated, awkward strides, the prisoner eagerly endeavouring to adjust his walking hands to their pace. The laughter of the onlookers gradually developed into a hideous howling.

There! The prisoner at last lost his strength. His stiff arms collapsed. The howling increased still more, as the Scharführer doggedly dragged their prisoner behind them at an even pace. Now their victim collapsed and fell with his face to the ground. They did not stop.

The howling gradually subsided. The poor devil once more succeeded in getting to his hands, but soon he fell again, his face to the ground; and then again, at ever shortening intervals. Each time the laughter grew thinner, until at last it stopped, for the poor wretch could no longer keep himself up, and the Scharführer dragged him along the ground at their will.

At first he allowed himself to be dragged on his chest, lifting his head backwards; but soon his face again fell to the ground. In place of the laughter, dead silence reigned.

The Scharführer dragged the body of their victim still further along the path. There were now only fifty paces to the gate, then only forty, then thirty, twenty, ten. A bloody trail marked the way. They dropped the prisoner alongside the stock, before walking over to the other Scharführer without a back glance at their victim.

The roll-call was taken. Keeping time with the camp band, the labour columns marched through the gate. No doubt one or another of the prisoners threw a quick glance as the man lay there, next to the stock, and saw a small pool of blood forming around the mutilated upper part of the body. . . .

I shall never quite forget this experience, but I am inexpressibly grateful and under an obligation to you, kind and gracious Nature, because you allowed me to rise above cruelty itself.

The May sun is shining, warm and kindly. The cloudless sky is a deep, mild blue. The trees in their dark fresh green are motionless before my window, and deep, promising, blissful peace has descended upon Nature. The sparrows are chirping, a tit is rendering its happy tune without intermission and the missel-thrush is still piping its song.

15. The Sanatorium and Nursing Home

On the journey to the concentration camp, I had met a comrade in Halle who had struck me specially by his reserved manner. He was a tall, strong, broad-shouldered man with a high forehead, refined features, and a tranquil appearance revealed the fact that its owner was a thinker.

Generally speaking, the prisoners in transit could be divided into two groups. The first consisted of those people whose whole behaviour indicated that they judged everything that happened around them only as far as they were personally concerned. The second group of people were quite different.

They were those who did not think of themselves alone, but considered themselves united by a common fate with their other comrades.

The first group were always intent on gaining an advantage for themselves, even to the detriment of their fellow-sufferers, while the others were constantly helpful, gave information and advice to the ignorant, and spread around them an atmosphere of calm and composure.

The prisoner I had observed, however, belonged to neither of these groups, but kept himself apart from everybody, although I saw that he attentively watched the groups which formed during our journey.

His good, well-cared-for clothing, too, was in contrast to those of the other prisoners. In fact, he looked as if he had been brought in to the prison yard from the road, straight from a Sunday walk.

The man interested me, and so I approached him unobtrusively and made a passing remark. At first he looked at me searchingly, waiting a few moments before he answered, in a strangely low, distinct and clear voice, "I am being taken to a concentration camp."

When I asked why, he replied in the same manner, "Because I expressed my Communist opinion."

I did not quite know how to interpret this man's demeanour, yet something about him appealed to me. True, I felt he was an outsider, yet there was something in him which made him appear congenial to me, an absolutely honest and straightforward person.

I learned that he had become a convinced Communist after studying Communist literature, although the only son of a well-situated middle-class family. When he had grown certain that his beliefs were right, he had felt bound to openly avow them.

He was sent to Block 36, as I was, and so for this reason I was often able to speak to him. A few days after our arrival, he was ordered to see the camp doctor. That evening he told me that the doctor had told him that he must be sterilised. The man had protested that he had been in several institutions for observation, despite which the Erbgesundheitsgericht had always refused sterilisation.

163

I could not form any picture of the real position behind this because at that time I was not so well acquainted with the subject. To my question as to whether he would be released from the camp after a possible operation, he replied in the negative. He had been sent there because of his Communist views and would probably have to remain to the end of his life.

Later, when I was transferred from Block 36, I lost sight of him.

One rainy autumn evening I was working alone in the surgery. The evening roll-call was over, and soon would start the first rush of prisoners for treatment. It was already getting lively outside on the landing, for there was some sort of commotion going on, although this was not unusual and did not disturb me at my work. I thought that some prisoner was probably being thrashed.

A little later I happened to walk across the landing, and in the darkness I saw a prisoner lying on a stretcher, with other men standing around. A nurse knelt alongside the stretcher, examining him. I walked by, without taking any further interest in him.

On returning, I noticed that the nurse was slapping the face of the man on the stretcher.

"The bloody liar!" the nurse yelled. "There's nothing wrong with him. He's perfectly all right; only pretending!" He went on slapping the prisoner's face, in an effort to make him get up.

I took a closer look at the man and noticed he was a Red. A Red? Now I was interested in the case; and in the bad light I recognised my comrade from Halle. I stopped the slapping at once, and he was then taken into the surgery.

During the time I had spent as the doctor's clerk, I had had enough opportunity to learn the symptoms of schizophrenia, and I saw at once that my old friend was suffering from this illness and was in a state of rigidity. During the time of his transfer the man had been ill and should have been in a sanatorium, not in a concentration camp.

I searched through the files and found medical reports and opinions about him from two sanatoria. There was no doubt that his was a case of harmless schizophrenia. Even the detailed observations of prolonged attacks gave no pretext whatever for carrying out sterilisation on him, especially as these always manifested themselves as a quickly passing state of rigidity, with no signs of even slightly dangerous activity. The minutely recorded history of the illness was so clear that even a very insufficiently trained psychiatrist could have immediately judged the case correctly.

And yet the Nazis had considered it correct to send this harmless sick man to the "Sanatorium Buchenwald".

16. Shot on Orders of the Reichsführer S.S.

AT times it happened that S.S. Oberscharführer Seehausen asked me to let him have a collection of forms necessary in cases of death.

At first I could not understand for what purpose these were required by him. I knew that, among other things, red forms in cases of suicide, and yellow forms for all other cases of death, were supposed to be filled in for the registrar, being required for statistical purposes and stating the cause of death.

Seehausen would sometimes fill in these forms in the surgery, although I never had the opportunity of investigating into the reason for his use of these forms himself, as he always put them out of sight in the brief case he constantly carried with him.

I hit upon a clue by chance one day, after Seehausen had against asked for a collection of forms. It was known to us that the Scharführer Uhlig, who used to be an orderly in the sick room and about whose fate I will write on other pages, had committed suicide in the detention barracks. It needed few reasoning powers to detect a connection between the events when Seehausen himself again filled in death certificates and red registry forms.

Once my attention had been attracted in this way, it was only a question of time before the accuracy of the deductions I had formed was confirmed.

I maintained a close friendship with a political prisoner who worked as a clerk in the camp laundry. Through him I got to know other political friends who had formerly held positions in the Leipziger Volkszeitung (Leipzig People's Newspaper). During our leisure hours we often got together, discussed our position, talked politics and philosophy, and were not lacking in humorous remarks which became more grotesque with us diehards as our difficulties became greater.

One of these friends was responsible for the registration and sorting of laundry. By chance, during a conversation, he once casually mentioned that he sometimes received blood-stained laundry and articles of clothing belonging to men who had been shot, despite the fact that nothing was known of any shootings in the camp. He asked me whether I knew anything more about cases like these, as he knew I had to prepare death certificates for those who had died or had been killed. I had to answer in the negative.

We agreed that he should at once inform me of any further cases of evident shooting; by paying special attention I might then observe something which would explain what secretly went on. We thought that the killings might have something to do with S.S. men who had fallen into disfavour.

Some time later, after my friend had told me of some evidence of shooting he had found in the laundry, S.S. Oberscharführer Seehausen again sent for a collection of death certificates. We knew now that the S.S. toughs also murdered people who had not even been brought into the camp as prisoners.

It did not take long to get the final proof we wanted. I succeeded in obtaining a form which Seehausen had filled in, and there I read, under the heading "Cause of death", "Shot by order of the Reichsführer S.S."

I willingly admit that this wording is clear, and with but one meaning. Within the framework of what went on in the concentration camp and in face of the many millions of murders attributable to the Nazi criminals, there is fundamentally nothing very special about all this.

Yet it is necessary to add a few remarks to show that it was in this that Nazi criminality obviously lifted its mask. That the accomplices of the greatest murderer of our time knew what was going on is proved by the fact that for a long time they endeavoured to keep this open wording a secret from me, a prisoner, from whom perforce few matters could be concealed. The criminals were normally extremely careful to see that their innumerable murders and cruelties could not be proved by witnesses, or by documents and the like.

Although a great proportion of the German people and the world knew that National Socialism had turned the once highly respected German judicature into a compliant tool for their criminal policy, it was generally believed that judgement could only be passed on people after properly conducted court proceedings, and that the sentence itself could only be pronounced after judgement.

At least outwardly the Nazis disguised their justice of blood and horror from the German people, who, for instance, were kept in the belief that the death sentence could only be carried out on a "fellow-countryman" after due court proceedings. But it was officially recorded that Herr Himmler was a law unto himself. Such a fact was nothing new to the initiated; it certainly was new that he had dared to have his order placed on record.

After the collapse and unmasking of Nazism, it is today comparatively easy to give the reasons for this blatancy. It was simply that Himmler, who did not shun any crime in order to remain in power, knew through the secret reports of his Gestapo far better than anybody else in Germany to what extent the edifice of National Socialism was cracking, so that even its firmest supports were beginning to rot.

For this reason the law of the S.S. itself was introduced. For this reason he had placed on record a small number of his personal orders to murder, in order to create the impression that he was master of the situation, and to warn all those who tried to break the ranks of his office.

It was known to every S.S. man that, until then, a murder needing an open consent could only be carried out on the express order and with the express approval of Hitler. Feared by every S.S. man who had stuck his nose a little further into the general affairs of Nazism than most, Himmler now let the entire S.S. know, with the speed of wildfire, that even S.S. men would be shot if it was considered expedient to do so.

Such shootings first of all concerned S.S. people of their

own rank and file who displeased their leaders, whose liquidation Himmler considered desirable, and on whom not even the German judicature could pass a death sentence, having been degraded to the status of a Nazi whore.

I know that every responsible person who meditates on the structure of a State will shudder at the fact that such conditions could be possible; but the reader may believe me that we concentrationers envied the deaths of these murdered people, for they were not slowly tortured to death, they did not suffer death by a starvation which dragged along for weeks and months and sometimes even for years; they were spared the hell of Buchenwald, and though their death was not perhaps always painless, it was at least a quick one.

17. The Green Hypodermic

How differently, for instance, did that poor wretch die who was sent to the camp in order to make him speak against himself.

One such case concerned a prisoner from Tellsruh, which is on the Upper Silesian–Polish border, who had undergone a term of imprisonment for repeated theft. He had committed the thefts with the aid of an accomplice, and during his imprisonment they were suspected of having shot a policeman in the prosecution of their crimes. But the evidence against them was not sufficient for sentence to be passed.

While his companion had succeeded in escaping to Poland, this man defended himself from the moment he heard of the accusation by persistently refusing to make any statement. His only words were: "Tellsruh", and "My name is —— no".

He understood everything said to him, he obeyed every order immediately and without objection, but nothing could induce him to make the necessary statement desired of him. He had remained silent during the course of his imprisonment, and still refused to talk even when he was taken to the camp, although he had no doubt endured the usual brutal treatment while there. Repeated whippings remained equally ineffectual.

He was handed to Dr. Ding, to whom, other methods having proved in vain, was delegated the task of making the prisoner speak. Ding set about his work with confidence.

Simple methods of intimidation and torment remained unsuccessful. Beating, hunger and torture while in the detention barracks were just as unsuccessful, as were the abrupt alternations between bullying and fatherly persuasion, between brutal torment and the "good-natured" cigarette. Still the prisoner remained silent.

Ding decided to inject in him a liberal dose from the "green needle" (Apomorphin). The prisoner himself bared the muscles of his buttocks without hesitation, and although Ding shouted at him diabolically, "You rotter, you will die now!" he did not resist as the needle was pushed into the muscle.

He instantly obeyed the order to stand outside the barracks with his knees in a half-bent position and his arms lifted sideways. After a short time the poison began to take effect on him. He stemmed the feeling of nausea with difficulty, obviously being afraid of dirtying the paved path.

The urge to vomit constantly increased. He kept painfully looking around him. Suddenly he could no longer prevent himself from being sick. He jumped aside towards a tree and vomited; but then instantly took up his previous position. Again and again he fought the urge to vomit, again and again he jumped to the tree, and at constantly shorter intervals. His knees at last gave way, as he was seized by convulsions. Supporting himself with his hands on the ground, he fell on his knees, retching uncontrollably.

His eyes protruded from their sockets, the mucus from his stomach smearing his painfully distorted face as he went on retching and vomiting. His features became more and more animal-like, until he finally resembled a raving dog rather than a human being.

Through all this Ding remained calm, laughing as the prisoner writhed in convulsions on the ground like a half-trodden worm. The doctor now ordered another prisoner to pour a few buckets of water over our tortured comrade. The vomiting slowly ceased. After about an hour he had so far recovered that he could again stand on his feet.

Ding called him in, tried to impress him with the necessity for telling all he knew, but still he remained silent.

The next morning, the prisoner having been brought in for further interrogation, Ding ordered a particularly appetising breakfast for him from the kitchen. Again he was asked whether he would now speak, and, after a short hesitation, he again answered: "My name is —— no."

"You have some idea now of the difference between the prison and the concentration camp," Ding retorted. "You can choose between them. Either you talk and you will be taken back to prison, or you do not talk, in which case you will become a mutilated corpse. I will give you half an hour to think it over. We will continue the treatment if you remain silent."

After the lapse of the given time, the prisoner still said: "My name is —— no."

Dr. Ding ordered his Scharführer to work on the prisoner with a complicated electrical apparatus. They began by pressing the two poles of the instrument into his hands and, beginning slowly, sent increasingly higher electrical energies through his body. He reeled with pain, terribly shaken by convulsive shudders. Yet still he answered none of the questions put to him.

Scharführer Hofmann, who was operating the apparatus, sent the current through it at short intervals, always increasing or reducing it according to the reaction of the victim. The current tormented the man in the most terrible manner. Perspiration poured down his face. His eyes remained closed for most of the time, but on the few occasions he opened them, the protruding eyeballs seemed enlarged, as if he suffered from Basedow disease in its advanced stages.

He struggled and twisted in terrible convulsions, particularly when all the available electrical energies were sent through his body. The torture became increasingly wanton, the tormented man "dancing" more and more frantically.

The Witches' Sabbath had now reached the stage where the Scharführer did not even notice how the tortured man, in his convulsions, moved further and further away from the apparatus. Soon he must pull down the whole machine, with all its wiring. Oh, if he would only do that! I prayed. Never in my life had I possessed a more ardent wish than this, for it was simply terrible to be a helpless witness to such torment.

Then something happened to me which I never before would have thought possible. Although I was aware of the laws and limitations of hypnotism, I still absurdly concentrated all my powers of thought on the electrical apparatus, in an effort to smash it to atoms at once, with that force which ignorant and credulous people attribute to Indian fakirs.

At last Hofmann switched off the apparatus. The prisoner stood in the centre of the room, breathing heavily and almost completely exhausted. He could not answer the questions even with his monotonous "Tellsruh. My name is —— no."

Previous prisoners who had been tortured with the electrical apparatus had without exception groaned and screamed, cried, begged, implored, finally to do everything demanded of them. Yet not a single sound had passed the tightly closed lips of the present victim.

On the orders of Dr. Ding, after a short interval the prisoner was obliged to undress and sit in a hip-bath half-filled with water. One pole was laid in the water and the other attached to a roller. He was then given an excruciating massage. Again he had to endure terrible tortures, his whole body quivering and rearing; but still he did not speak.

S.S. Scharführer Hofmann now passed the roller over the man's arms, chest and body, so that he jerked and kicked more and more savagely. As Hofmann passed the roller over the left side of the chest, the prisoner reared up with one terrific jerk. He shot from the bath like a pike, in doing which both his arms struck out in a wide semi-circular movement. And then —he collapsed over the bath, completely limp and lifeless.

Every onlooker was astounded by this sudden change in the situation—Dr. Ding, Seehausen, Hofmann, a third orderly and yet another prisoner. All stood as if they had been struck dead. It seemed to me as if we stood there endlessly.

The most benumbed of us was Hofmann. He stood with trembling knees, roller held loosely in his right hand, gazing at the body with terror-stricken eyes, his mouth half open. This was undoubtedly his first direct murder, perhaps his last, for he was fundamentally of good stock, although that type of person was bound to deteriorate in a Nazi atmosphere.

That evening I wavered in my resolutions more than any other time of my imprisonment, when I considered the almost complete hopelessness of leading a purposeful life again, and reflected upon the sorrow which I now still had to go through.

18. Criminal Surroundings

GREENS were among the first batch of concentrationers to arrive in 1937 in order to erect the camp on the Ettersberg. These were prisoners who, despite suspected criminal activities, could not legally be imprisoned or placed under protective custody; so were taken to a concentration camp instead.

It was one of the greatest mental agonies I suffered that I was treated in the same way as the criminal elements during my entire imprisonment. It is true that I got to know some splendid men among the criminals, even, strange as it may seem, some of high moral standards, men who unreservedly behaved as good comrades would. Most of them were, however, an untidy, dirty, unprincipled, tramp-like mob against whose direct and indirect harassing one could only defend oneself through isolation, difficult in the circumstances.

Even in the dark middle ages, it was at all times recognised that political prisoners were not put together with ordinary criminals. Why National Socialism did this is quite simply explained.

I know very well that my explanation will not appear plausible to some credulous people. It is nevertheless true, as true as the change of day and night, as true as is every law of Nature, the unavoidability and unchangeability of which we perceive every second of our lives.

As expressly and openly stated by Goebbels, political offenders constituted an ordinary criminal problem to the National Socialist clique of leaders because they were not in a position to differentiate between ordinary and political criminals, because their ideology was based on pseudo-knowledge and half-truths, that cancer of the human race. They were prisoners of their thoughtless propaganda, which continued to find more and more appealing yet dangerous slogans, which disarmed and captivated unpolitically trained people. Every German must surely now realise the truth that these leaders were not really politicians but unscrupulous criminals, who wrapped a political cloak around them like a fraudulent impersonator wearing a dinner suit for some nefarious purpose.

Although, during our term of imprisonment and our time in the concentration camp, we politicals were forced to share our cells, tables and work with dubious criminal elements, I can count on the fingers of one hand the number of superiors and guards who did not themselves differentiate between me personally and an ordinary criminal.

Despite express prohibition, I noticed again and again that my guards treated me more courteously, more decently, more objectively, than they did the real criminals, and this was an attitude shared with other political comrades.

Even some of those S.S. myrmidons who took great pains to act in accordance with instructions could not conceal the fact that they were unable fully to comprehend the demand of their leaders to treat us like real criminals. This circumstance is certainly one of the reasons why influential positions in the camp passed more and more into the hands of the political prisoners.

It came about, however, that two Greens became camp seniors when the camp was first established, and all lower and Kapo positions were soon also occupied by Greens. This was a hard blow to us politicals, and even to the camp life as a whole.

It must be realised that a Kapo had tremendous power over his fellow-prisoners, a power so great that he could even decide on their life and death. The camp management deliberately gave the Kapos such positions of authority because in this way they found willing tools for their brutal policy of destruction even in the ranks of the prisoners themselves.

Naturally, as easy as it was for the camp management to remove a Kapo who displeased them, it was as difficult for fellow-prisoners to do so. In view of the natural antipathy of the criminal elements towards the political prisoners, and considering the opposite nature of their two worlds, it was a long and tedious fight before the Kapo positions could be wrested from the criminals.

A Green by the name of Richter was the camp senior when I first arrived at the camp. He held that position when the camp had been established. Then he was with the punitive company for some time, until he was again appointed a camp senior. He was a stocky, broad-shouldered, crafty-looking fellow. I think I can sufficiently plainly reveal the kind of man he was by two facts.

It was Richter who had given us newcomers the clumsy instructive talk in the square on the day I first arrived there. Generally speaking he had correctly described camp conditions, though at that time we found them unbelievable, while his remark that he himself would carry out the hanging of recalcitrant prisoners was not a boastful exaggeration but quite in keeping with the facts.

The second prisoner who had arrived while Richter was addressing us, and had caused him to become uneasy, had been Hans Schulenberg, who was a camp policeman at the time and enjoyed great popularity because of his correct conduct. Having a great deal on his conscience, Richter knew that he was in Hans Schulenburg's hands, although the latter did not denounce him because of his fundamental principles.

Richter himself knew nothing of the fundamental principles of a political prisoner. He thought he could attain personal favour by subservient toadyism. He had what we prisoners called a "cyclist's" nature, showing a bent back subserviently to those above him, and treading down those below him.

When Richter finally met his fate and died, the Buchenwald Song was sung with the following variation:

> The forest is black and the sky is red
> Now Richter cannot beat Blacks till they're dead.

I believe these points suffice to indicate Richter's character. But I have more to tell of him.

Shortly after I had been detailed to the sick ward, I noticed a peculiar unrest among my old comrades. It was not until later that I was able to understand the reason for this, and even then it was only with great difficulty that I found this out. I was still too new in the camp to be told everything. Experience would first have to prove to the old comrades that I could be trusted without reservation. My political past, the fact that I had undergone long years of imprisonment on their behalf, and had been sent to the concentration camp, three factors which would normally have rendered me trustworthy, counted for very little here in the camp, and it was customary to wait for a crucial test before trusting a newcomer.

Although our lives hung by a thread, situations still arose in which one could risk even more than these for one's comrades. Whoever passed a crucial test was considered worthy of trust, and I had not yet done so.

Although, therefore, I was told little, I did get to know that the cook from the camp kitchen and the Kapo who dealt with the corpses were mixed up in some affair, together with a prisoner who was a dentist by profession and carried out all kinds of dental treatment in the sick ward. The first two were Greens, the dentist being a Black.

For a long time the Kapo who dealt with the corpses had obtained possession of gold by extracting gold fillings from the teeth of dead prisoners, after having stolen a pair of dentists' pliers from the sick ward.

He had three methods of getting the gold out of the camp. Firstly, he hammered the gold crowns into small lumps which he intended to swallow should he be discharged one day, for as an old crook he was familiar with such matters. Secondly, through the cook in the sick ward, he succeeded in contacting S.S. Scharführer Uhlig, who declared his willingness to get the gold out of the camp if he shared in the proceeds. Finally, he persuaded the dentist to produce massive gold teeth and crowns in tedious night work, which he fitted for individual prisoners by removing their healthy teeth, if necessary.

This peculiar business may in the beginning have been comparatively small; but the Kapo later had gold literally en masse, particularly when the Jewish pogrom of 1938 brought with it deteriorating conditions and the death rate rose sharply, steadily increasing from then on.

I did not know Scharführer Uhlig very well, but he was a

young, good-looking fellow, with careless daredevil manners, pert, often inclined to crack jokes, and romp in a boyish manner even with the prisoners. But he was also moody, which was inevitable in such an undisciplined person, especially in view of the authority he exercised as a camp Scharführer. Most of the prisoners avoided him for this reason and only frolicked with him when they could not avoid doing so.

Although it was forbidden to do so, he regularly ate his breakfast in the kitchen of the sick ward, for meals there were cheap, convenient and tasty. The Green who was cook of the sick ward saw to this, even at the expense of the sick.

Suddenly the dentist was put under arrest. This was the signal for all concerned in the affair to wipe out any traces of their misdeeds, and, if necessary, to prepare a combined plan for their statements. Nothing happened for two days, then further arrests were made.

The criminals wondered if the dentist would "split"—that is, whether he would talk, or if not, how long he would refrain from doing so. It would not be possible to cover the Kapo, for the camp management would certainly trace the source of the gold to him.

The criminals concluded that the arrested men were without exception people who could not "squeal". Their forecast was, "The tooth plumber has heart; he sings deliberately." (The dentist has courage and what he discloses is well considered.)

The Kapo promised that should he be "for the jump", he would unpack carefully, remaining as inconspicuous as possible. In all circumstances he would keep quiet about certain aspects of the case, one of them being Uhlig's connection. The motive for this promise was not of course the protection of the S.S. Scharführer, but self-preservation, because he knew perfectly well that he would inevitably die if the wangle with Uhlig were discovered.

There was a slight chance of those concerned in the whole affair getting off lightly, for they were criminals towards whom the camp management willingly exercised a certain degree of clemency involving purely criminal derelictions, on the principle that brothers in crime stick together.

The Kapo hoped to be further excused on the plea that

"only the teeth of the dirty Jewish swine had been extracted and they, in any event, had stolen the gold from the Aryans in the first place". With such an explanation he gambled on mitigating circumstances, and had good reason to assume that he would succeed.

Finally, there was a consideration which was as bold as it was perhaps effective. It was intended to point out that those prisoners who were discharged from the camp with such dental repairs as they had received would be excellent evidence against the "fairy tales" of atrocities circulated about the camp.

The Kapo was duly sent for. On the third day it became known that he had either hanged himself, or had been hanged, in his cell. This was a bad sign. Uneasiness increased among those concerned. A few days passed without further incident, however. Had the Kapo settled the affair in order to protect his confederates?

One day Rödl came into the sick ward. He walked through every room, staying in each for a short time. Nothing indicated that this inspection had anything to do with the matter of the gold teeth.

The men who had previously acted as bearers were summarily dismissed, a harmless Black became Kapo, and without exception political Jews were given jobs as bearers, and they considered this sad and unpleasant task to be a privilege.

A few days later the cook of the sick ward was taken away, and at the same time we heard that S.S. Scharführer Uhlig was under arrest.

After his service revolver had been returned to him in his cell in no uncertain manner, Uhlig committed suicide.

A few days after these events, I noticed that Ding was filling a hypodermic needle, which he then handed to Seehausen. The latter placed it in his brief case, and left us for about half an hour. He whispered something to Ding on his return. I could not hear what he said, except for the words, "With it a little air too." At the time I was still too inexperienced and new to the camp to realise that Seehausen had liquidated the cook.

I still suspected nothing even the next day, when I had to fill in the cook's death certificate. Why, even when I heard from the bearers that the cook had obviously been killed with

177

an injection in the arm, I assumed the murder had been committed by S.S. Scharführer Sommer, who was in charge of the detention barracks and who had the features of a brutal hangman. Seehausen himself had the physiognomy of a clumsy yet straightforward man.

Within a few weeks, however, I gained enough experience to understand the real facts. Seehausen was the man who could best commit the murder without meeting any resistance, for he had often enough had his breakfast with Uhlig in the sick ward kitchen. The cook would assume that Seehausen was really injecting a heart restorative into him, and not the poison it really was.

The affair of the teeth soon died down. After some weeks the dentist was released from arrest, and the other prisoners mixed up in the business but not yet arrested, were now certain that their names were not known to the camp management. Among these was the camp senior Richter, who had hidden the greatest part of his treasure in the heels of his boots and whose mouth was literally full of gold.

Some time later his destiny was fulfilled. He had become in the end a nuisance to the camp management, because of his many crooked dealings. The services he had no doubt rendered them stood in no reasonable relationship to the trouble he caused.

Richter was still very confident on the morning of the day which brought down the final curtain on his life. He had wriggled out of innumerable situations and had always found that the camp management protected him, and was so accustomed to death that he probably did not fear it for himself.

I do not know the immediate reasons for his being relieved of his position as camp senior. In any case, this point is unimportant, for Richter had so many scores against him that any one of them would have been sufficient to liquidate another man.

To begin with, Richter knew that he would go over the stock that day, and so he reported himself sick. The head nurse did not quite know what to do, knowing that if he received Richter into the sick ward the camp management would ask for an explanation of an obviously shady arrangement. On the other hand, he did not like to refuse Richter, there always

178

being the possibility that the man would work his way out of his difficulty and even receive an influential position again.

He therefore held the acceptance in abeyance, saying that he had more important matters to settle first.

In the meantime, two Scharführer had come to look for Richter.

He protested against being taken to the gate, saying that he was seriously ill and would first have to see the doctor; but the Scharführer smiled in amusement, ignoring his protests. Those who witnessed the scene were also amused, knowing that Richter was receiving his just reward.

He was then placed under detention and several times suffered punishment on the stock. From this fact it was concluded that he had not "squealed" about the affair of the teeth, especially as no arrests were made which could have been connected with him.

He died during the night the S.S. officers had a wild drinking party in their mess. That day Ding, looking very seedy although not normally a drinker, dictated his death report to me. Cause of death: syphilitic inflammation of the jugular vein. The result, which was premeditated, preceded the post-mortem, which had not yet been carried out.

The bearers could discover no traces of a venous injection, when they collected the body from the detention barracks. Traces of an injection would in any case have been difficult to detect, in view of the very badly mauled body. They did see, however, that somebody had already extracted the many gold teeth from the jaw, and knew that a prisoner could not have carried out this work.

19. The Black-out Barracks

ONE day, on Rödl's orders, an old, rather isolated wooden barracks which was to be demolished in order to make room for a stone building, was cleared of all its furniture. The doors and windows were exceptionally well barricaded and the inside of the barracks was completely blacked out. In this way the Black-out Barracks was established at Rödl's instigation, for he felt that the numerous other methods of punishment at his disposal were no longer sufficient for his purposes.

The following orders were issued: 1. I (Rödl) will determine the period of confinement in darkness to be given to any prisoner as punishment. 2. There will be no interruption of imprisonment in darkness for health reasons or such. 3. Food will consist only of bread and water, each prisoner to receive 200 grammes of bread per day. 4. Any communication with the prisoners concerned is strictly forbidden.

When the barracks was ready, twenty-three prisoners were moved in for a period of four weeks' confinement in darkness; two days later, three more followed, and after eight days another eleven, so that there were altogether thirty-seven men locked up in the new Black-out Barracks. No further arrests followed.

I am unable to say in detail what took place there, nor do I know whether this tragedy will ever be disclosed, for it seems unlikely that any of the victims are still alive. But I can describe what I saw, and even if words can only indicate the actual facts, I hope that they will be sufficiently impressive to create some idea of the true picture of what happened.

On Rödl's orders, a large board was put up in the entrance room of the Black-out Barracks, and on this were written the names of the prisoners and their period of imprisonment. One morning, about four weeks after they had been taken there, the Scharführer in charge of their bread ration called out the first twenty-three prisoners; but only four actually emerged. They wandered into the light like walking corpses, to instantly collapse outside the barracks.

Four stretcher-bearers were ordered to report immediately at the Black-out Barracks. Walter Krämer, the senior nurse, at once proceeded there with four stretchers and bearers. The Scharführer had meanwhile entered the barracks and, with the aid of a torch, had ascertained that a large number of the prisoners were already dead, that others were obviously dying, and that the rest appeared to be in a state of exhaustion or were completely mad.

Krämer had the four prisoners outside carried to the sick

ward, then also entered the barracks, having ordered all bearers to come there with every available stretcher.

It was still early in the morning. Ding and the orderlies were not expected to arrive in the camp for some time, and so I joined the column of stretcher-bearers, with a deep foreboding of tragedy.

Krämer came towards me. I saw at once that he must have had a terrible experience. He looked at me with eyes which reflected unspeakable horror, although he had seen so much misery, suffering and cruelty, possessing almost phenomenal powers of resistance which I had admired again and again, always remaining calm even in the face of the most dreadful calamities.

We exchanged a few words, and he told me that the Scharführer had agreed to his removing the dead and dying from the barracks.

The Scharführer stood at the door, his face expressing cold horror.

He even stepped aside when Krämer and I entered the barracks.

We were met by the putrid stench of combined excrement, rot and corpses. Krämer shone his torch into the depths of the room. The floor was damp and smeared over with dirt and filth. On the left, the torch's thin weak beam touched a row of dead prisoners, starved, cramped corpses, apparently laid side by side by their comrades.

The beam of the torch wandered to the right. There, the dead and dying were lying in a jumbled heap. The beam glided from one skeleton to the other.

It was a good thing that the light of the torch was so weak, for thus it could not reveal the whole tragedy to us at once. One of the prisoners lay breathing feebly, sometimes seized by convulsion, beside him six, seven or eight bread rations.

There, another corpse was huddled against the wall, water mug and bread still in his hand. There, the others, the living, sat on the bare floor with their backs against the wall, apathetic, exhausted, gazing stupidly before them. One of them had completely undressed himself and squatted on his clothes, like a monkey in the Zoo. Another, apparently a gypsy, sat in a corner, quite calm and serene, continuously smiling, the light of our torch bringing no single reaction from him.

Others lifted their hands to their eyes or, being dazzled, lowered their heads when we directed the light towards them. Strangely, none spoke to us; it was as if they had lost all powers of speech. It was not until later that we realised the real reason for this fact. Face to face with all the horrors, we had ourselves forgotten to speak to them, forgetting that they could not see us because we were standing behind the dazzling light, so that they assumed we were Scharführer and not fellow-prisoners.

We carried from the barracks nineteen dead and seven dying. Dr. Ding had meanwhile arrived and he immediately ordered the barracks to be completely cleared. Four prisoners were discharged to their living quarters, the other seven being admitted to the sick ward for treatment. All seven died, despite the fact that the nurses did everything possible for them.

Dr. Ding had obviously cleared the barracks of his own accord. As we knew that the establishment of the Black-out Barracks was Rödl's personal work, we assumed that a clash would now ensue between the two men, Dr. Ding, as subordinate, getting the worst of it; but nothing of the kind occurred.

When, some time afterwards, I asked Dr. Ding how he had settled this affair with the Obersturmbannführer, he said to me, "Oh, he! Fourteen days later that idiot had completely forgotten the matter. If I had told him that the barracks had been abolished, he would only then have remembered that he had ever established it!"

20. The Rev. Paul Schneider

PERHAPS only former inmates of the camp will fully understand that I can remember only the rough outlines of my many horrible experiences in Buchenwald, and these some times dimly. Those Americans and Germans who spoke to the inmates still remaining in the camp immediately after it was opened, and saw to what spiritual cripples the Nazi gangsters had reduced even intelligent people, will also understand how impossible it is to give minute descriptions of all the horrors perpetrated by the infernally diabolical S.S.

Those who would be well served by this fact need not rejoice, for enough is remembered to spell the right sentence for them!

The Vicar Paul Schneider, from Dickenschied, had been in Buchenwald for two years. He was a well-known leader of the practising Christians of Germany, along with Pastor Niemöller, who was in the concentration camp of Oranienburg at the same time.

He was put on the stock and punished with twenty-five strokes of the cane when, at a roll-call, he refused to salute the murder flag of that Reich which was to last a thousand years; and because he steadfastly persisted in his refusal, was locked in the detention barracks.

That was the beginning of the end. Schneider enjoyed great popularity and general respect because, from the first day of his time in the camp, he had shared literally everything with his fellow-prisoners, even the bread and the little money he had. We knew, however, that because he made no secret of his Christian views and his opposition to Nazism, the death sentence had almost certainly been passed on him. None suspected that day that this would not be carried out until more than an endlessly long year had passed.

Schneider's voice was often heard loudly and clearly, resounding from the detention barracks across almost the entire square when the tens of thousands had fallen in for roll-call.

"Comrades, listen to me," he would call. "This is Vicar Paul Schneider speaking. They torture and murder here. For the sake of Christ, have mercy. Pray to God. Remain steadfast and true. God the almighty Father will take the evil from us."

It was clear to all of us that Paul Schneider was fanatical in his faith, a deeply religious man who found comfort in the passion of his religious ideal, with the strength to suffer hardships and even death. He believed in salvation through God. He very well knew what would inevitably happen to him after his sermon, but his moral principles forced him to act in a way typically courageous.

After each sermon of this sort, Schneider was invariably brought out of his cell, whipped until the blood soaked through his clothes, then dragged back to the detention barracks, almost unconscious.

I do not know what else Schneider had to endure in his cell, but his sufferings must have been terrible. There, he was in the hands of the jailer, the unbelievably sadistic S.S. Scharführer Sommer, who carried out thrashings with lust, tree-hanging with perverse joy, and again and again sent for poison from the sick ward's chemist, after which cases of death in the detention barracks were always registered.

I met Paul Schneider face to face for the first time in the summer of 1939. He was brought to the sick ward by Sommer himself.

What a heartrending sight he was! Never have I felt more strongly the deep tragedy of Pilate's words, "Ecce homo". The noble face was full of grief, and the clear, honest eyes full of that ecstasy which the noblest qualities in man and a determined will had imprinted in them. The body was emaciated to a skeleton, the arms shapelessly swollen and blue-red, and green and bloody the signs of fetters on his wrists. And the legs!—they were not human legs!—they were the legs of an elephant!

Having seen many prisoners die of embolism we were puzzled that this man could still be alive. In such a condition, how could he have covered the distance across the large square, through the long rows of barracks and through the wood, down to the sick ward.

His dirty face and its stupid, brutal features contrasting abominably with that of his companion, Sommer did not for a moment move from Schneider's side, so that we found no opportunity to speak to our comrade in order to learn the details of his sufferings.

We wondered what was to happen. Another murder? Somehow the thought stirred us deeply, although we had grown indifferent towards the daily mass deaths we had witnessed.

Paul Schneider, however, was no nameless, unknown prisoner, but was one of those whose death would affect wide circles, in Holland, England, Sweden and America. He was our comrade, and although his opinions were not always ours, his uprightness and Christian way of life were beyond all doubt.

We tried not to show our feelings to Sommer. Only the most trusted prisoners exchanged glances between themselves, telling the initiated what we felt and how moved we were. Not for a fraction of a second did we interrupt our allotted work, and slowly Sommer's lynx-like scrutiny of our faces for signs of pity ceased.

Dr. Ding arrived at last.

"Why did you not report yourself sick, Schneider?" the doctor addressed him in calm, professional tones.

Paul Schneider wanted to get up from the bench on which he had been allowed to sit, but Ding immediately said, "Remain seated."

Schneider now looked somewhat helplessly at the doctor, apparently surprised by the manner in which Ding had spoken to him; but his eyes revealed suspicion. He made a gesture with his right hand, as if he did not know quite what to answer.

Ding repeated again, almost persuasively, "You are sick! You must report yourself if you do not feel well."

Schneider did not answer. Was this doctor not of the concentration camp Buchenwald but an unsuspecting angel from another world? Did he not see how obviously he had been tortured, almost to death?

"Come along with me," Ding went on. "I will examine you."

Schneider got up painfully and staggered to another room behind Ding, where he was thoroughly examined through a stethoscope.

Would Ding give him the needle now? I wondered.

No! He did not!

Instead, he ordered, "Bandages and ointment for the wrists. Grape-sugar. A heart restorative. Careful massage. Ultra-violet-ray treatment for the bruises on the back, the buttocks and the thighs."

He left it to the prisoner-nurses to carry out his instructions.

What was going on? Could there really be a change, and Paul Schneider to receive different treatment?—worthy of a human being?—in keeping with all laws and standards?

The nurses went to great trouble with Paul Schneider, but they could not exchange a single word with him which would explain this behaviour, for Sommer would not move from his side.

Before leaving the room, Ding said, "Treatment will continue tomorrow. Sommer, immediately after roll-call in the morning you will bring Schneider into the surgery again."

This treatment continued for about eight to ten days, and Schneider recovered surprisingly quickly.

During this period, in my presence Ding once asked him, "Well, Schneider, how do you feel now?"

Schneider smiled. "All right, Herr Sturmführer."

Ding said, "Have you a proper camp bed in your cell?"

"Yes, Herr Sturmführer," Schneider replied.

"Why don't you give up your nonsense, Schneider?" Ding said. "You can see you will be treated correctly if you comply with the camp discipline."

Paul Schneider did not answer, merely smiling, but his eyes glistened.

"I will speak to the Standartenführer as to whether you can be released from arrest," Ding promised.

In the meantime, the nurses had found some opportunity to speak to Schneider. He told them that he had been tied to a cross in his cell for a fortnight, day and night without a break. Scharführer Sommer, whom he described as a murderer and torturer, had always ill-treated him terribly, particularly during this period. He could not understand why he was now suddenly being treated so decently, whether he was to be discharged, or what?

The treatment at an end, with some striking results, Ding again carried out a thorough physical examination of Schneider's heart and lungs.

"There you are, Schneider," he said; "you have recovered splendidly. Only suffering a little from after-effects. Well, that's understandable, in view of the whole business. We'll settle that too. Let us inject a heart restorative."

He fetched a phial from the chemist, filled the hypodermic,

and injected his patient. I was not present the next day when Sommer brought Schneider back to the surgery. According to the reports of the nurses, Ding asked Schneider how he felt after yesterday's injection. Schneider answered that he felt quite well, apart from a little giddiness. That should not have occurred, Ding replied, but perhaps Schneider suffered a certain amount of allergy towards the medicine, from which he had otherwise always had good results. "We will try some other medicine and see how it agrees with you."

Ding was not present when I myself entered the surgery. Schneider was sitting under the ultra-violet rays. He replied with a smile to my "Good morning." He had certainly recovered well. His arms and legs were normal again, though his body was still very thin, but his chest was broad and strong and his bearing as upright as of old.

Ding came into the room, a filled hypodermic in his hand. He was surprisingly lively, and, knowing this trait in him, within a moment all was clear to me. I could not be any part of the farce, and left to walk over to the doctor's room.

I was quite overcome by my reactions. I had almost begun to believe that Schneider could last out in Buchenwald. And now this sudden change! Following some inner prompting, mechanically and unwillingly I walked over to the wastepaper basket, in which I knew Ding usually threw his empty phials. There I saw five empty strophantin phials, two of which alone would, if injected together, prove fatal.

Shortly afterwards Ding came into the room, sat down at his writing desk, and I gave him a file for signatures.

He signed them all, without reading a single paper, for his thoughts were obviously elsewhere.

Peix, the nurse of the in-patient ward, came into the room. Now more of the farce was to be played out. Ding pretended to be busy. I looked at Peix. The moment was like an eternity.

"Herr Doctor," said Peix, "is Schneider to return to his cell again?"

"What?" said Ding, quite surprised. For a moment he gazed before him, thinking quickly. "What?—Ah—Yes—No," he stammered.

There was an atmosphere of breathless expectancy as Ding

gazed into space. Then he said, as if referring to a harmless case of therapeutics, "No, let him lie under the light for another half hour."

Peix left the room and Ding continued to sign the papers I put before him. Could I have been mistaken? I wondered. It was not possible for any human heart to withstand such a dose of poison for more than a few minutes! Was I already seeing ghosts?

Ding himself was quite calm. He put questions to me and talked about this and that. I thought I must have been mistaken!

Suddenly, Peix came running into the room. "Herr Sturm-führer, please come quickly!"

Ding jumped up. He made no attempt to ask what had happened, but followed the nurse. I had to steady myself by holding on to the table for a moment, before I followed them.

Stretched out on the floor, Paul Schneider lay dead. Ding knelt by the body and opened the closed eyelids. Peix stood by his side like a statue.

I learned later that Schneider had complained about being giddy under the rays. The nurse had taken the apparatus away, but Schneider collapsed as he began to walk towards the chair where his clothes were.

Ding dictated to me an imaginary history of the illness from which Schneider was supposed to have suffered. Even a temperature chart was drawn up, despite the fact that Schneider had never been treated as an in-patient. His death certificate stated that he had been discharged from the sick ward and had been undergoing treatment as an out-patient. He had died suddenly, after treatment in the surgery, heart failure being the probable cause of death.

Camp commandant Koch was immediately informed of the occurrence. It was the first time such a thing had happened. Berlin was informed by wire. The forged papers concerning the illness, with their lies of several kinds of treatment in the sick ward, were carefully compiled for dispatch to Berlin on demand. Berlin did demand these documents.

While the bearers were carrying the body into the morgue, I racked my brains, wondering at this expense, when there was usually a far shorter process of disposal. Even a post-mortem was ordered, which made the puzzle still more confusing to me.

The dissector of the pathological institute of the University of Jena arrived next day. I was asked to write a report of the post-mortem. Once more I saw Paul Schneider on the stretcher. There was no sign on him of any kind of ill-treatment, no sign at all of all the sorrow this man had been compelled to endure. In the bend of the right arm a small prick was hardly visible, but here was the spot where the murderer had injected poison into the bloodstream, the poison which would not work, who knows for what reason, until it had eventually acted under the heart-weakening heat rays.

The body was opened and all the organs found to be sound, with no traces of an illness which could have caused death. The heart was opened, that great, strong, faithful heart, and the post-mortem report ended with the words: "Cause of death, heart failure."

Here is the epilogue, which also answers the questions which had puzzled me for so long.

Schneider's body was not taken to the crematorium in Weimar!

Peix and I were ordered to be present a few days later, when the body was collected.

In the mortuary we had to pull Schneider's corpse down from a heap of others. Maggots were crawling in the dead man's nostrils. The lower lips and chin were smeared with blood and lymph. The man who had conducted the post-mortem on loosening the gag had clumsily cut the lips. Peix wiped the dead man's face with a scrap of paper which he had found in the corner of the hut. When we laid him in the coffin his cranium slipped backwards. The post-mortem orderly, as cold-blooded and indolent as the doctor, had forgotten to nail the skull together, as is usual, with wire tacks. As a result, there was an ulcerous flaw on the forehead above the eyebrows. We placed a bolster of straw under Paul Schneider's head so that the forehead was smooth once more. The coarse five or six inches of the flesh incision from ear to ear could be seen because Paul Schneider, like the rest of us, had his head close shaved.

Once again we witnessed the most despicable theatricals.

Never before in the history of Buchenwald had a body been laid out in state. On the contrary, all bodies were normally pushed into primitive coffins in the most shameful manner and were taken in heaps to the furnaces of the crematorium.

Yet on the orders of the man in charge of the concentration camp, S.S. Obersturmbannführer Rödl, recipient of the golden Party Badge and the Blood Order, drunkard, sadist, murderer, a man who brutally tortured to death, or allowed to be tortured to death, many, many thousands of defenceless people under protective custody; on the orders of this beast in human shape a garage was cleared on the Karacho Way so that the body of Paul Schneider could lie in state. To fill the cup of mockery to the brim, Rödl even ordered flowers from the nursery, and had them placed on both sides of the bier! In this way the sewing up of the skin on the bald skull was hidden in shadow.

I was present when Frau Schneider arrived, accompanied by a friend—this woman whose husband, the father of her six young children, had been murdered. Dr. Ding, the murderer, shook the unsuspecting woman hypocritically by the hand.

The body was transferred to the coffin they had brought along, and this was sealed. But Frau Schneider received instructions that the coffin was not to be opened under any circumstances. An untrue rumour which would not be silenced ran round the camp that Paul Schneider's corpse had been made up and given a wig.

21. Conviction and Bearing

DURING my time of imprisonment I experienced many terrible things which have impressed themselves on my mind and will never be forgotten. Yet these inhuman atrocities were not alone the cause which often brought me to the very limit of my powers of resistance, threatening to crush me.

Who does not know the importance of beliefs in preserving the stability of human society? One's beliefs are usually one's first standard in judging and assessing, trusting or not trusting another person.

I have met many splendid people whose convictions were by no means identical with mine, yet whose self-discipline and moral demands in following a strict general regimen were the most fruitful basis for the establishment and cultivation of an ordered society. But I have also experienced many bitter disappointments, which weigh heavily upon me.

Genuine conviction is always the result of long and difficult struggles with oneself, ardent study, most critical soul-searching and real tolerance towards others. Only he can have convictions who forms his own opinions and adjusts his daily mode of life to that driving force which may be formulated differently by different people but the essence of which is nearly always the same.

How often have I met people whose convictions consisted of a set of phrases, who pretended faith in order to gain some personal advantage; who put forward wild assertions before retiring to their own circle, self-satisfied and presumptuous even when such assertions were unmasked, or were threatened with unmasking, as empty dreams by the force of facts or by the power of logic.

Some people were themselves not of much use yet were always ready to mercilessly deride others. They did mean things under the pretence of unselfishness, or did not bother to judge their fellows by the best intellectual and spiritual standards, being only concerned in having as many followers as possible, never shrinking from giving power over their fellow men to unworthy individuals who knew how to pretend to convictions they did not really possess.

And how seldom have I met people who first looked for the good in their fellow-creatures to see what spiritual qualities, what talents and aptitudes they possessed, before utilising them for the general good.

Although I have met such people comparatively seldom, I have met them! And I have always noticed that, whatever their convictions, they had enjoyed general respect and esteem, the dirty slanderer with petty hatred or mean suspicion never being able to approach their level.

These were the born leaders.

At the time of the Weimar Republic many such people went their own way, upright and proud, ignoring the poison which the clique of obscure politicians flung at them from a thousand dark corners, often in mean and vile ways; and yet they were finally the victims of this clique, for there is no fighting against fearful odds.

Any democracy which again opens the door for the exploitation of such methods can be no true one. The builders of our future state should consider it their first task to forge the weapon which will break the poisonous influence of evil characters and idlers, wherever they make themselves noticeable in any sphere of public, social, political, cultural or economic life.

I could give high praise to those political prisoners of all kinds whom I met in prison and in the concentration camp who, even when beaten and outcast, lived and acted according to their own moral standards.

But I do not think the time is ripe for public mention of these men. I would probably not act according to their ideas were I to surround them with the glory they have earned a thousandfold. They are not Hitler's kind, who let themselves be fulsomely praised to the point of blasphemy, and even publicly flattered themselves. If at some time it should be required of me, I will sing their praises, if only to show of what mettle those men and women must be who are called upon to take the lead, the sole lead, in the state of our dreams.

Yet on the other hand, what shall I say about a political prisoner who was once a leading official and became a willing tool of the murder machine which existed in the concentration camp? What shall I say about a political Kapo who beat and tortured his fellow-prisoners, and reported them for punishment to the camp management in order to avoid being himself beaten and tortured? What shall I say about a political Kapo who accepted bribes for exercising favouritism?

As I have already indicated, it was an unwritten law that every political prisoner who had not shown himself to be an undesirable character was to enjoy preferential treatment and assistance from all other politicals in the camp. Yet what shall I say to the following?

One thousand prisoners were to be transferred from Buchenwald to the concentration camp of Mauthausen. Mauthausen was called Murderhausen by us, because it was known that any transfer to that place meant certain death, as later discoveries confirmed. What shall I say, then, of a political clique within the camp who actually managed to put on the dispatch list the name of a former workers' leader whom they themselves described as a lackey of Hitler and a social fascist, despite the fact that he had proved himself to be an arch-enemy of the Nazis by undergoing years of imprisonment, followed by his deportation to Buchenwald!

It was an unwritten law in the camp that vacant positions of trust were to be filled, where possible, by suitable political prisoners. In this direction we prisoners could often exert an influence on a decision. It was a matter of course among the decent prisoners to watch for personal aptitude in that connection and to disregard a person's political past. But time and again I found that a political clique only got their people into such positions, often despite lack of qualifications for the job.

Such people were not true politicians but are the gravediggers of freedom, National Socialists in reverse, with the accent on their own special brand of Socialism rather than on Nationalism.

*   *   *

I had many interesting and enlightening discussions with the former Communist Deputy Walter Stoecker, who was a prisoner in the camp. Stoecker was a very reserved person who worked with the men who laid the floors, and as opposed, for instance, to the case of Ernst Heilmann, was not especially harassed by the camp management but treated like any other prisoner—just as other prominent people received no special attention, prisoners such as Theo Neubauer, Carlo Mierendorff, the son of Eisner Benedikt Kautsky and others.

I got to know Walter Stoecker better when he came to the sick ward because of a sudden attack of facial paralysis; after he had been cured, Dr. Ding agreed to his remaining for some time to recuperate.

I had never heard Stoecker speaking at public meetings, and so did not know his methods or how he argued his cause

193

on such occasions. In personal conversation with me he showed himself to be educated, well-read and capable of objective thinking, with none of the unpleasant, presumptuous and biased manners of a zealot unfortunately so often met with in agitators of his political colour.

We not only discussed social, economic and political problems, but also spoke in detail about cultural, philosophical, artistic, religious, scientific, technical and educational matters, our views and aims almost always corresponding.

It was a pleasure to hold discussions with the man, although I cannot deny that our views on tactics differed considerably. These are the tactical differences which require further elucidation, and will be a matter for the German people to settle in the difficult years ahead, for on their settlement will depend how we heal the injuries of war towards a better way of life.

There is a particular tragedy connected with Walter Stoecker's death.

A typhus epidemic had broken out in the camp and the vaccination of all prisoners was ordered. This was carried out by prisoner-nurses without supervision by the S.S., so that we could make the vaccination optional for those who could be trusted to keep strictly to the regulations prescribed for the prevention of infection. Most of the prisoners refrained from being vaccinated; but Walter Stoecker, who was in the sick ward, did not.

The typhus bacillus has an incubation period of seven to nine days, so that there is this period between the actual infection and the first signs of the illness, which is particularly severe if the infected person has been vaccinated during this time.

Walter Stoecker had already been infected when he was vaccinated at his own request. He really died because he wanted to be kept alive. The news in foreign newspapers at the time suggesting that he had been murdered in Buchenwald was not correct, possibly one of the rare cases where death could not be fully blamed on the S.S. there.

22. The Tree-hanging

"THERE is someone hanging on the wire on the north side between the towers!" This alarming message was given to me by one of the bearers, whom I had requested to let me know when any of the men committed suicide through contact with the high-tension wires.

I had not seen such a case before, although this kind of suicide was not rare, due to the fact that those who tired of life for obvious reasons nearly always chose to die in places off the beaten track. Even from the watch-towers a mere short stretch of wire fencing running round the huge camp could be overlooked.

Before I had become a doctor's clerk I could not have risked leaving my place of work. Now, however, in view of the independence I had managed for myself, first because of the peculiar circumstances of my work and later by my own initiative, I could undertake informative trips and private errands without much risk to myself.

I went through the wood towards the spot indicated to me. Then I saw Scharführer Sommer with a group of prisoners, coming along the main path which ran between the rows of barracks. This made me hurry, and I did so as if I were particularly busy.

I found that the prisoner had met his death almost exactly between the two watch-towers. At this spot, and for about sixty feet in front of it, the electrically charged wire was protected by barbed wire to a width of about nine feet. I saw that I could climb over this, with the aid of the plank our comrade had probably collected from a nearby pile of boards to put over the wire.

Under threat of being shot by the guards in the watch-towers, prisoners were forbidden to cross the wire entanglement. But as I was interested in having a closer look at the man hanging on the wire, and was clearly recognisable as a prisoner-nurse in my white uniform, I took a chance and climbed the plank, over the wire entanglement.

In our clean suits, snow-white and well cared for, we nurses

195

made so sharp a contrast to the other camp inmates that even the S.S. men were impressed by us. We were considered a special breed, with whom it was not so easy to deal, and so were mostly left alone, even when, taking due precautions, we did things as a matter of course for which other prisoners would have been beaten to a pulp. "Fine feathers make fine birds" was a proverb which had not quite lost its validity even in the concentration camp.

There was a double row of chevaux-de-frise immediately in front of the wire fencing. These the suicide had had to negotiate in order to touch the charge wire. As I drew closer, the guard from the watch-tower called out, "Careful! The electric current hasn't been switched off yet!"

What a difference my clothes made, I thought. Had I been wearing ordinary camp clothing a few bullets from the fat-squirters would have penetrated my body long ago. Now the worthy citizen up there was even worried about my well-being!

The suicide hung on the wire in a cramped position, with a wax-like face, and was barefooted. I could see by the condition of his naked feet that he had run across the chevaux-de-frise, and I realised the desperation he must have felt to ignore the pain he had received in doing so.

I was still standing by the body when I heard pitiable cries of pain, which came from the wood behind me. At first they were very loud, but soon they became weaker, and eventually died away altogether. The sounds resembled the cries of an animal which is being slaughtered by an inexperienced slaughterer, without having first been rendered unconscious.

Soon afterwards I heard similar cries of pain, this time fainter but somehow even more heartrending than they had been before. Intermingled with the sounds was a high-pitched, terribly despairing wail, as if someone were crying for his life in face of dreadful agony and death.

I quickly realised that some punishment was being carried out nearby, and, although it was always advisable to avoid such places if one did not wish to risk being treated in a similar manner, I decided out of curiosity to walk back in the direction of the sounds.

It was not long before I discovered the place of execution. Already four or five prisoners were hanging on a group of trees, while about the same number were standing a little aside, obviously waiting for their turn to suffer. Thus, I became a witness of the tree-hanging, of which I had heard so much and which was so dreaded by the prisoners.

This system of punishment had been developed by the gentlemen of National Socialism from the tree-tying, as it is so nicely described. The Fridericus-Rex legend died hard. From it, the militarists had cleverly whipped up their pernicious policy to blind demoniacal possession by describing all brutality as humanity, all the undignified conduct of that Prussian king as Prussian honour, and all spiritual bondage, with which they kept themselves in power, as freedom and tolerance. From this legend it was known that it had been customary for the Prussian king to have had delinquents tied to a wheel or a tree. Just as the Nazis, his spiritual kindred, developed running the gauntlet into birching, so they developed the tree-tying into tree-hanging.

This consisted of tying the offender's hands behind his back, and in this way hanging him from a tree into which a nail had been driven. Those who cannot imagine what this means should experiment a little on their own bodies. I could then save myself the trouble of a detailed description. I advise them, however, to tie their hands crosswise, and that should be sufficiently instructive for them. The S.S. Scharführer Sommer preferred to tie the prisoners' hands parallel to each other, as he found that made for some extra pain.

I had to appear uninterested in this sight, and for the sake of caution I had to unpass the place of execution at a suitable distance; but I saw and heard more than enough. Screaming, whining, cursing, begging, praying, groaning, bellowing, crying and yelling in all shades and intensities of tones came from those poor devils, whose attitude varied from the stoical endeavour not to let a sound pass the lips to an abandoned screaming that ebbed to a whine and the final death rattle.

The hanging men tried to alleviate their pain by indulging in various jerky movements of their bodies, only to become more and more limp, until they finally hung, apparently lifeless, often unconscious, sometimes even dead.

Long before I witnessed this tree-hanging, I had once spoken to my friends on a Sunday, during our leisure hour, about the remarkable absence of birds in these woods, although there were coniferous and beech woods, high and low-lying forests, as well as brushwood in and around the camp. Among us was an ornithologist who suggested many plausible reasons for this fact.

In the camps of Neusustrum and Börgermoor, however, I had noticed that the birds which were previously not at home in the inhospitable areas soon settled down to live there. The reason for this fact was, I think, because of a kind of herd instinct which was due to the knowledge that the birds could depend on finding food about the camps.

Our ornithologist could not really explain the absence of birds in Buchenwald, despite the enlivenment of the inhospitable forest by human beings and great stables of all kinds, and as a responsible scientist he would not make a mere assumption an assertion.

After I witnessed the tree-hanging I needed no further explanation as to why the birds stayed away from this hellish place.

23. The Political Files

IN accordance with regulations, after three months the camp management had to make an initial report on every prisoner's conduct, and further reports after every six months. During my time in the camp I was able to ascertain exactly how important these reports were regarded.

It frequently happened that the political files were put at the disposal of the camp doctor, being files which were compiled in the political department for every prisoner. In the beginning the Scharführer would not part with the files, which were kept under lock and key, the rule being that, if the doctor wished to inspect them, they were brought and collected by a Scharführer from the political department, and then returned immediately.

This procedure was based on a strict regulation by the camp

management who, for good reasons, had expressly ordered that no files were to be removed in any circumstances from the political department, where they were kept in steel cabinets.

Only members of the political department, the camp commandant and the camp doctor were allowed to inspect them, and then by special authorisation of the chief of the political department, S.S. Obersturmführer Frerich, who held them responsible for their safe-keeping.

It was a long time, therefore, before I had the opportunity to look at a political file, and still longer before I was able to look through one in detail. Later, however, the situation changed and I even had such files in my own charge, but when this took place, the camp doctor told me not to reveal the confidence he showed in me to any other person.

I knew quite well what would happen to me should the camp management hear of this matter, although it did not appear particularly dangerous to me.

Only once was the situation somewhat delicate. Rödl came into the sick ward when the doctor was not there. After my report, "Prisoner-clerk 996 engaged on filing", and his usual "Carry on!" Rödl remained in the room.

I felt he was watching me attentively to see what I was doing, but was too well seasoned to let myself be disturbed by that fact.

"Is the doctor not here?" he asked me at last.

"No, Herr Obersturmbannführer. Herr Sturmführer" (a nurse was given five strokes of the birch once because he had said "Herr Doktor"!) "told me that he had something to do in the S.S. sick ward today, before he came to the camp."

After a while, Rödl said, "Give me File Huber, Franz."

Alas! that was the name of a prisoner whose political file lay in the drawer of the doctor's table, to which I had the key. However, I did not hesitate for a moment.

"Very well, Herr Obersturmbannführer," I said, and walked calmly over to one of the cabinets in which were kept the files of the sick ward, picked out a file and handed it to Rödl.

"Not that!—the other one, the one from the political department!" he yelled impatiently.

I acted as if I were stupid. "The political file, Herr Obersturmbannführer?"

"Yes, yes, that's it! Aren't they here?"

"I don't know, Herr Obersturmbannführer."

Rödl pointed to the doctor's writing desk. "Not in there?"

"I don't know about that, Herr Obersturmbannführer," I returned meekly.

Rödl was satisfied, and left. Ding was also happy, when I made my report to him.

The political file was often poor enough, consisting usually of the so-called "order for protective custody", that red form which was also handed to the prisoner, the political question-naire which was a short history of the prisoner's life and had to be filled in under threat of severe punishment immediately upon arrival at the camp, and the conduct report, made out after the first period of protective custody, being in every case an adverse one. Sometimes, but only rarely, a copy was added of the penal register of criminal prisoners.

In addition, I found various pieces of correspondence with the Chief Security Officer in Berlin, records of floggings, let-ters which were withheld by the censor and the like. I found the files of prisoners who had been in the camp for years to be no fuller than those of comparative newcomers. At the most, they may have contained one or two more conduct reports demanded by Berlin.

I soon noticed that these conduct reports were all exactly alike. The anti-social prisoner was still lazy, the criminal had also committed punishable offences in the camp, the political still showed no change of heart, the expounder of the scrip-tures was still not prepared to give up his faith, and so on. Even so, it was some time before I discovered that many prisoners whose conduct reports stated that disciplinary action had lately to be taken against them, had not been punished at all.

Then I obtained the political file of the prisoner Melingo. We others called him Melingo but his full name was Edler von Melingo. He had constantly been in the sick ward, even from the very first day of his arrival in the camp. He had the most tiresome illnesses, and over and over again he was on the verge of death, although the nurses always managed to save him from dying.

That is why Melingo became an habitué of the sick ward

and—pardon my comparison—something like the mascot of the company. Something would have been missing as far as we were concerned had Melingo not been in the sick ward. Had Melingo not contracted, say, appendicitis, after surviving inflammation of the lungs, we would not have felt all was right.

Once, when things just would not go right and death was on his doorstep, Perth—the Jewish doctor I have previously mentioned, who was actually not allowed to practise in the sick ward—carried out the only blood transfusion for healing purposes ever made in Buchenwald during my time. Ding watched, not having seen the operation before. Melingo's life was saved.

When he was lying for weeks with pleurisy, with a tube from which pus was constantly oozing, and food sanctions were passed on the camp for eight days, we gave him our last bits because it had become a matter of honour to keep Melingo alive.

Yet what did I discover in Melingo's political file? This was a somewhat larger one than usual. Repeated correspondence about him had taken place with the Chief Security Office in Berlin. Various quarters had probably tried for his release, so that several reports had been made concerning his conduct.

It was stated that he was extremely lazy at his work, that he still showed no signs of moral improvement, and that lately he had even had to be punished, despite several warnings. As if there were anything like warnings in the camp! Then again: Melingo still showed no ardour at his work, had to be cautioned again and again, and only worked under strict supervision.

Melingo? Our bundle of worry?—only worked under strict supervision? But look at the man, lying there, dangerously ill in bed! He could not work and had never yet performed any in the camp. Yet in black and white were the words: "only works under strict supervision"! Could it have been made clearer to me from what unscrupulous lies these reports on "conduct" were compiled?

How many times was I then to establish how all such reports stank with lies! I do not doubt that the report on my own conduct was similarly concocted, although I had never been cautioned or punished or had otherwise aroused disparaging attention.

Once, our comrade Ernst Utrott, who was engaged as a clerk in the office, received a letter full of reproach from his wife. She had been waiting for him for over five years. Shortly before the end of his term of imprisonment, he had faithfully promised to adapt himself to the new political conditions, and yet, when she now applied to the Gestapo for his release, she had been told that he was still carrying out political agitation. In such circumstances she was forced to apply for a divorce. Obviously this letter had slipped past the censors.

The matter was quite clear to me. A report of his conduct had been concocted in the usual way, despite the fact that Ernst Utrott had given as little cause for attention as I had, and was only a number in the political department.

I spoke to Ding about him, and he sent for the file. There it was, in black and white, "Demand for a report on Utrott's conduct", with its reply, "Because of political agitation in the camp Utrott had to be repeatedly cautioned"!

This was written about a prisoner who kept to himself, had never been cautioned and who was extremely conscientious and diligent at his work.

Ding made no reply when I complained that such reports destroyed the prisoner's family life, and queried whether it were possible to avoid such a calamity at least by submitting more neutral reports.

24. Shot While Escaping

By far the greatest number of prisoners were forced to work daily outside the camp. The places of work were cordoned off by members of the S.S. Totenkopf Units, who received their military training in barracks built by prisoners.

Almost all these places were within the death zone or away from public traffic. There were new buildings for barracks and garages, splendid villas for S.S. officers and more modest settlements for S.S. N.C.O.s and men, and construction of and repairs to roads, site clearances, brick works, water supplies, etc., etc.

The official task of the S.S. Totenkopf Units was to guard the prisoners. They had orders to make ruthless use of fire-arms at any sign of attempted escapes. Because no such attempts were made, they acted as villains and torturers and continually amused themselves by inventing and carrying out new tortures.

Any attempt to escape meant death in any case, and to my knowledge such attempts were made only three or four times. Indeed, during my time in the camp, not one single prisoner tried to escape from his place of work. Those who were "shot while escaping" were either shot for sheer amusement during S.S. tortures or knowingly chose this as a form of suicide, no longer able to endure the terrible torment they suffered.

A good comrade of mine chose the death shot while escaping. His name was Rudi Arndt. He had formerly been a member of the Central Committee of the Communist Youth Association, and had been in protective custody since 1933. He had six long and difficult years behind him when he decided on suicide, or at least the decision was forced on him.

He was an old inmate who had passed through the hard school of S.S. brutality and had thereby himself been hardened. During the last few years he had a job which was to some extent tolerable to him.

He belonged to that circle of political prisoners in Buchenwald who were, where possible, screened by their fellows. He worked in the clothing department, and because of this fact was removed from the immediate attention of the camp management. In the end, however, fate took its course.

Something or other had exploded. That is, the camp management had obtained knowledge of something which in their opinion offended against camp discipline. That it was nothing dishonourable is only mentioned by the way. But our comrade was mixed up in the incident. He fell into the clutches of Rödl, who first of all had him flogged, and then sent him to a punitive company which had to perform particularly hard work outside the camp, where there was always "fun", as the S.S. men used to say.

We were experienced enough to realise that he had met his fate, and certainly he was not to be released alive from Rödl's clutches. The only thing he could still do was to spare himself the agony of enduring horrible tortures.

That same day, therefore, he walked slowly towards the chain of guards who were placed around the punitive company, and ignoring their challenge, walked through their cordon. The first round fired by the guard missed him, and he continued calmly on his way. But he collapsed after the second shot.

Yet he was not dead. The S.S. men used dum-dum bullets and one had entered the lower part of his back, literally tearing the abdomen wide open, the intestines partly laid bare.

He was still fully conscious when he was placed on the stretcher. With great will-power he courageously bore in silence the pain which tore at him. He even gave his own particulars at the gate in the normal procedure, and not until he was on his way to the sick ward did he lose consciousness.

There, we saw at once that nothing could be done for him. The intestines were torn in several places, the inside of the abdomen was filled with a bloody slimy mass interspersed with excrement, and part of the intestines were lying coiled on the outside of his stomach.

Walter Krämer, a close friend of his, spoke to him several times, to no avail. Krämer put aside the morphia needle with which he had been going to relieve his friend at least of his last agonies.

We stood around the stretcher, helplessly, waiting for the moment when the still beating heart would stop for ever. The stretcher-bearers related in detail what had happened, and our comrade's identity was given to one of our number who did not know him.

Someone asked the stretcher-bearers whether he had said anything while still conscious, and then the dying man, to our surprise, suddenly opened his eyes and slowly shook his head. We had not noticed that he had regained consciousness.

When Krämer, his fingers on the man's pulse, saw this, he spoke to him. "Can you hear us?"

He closed his eyes but nodded his head very faintly.

"Have you any pain?" Krämer asked, and again he shook his head, very slowly.

Then one of the S.S. assistant doctors came into the room. He looked at the terrible injury, and seeing that parts of the intestines protruding from the abdomen were still active, he seized them with his bare hands.

We saw our comrade now obviously suffering pain, and Krämer said quietly, "Sturmführer, he is still conscious."

"What? He, still conscious?" the S.S. medical man growled, without any feeling. His stupidity was great enough to be evident to a person of the meanest intelligence. "What? He? Impossible!" Then, louder and still more objectionably, he cried, "Hey! You there! What's your name?—Well, what about an answer?"

Then our comrade opened his lips, until now tightly closed, and slowly, weakly, as if already speaking from another world, he said in a low voice, yet audible to everyone, "Let—me—die—in—peace."

He opened his eyes, looked at the S.S. doctor as if he wished to impress his features upon his memory, and, turning to Walter Krämer, gave him a pleading look.

Krämer understood, and before the S.S. doctor could compose him again, performed the last service for his friend.

25. Building

WHEN all the prisoners were in it, the camp could more or less be compared with a lazy, creeping, crawling ant-hill in which at times there was some measure of excitement, as if someone had prodded it with a stick.

It was considerably quieter during the day while the labour columns were outside, but of course it was not deserted, for work was carried out on paths within the camp itself, on barracks and workshops. Work went on in the vegetable garden, the laundry and the stables. There was great activity in the camp kitchen. Columns of prisoners worked in the timber yard and in the woods. There was the building office, the sick ward, the mail centre and the clothing department. The room orderlies, the block and camp seniors and the camp police all performed their separate duties. Everybody had work to do, but there was a marked difference between that which was done within the camp and that outside.

This was primarily due to the fact that no chain of S.S. men guarded the labour column inside the camp. True, even here some of the Kapos provided unpleasant methods of activity, often "entertaining" to S.S. Scharführer or S.S. officers when they appeared; but on the whole work within the camp was considerably quieter; and if one succeeded in finding a job there, he did not hang on one but two fine threads. The sword of Damocles, always dancing wildly over the heads of the labour columns outside, hung quietly here, only occasionally swaying dangerously above us.

Although the camp kitchen was provided with modern cooking facilities, it was comparatively poorly equipped. The laundry, built at a later date, was better and more to the purpose, although it too showed deficiencies, especially in its building; yet it could be shown off, when necessary.

There were abundant sums of money available for the extension of barracks and camp, and the building management had spared no expense in erecting the laundry, which was meant for the use of all the troops in the camp.

The laundry had everything, from the most up-to-date water-softening plant to the centrifugal drying machine and the drying chambers. Its capacity was astonishing. It was by no means fully employed during my time, but it could have coped with the entire washing of a town of forty to fifty thousand inhabitants, with only a small amount of labour.

In another sense, too, Buchenwald could be a convincing object lesson of a model prison. In our rare hours of leisure we prisoners sometimes discussed this matter. We imagined what an unsuspicious and unbiased visitor would say if he saw this Buchenwald and its surroundings without any of its inmates.

He would, in our opinion, have been simply amazed had he seen what had been hewn out of the ground in so short a time—the huge new barracks, these roads and paths, the settlements and villas, the workshops and the laundry, the stables, and, down in the valley, the brickworks, one of the largest and most modern in Germany, which had an extraordinarily large output.

Then we would close our eyes and think of the gigantic power which technical science had created, and visualise the task of the future, which would tame such a science and place it exclusively at the service of mankind, not for the purposes of destruction but for peaceful construction and development, not to exploit man and thereby prostitute itself, but to make life more worthwhile for everyone.

From such buildings one could, of course, without any difficulty ascertain the two most notable characteristics of the National Socialist "Führer" clique—stupidity and base principles. It is certainly no overstatement to say that nearly all this extensive planning and the really practical execution carried out was not due to the knowledge and work of leading Nazis but to prisoners harnessed everywhere, beginning with the building office and the building management staff to the foremen and down the scale, to the last skilled and unskilled labourer.

Where, in the initial stages, prisoners could not be used for these constructions, huge sums of money were squandered to an almost incredible extent on instructing the Nazis, and on unnecessary building. Often whole parts of buildings were torn down again after having been built, plans were frequently and fundamentally changed while building was still in progress, and half-finished projects were dropped.

Not only stupidity and incompetence celebrated orgies, but profiteering and corruption thrived, beginning with small private favours to profiteering on a large scale, when goods and money amounting to tens of thousands of Marks and more were juggled from the pockets of the State into the private possession of S.S. men.

The best and rarest materials were only just good enough for these wangles—chrome, nickel, wolfram and molybdenum steel, the most expensive dies, the best clinkers, the most valuable timber. It cost nothing for the labour and the technical and artistic talents which had to produce the houses and finished articles of all kinds from this material!

Of course profiteering was graded according to rank. The S.S. man had only a dress dagger of molybdenum steel made for himself, but the camp commandant wangled furniture worthy of a millionaire, the Scharführer juggled a few ten-thousand Mark notes for himself, the Sturmführer reached the hundred-thousand Mark line, and the higher S.S. officers did not know what their maximum limit was.

Goodness knows how these S.S. men covered up their manipulations, although I believe it was not difficult to do so, for base principles were the general rule, and auditors for the German Reich did not exist, as they had in the time of the Monarchy and the Republic.

Several hundred thousand Marks of the estimated cost for the projected prisoners' sick ward had already been used up in my time. There was not much to show for this sum of money, which had already been expended for the provisional sick ward consisting of two wooden barracks, each seventy feet long and twenty-two feet wide, one of which was more normally in use for administrative and surgery purposes.

The excavations were visible, of course, though unfortunately they were half filled again, because for more important reasons work on this had been stopped for some time. In one corner was a wall, half in ruins, yet with a little imagination it could be recognised as the beginnings of a foundation.

"And, in confidence, comrade, this is only the prisoners' sick ward. You should see the S.S. sick ward. That is wonderful and has all the latest gadgets. Not one request of the doctors and surgeons has been ignored. There we have to prove what we can do!"

Buchenwald was built in 1937. I was there from 1938 until 1940. The first Americans entered the camp on 11th April, 1945. The prisoners' sick ward was still in the process of construction!

When S.S. Standartenführer Koch, the camp commandant, discovered that buildings came into being which had not even been provided for in the original building plan, he issued strict orders that no erections whatever were to be put up without his express approval.

The S.S. Medical Office, Berlin, from which all medicines, bandages and surgical instruments had to be ordered, had once complained that the packing cases had not been returned in good condition. Investigation proved that, while the prisoners had emptied the cases immediately and had prepared them for return according to regulations, the S.S. men transporting them to the rail goods yard in Weimar were unable to complete their task, and the cases had to remain for several days in wind and weather, there being no facilities for placing them under cover.

Referring to this complaint by the S.S. Medical Office, approval was asked to erect a simple storeroom. Koch gave it on condition that the storeroom was of the simplest form and made of timber.

Approval having been obtained, Walter Krämer began to organise the task of erection. After a short time, a small solid hut containing various rooms stood hidden behind the sick barracks. Now laundry and bandages for the sick ward could be stored here, and the clothing of the sick could be primitively but properly sterilised.

When the hut for disinfection was ready, we nearly forgot to store the cases for the medical office, after all! I can leave it to the reader to draw his own conclusions from this little episode, in judging the S.S. and their prisoners.

Another episode.

In view of the lack of food and insufficient clothing for the prisoners, it was understandable that, during the cold winter months, the camp inmates suffered severely under the adverse weather conditions.

All types of frostbite were common occurrences, the Jews and gypsies suffering most. We prisoners had no powers to remove the cause of these frostbites, and nothing could be done for the worst cases. Even the most efficient doctors would have left the last word to the incinerators, as we did.

Still, we had a slight chance if at least combating the medium and less severe forms of frostbite, and we naturally did so with all the vigour at our command. Ointments and bandages were in short supply, with not enough for all the severe cases, but we had hot and cold water and could apply the alternating bath therapy.

The results were good; in fact, so good that Dr. Ding began to be interested in our work, probably because he scented something that might make an impression upon his colleagues in view of the fact that ours was so cheap a method of treatment.

There were hundreds of sick cases, making the already overcrowded sick ward too small to carry out any special treatments. It was obvious that these could not be done in the open, so, with Dr. Ding to help us out, we made an application for a barracks. We duly received approval of our plan. Encouraged by his former success with the medical storeroom, Walter Krämer now had a further opportunity of showing his organising abilities.

Of course the new barracks had to be erected close to the sick ward. We chose a spot on the sloping terrain, which necessitated a levelled foundation. We were sure of the assistance of certain Kapos and the prisoners, and within a short time the washroom was installed in the basement. We were able to place a few more beds in the barracks itself, making this a second sick ward. Why, we even arranged for a small mortuary in the basement, so that we would no longer have the dead, the dying and the living lying together in confusion in the main sick ward.

26. The Company of the Witless

THE barracks were heated by round iron stoves in which briquettes were mainly used, and it was the duty of the room orderly to fetch the fuel from the coal yard. The so-called administration barracks, which included our sick ward, were supplied with wood and briquettes by a labour column especially striking even in this unusual camp.

If one saw this column of men in the distance, as they marched through the camp with their Kapo, one received an immediate impression of a herd of small elephants lumbering one behind the other. While other columns of prisoners always proceeded at a quick pace, work outside the camp being frequently carried on at the double all day long, this group of men never hurried, and marched more slowly than a funeral procession, with almost robot-like precision.

A closer look would disclose that practically every prisoner here looked unusually stupid, wearing on his sleeve an armlet with the inscription "Stupid" or "Daft" written on it.

S.S. Obersturmbannführer Rödl had personally formed this column and so was particularly proud of it, not realising that its formation was not only an impressive accusation against Nazism but that the whole idea was really stupid in itself.

He called the column "The Company of the Witches". Its members were to a certain extent taboo even in the camp. They were not exempted from the general conditions prevailing in the camp, having to suffer hunger and cold, and to live under the inhuman hardships as the others; they had to bear their share of the punishments which fell upon the camp. But they were not driven or beaten at their work, and at the most their Kapo only occasionally treated them with severity. They were not punished individually, not even when they offended against camp discipline. Briefly, they were treated with consideration, both by the S.S. men and the prisoners.

Rödl himself decided which of the men joined the company of the daft, as its appearance showed. He might order a completely normal prisoner to wear the "Stupid" armlet; or he might even refuse to accept a prisoner whom some room orderly led before him as being quite obviously daft, the latter usually shortly succumbing to the difficult camp existence.

At their work, it was surprising to see the kind of stupid stubbornness with which they executed their tasks once they had been trained to do them. The "witless" prisoner would come into the registry office of the sick ward, shoes wiped, cap in hand, haversack slung on back, and immediately make for the briquette scuttle; he would lift the lid, look inside, and retreat in order to bring back the number of briquettes required.

Usually we overlooked the matter when such a man forgot to wipe his shoes, or did not take off his cap; but if someone reminded him of his omissions by silently pointing to shoes or cap, the "witless" automatically pulled off his cap or wiped his shoes with the cap if he held it in his hand, before calmly putting that back on his head, sometimes spreading mud over his face as he did so.

On the whole, the company of the daft led a life fairly free from interference, and only occasionally, when the column grew too big as a result of Rödl's intelligence, did the camp doctor come along and arrange dismissals from among the men.

During the summer of 1939, Dr. Ding had the sudden idea of carrying out the Cardiazol Test among the prisoners of this company. He had read that, by injecting epileptics with a certain amount of Cardiazol, an epileptic fit could be brought about; while the injection would also establish the presence of real epilepsy in those cases which did not lead to open fits of this kind but manifesting themselves only in a condition of mental disorder varying from a state of excitement to acute depression.

The Cardiazol Test proved that almost all the prisoners of the company suffered from epilepsy and should have been in nursing homes. Ding did arrange for the transfer of a number of these prisoners to such homes, but I do not know whether he realised that, under the National Socialist regime, sick persons like these were automatically liquidated.

27. Prisoner-nurse

In addition to the X-ray room, the chemist, the operating theatre, the laboratory, the registry and the doctor's room, the surgery was also situated in the administrative barracks of the sick ward. It was divided into an outer and an inner surgery. Prisoner-nurses were employed, as well as men with first-aid experience and other adaptable and interested prisoners who could be trained to act without a doctor's supervision.

The doctor and the layman with some idea of medical science may be shocked by this arrangement. They will be still more shocked when they hear to what extent difficult diagnoses and prognoses, operations and amputations were carried out by raw beginners.

They will not only be utterly shocked but simply speechless when they learn of the boundless stupidity, unscrupulousness, laziness and frivolity with which so-called S.S. doctors exercised their profession in this camp, and with what nonchalance they placed the little knowledge they had at the service of the criminal, sadistic and murderous Nazi ideology.

Of course there were exceptions. I need only mention Dr. Blies from Offenbach on Main and Dr. Zahel from Austria, the one a physician, the other a surgeon, two doctors who were in the camp for far too short a time, performing their medical duties without regard to what a person had done.

The nurses in the surgery were kept busy from morning till night. Only during roll-call were the rooms deserted, but the main rush of prisoners began immediately after the evening roll-call was over.

There were three types. The first to arrive were those who could still walk fairly well, and therefore quickly covered the distance from the square to the sick barracks. Then came those prisoners who could no longer walk alone, assisted by fellow-prisoners and stretcher-bearers. Finally, there were those who were more or less still able to drag themselves to the sick ward for medical attention.

No sooner had the first patient arrived than there began the cleaning of wounds, bandaging, cutting, the application of plasters, the examination of eyes, ears and throats, the testing of hearts and lungs, the X-rays and heat treatments, the vaccinations, and all kinds of injections.

Plasters, ointments, tablets, medicines and drugs of all descriptions were handed out where required. Here a prisoner was detained for treatment, there the death of another was reported; one had to be told that he was not sick at all, and another warned not to consider his illness too lightly. On the one hand, treatment was carried out with almost intuitive talent, on the other, very bad mistakes were made.

One endless stream of patients kept coming, waiting, being treated, and going, and when the last patient had left the surgery shortly before the curfew, the nurses would sink back into their chairs, completely exhausted by their work. They rested a while to regain their breath, then tidied the surgery, before sinking on their damp beds, dead tired.

213

The unselfish work the prisoner-nurses performed in sooth-ing pain, in allaying sorrow, in saving lives, will never be ascertained, and what they did was certainly neither on the instructions of the camp management nor according to the intentions of those people. Their justification lay in what was required of them by common humanity. Sometimes they risked their lives for their comrades, and even lost them.

They were the tremendous force of goodness which again and again breaks through the powers of evil—a thousand times blighted, a thousand times shattered, only to rise again, in-defatigable and effective.

In order to assist their comrades, they had to avail them-selves of tricks, devious methods and camouflage. Every weak-ness, every stupidity, every embarrassing situation of camp management and S.S. men had to be exploited.

It was hard work, work which had to be improvised with insufficient means and inadequate knowledge. Yet it had its successes. They possessed the halo which for all times will shine, invisible to many, but visible to all those who know the camp which was once the scene of the lowest humiliation of mankind.

28. The Nightmare Camp

DURING February, 1939, the inner camp was erected within the camp, on the east side of the square. Three large tents were pitched parallel to each other, like the stables of a circus, and a barracks was built at some distance from the tents, forming a yard between these and the barracks. All this was surrounded by high barbed wire.

None of us had any idea for what purpose the new camp was to be used. Was a new pogrom to be staged? we won-dered. Yet the special camp seemed too small to hold the vic-tims of such a venture. If plank beds were indicated by the wooden planks nailed together in the tents, looking like racks for bottles in the cellar of a wine dealer, then, measured by

Buchenwald standards, the new camp was only destined for two to two hundred and fifty prisoners.

Only a few of the criminal intriguers involved probably knew that this special camp was connected with events which would "spontaneously" take place a month later.

What was the political situation at the time? A year previously, fate had taken its course when Hitler carried out his badly camouflaged attack on Austria, without any signs of a determined protest on their part against his deed. One should recall that on the 12th February, 1938, in the Berchtesgaden agreement the Reich once again "solemnly guaranteed the independence and sovereignty of the Austrian brother people"; yet on the 10th March, 1938, Hitler's war machine trundled for the first time along the "roads of peace", the Reich's Autobahn, of which the stretch from Munich to the Reich frontier was one of the first to be completed and the first to be dedicated to its real purpose.

The armour rolled according to precise marching orders, and not a soul seemed to notice that the Austrian people "revolted" on the very next day, and called in the German Wehrmacht for assistance. On the 12th March, Hitler was spontaneously welcomed as the "saviour of Austria". On the 13th March the annexation of Austria was completed. On the 10th April a people's referendum was staged, resulting in 99.9 per cent. yes-votes.

Could not a blind man with his stick feel what was really happening here? How was it possible that the politically experienced world did not then see where the path of the criminal Nazi clique led? Why did nobody call a halt to these obvious manoeuvres?

Now, a year later, almost to the day, Hitler embarked upon his second venture. Remember: 23rd September, 1938—Godesberg memorandum; 29th September, 1938—Munich agreement; 5th October, 1938—resignation of Benes; 2nd November, 1938—Vienna arbitration; 30th November, 1938 —Hacha became President; 14th March, 1939—German troops entered Slovakia, and on the 16th March, 1939— Decree concerning the Protectorate of Bohemia and Moravia.

On the 14th March, 1939, on Hitler's orders, the German army marched on Prague because "Hacha suddenly and unexpectedly called for his assistance". One month previously, however, Hitler had made preparations in the concentration camp of Buchenwald to liquidate certain of the people whom he would arrest on the 15th March.

What we inmates experienced at Buchenwald was only a small and rather unimportant part of the full object lesson. There are many hard facts available which are far more convincing as to whom the war guilt belonged. But to me, seeing what happened at Buchenwald, it is obvious that never in history has the blame for making war ever been more clearly, convincingly and justifiably attributed to one single man!

Hitler wanted war! His attack on Austria was the first step towards this end—the second, his entry into Prague. A few weeks later, when he overran Poland in eighteen days, the forces which had long been set in motion were continued in their course.

The first batch of those prisoners intended for the special camp arrived only a few days after the troops had entered Czechoslovakia. The only thing we could learn about them was that they were Jews, among them inmates of a Jewish home for the aged, very old men, the oldest being ninety-three years old, with many orphans of eight to fourteen years of age. Yet within eight weeks the camp was totally liquidated, except for a few children whom we were able to transfer to the general camp before the final tragedy took place.

I can hardly describe what happened. It was all so horrible and dreadful, so turbulent, that one did not notice the individual in this camp, merely the whole pathetic group.

Approximately 1,200 to 1,400 prisoners were crowded into the camp. As they were not made to work, their rations consisted of one pint of thin watery soup and a slice of bread per day—too much for immediate starvation, far too little to help them keep alive.

The great dying actually began during the transport to the camp and increased daily in numbers and in horror. No medical attention and no nursing services were permitted them, medicines and bandages not being allowed into their camp. No one could leave it, no one enter.

At first we could only guess what was going on there, when, for instance, we saw the scenes which occurred during the food distribution in the square; for at these times the prisoners behaved like a hungry, half-mad pack of wolves, the Scharführer rushing among them with whips and striking them with sticks and pistols.

After about four weeks, Dr. Ding entered this place for the first time, after a Scharführer had told him that many prisoners had lately died for no apparent reason. The Scharführer assumed that some kind of epidemic was abroad in the camp, not knowing that death could result from starvation.

I had to accompany Ding.

About four hundred prisoners had already died before I entered the camp. Despite this fact, the other prisoners in the tents (which they could only leave to fetch food and relieve nature) were literally lying on top of each other, the living with the dead, the healthy with the sick, old men with children, the timid with the fatalists. There was unbelievable stench, indescribable dirt, humans rotting alive, insane, twisting with cramp, some in comas no brain can imagine, no pen describe.

Only the faintest of lights penetrated through the tents, as if the kindness of the light itself hesitated to reveal the madness here taking place. A woollen blanket hung in one corner. We looked behind it, but found nothing. One of the children we later transferred to the main camp told me that those who intended to end their lives with a rope retired behind this blanket. The rope was then removed from the dead man, and hung on a nail for the next candidate for death, this being the one rope available for this purpose.

Eight days later I again entered the camp, but I could not raise the courage to walk into the tents. Food was just being given out, the distribution proceeding far more quietly than before, although only those ate who collected their portion for themselves.

All the prisoners were in a state of semi-starvation. Many could hardly keep on their feet. It was only by dint of great effort that they could turn up at the barracks for food, with dented food bowl, an old tin or any other receptacle in their hands. Others seemed more certain on their feet, but even they were terribly thin, like wandering skeletons.

Two such skeletons dragged a comrade, apparently in a

faint, to the place where food was being distributed, and were given three portions of the thin watery soup. After they had received their food, one of them shouldered his unconscious comrade and carried him back to the tent, the other guarding the soup with care. As the first man passed me with his burden, I saw that he was carrying a corpse.

At that moment Ding called my attention elsewhere. Hardly five or six yards from where the food was being distributed, a man sat in front of another, apparently feeding him, as the latter sat on the ground, leaning against the barracks wall. Each time he held the spoon to the other's mouth, he looked left and right, and then pushed the spoon quickly into his own mouth.

We watched him for some time, before Ding went up to him. The moment the feeder saw him, he threw away the bowl of soup, jumped up and quickly disappeared into one of the tents. The other prisoner did not move, and Ding pushed him. He fell over, a lifeless corpse, dead for at least two days, rigor mortis no longer being present.

After the eighth week, the special camp was strangely quiet, for, with the exception of about one hundred people, among them a surprisingly large number of children, all were dead.

On Ding's instructions the children, whose physical condition probably permitted their recuperation, were transferred to the general camp. There, we collected them, bathed them and gave them food and clean clothes. "Oh," one of them exclaimed. "Is it true? Are there really still such good people? I can't believe it!"

Within a few days, the last of the adult inmates of the special camp had closed his eyes. The camp was cleaned, disinfected and put in order again. Three months later it was used for the second time.

MEDICAL BLOCK, BUCHENWALD

29. Money is Money

According to tradition, it was the Roman Emperor Titus Flavius Vespasianus who coined the expression "non olet" which he was reproached in connection with the profits he had derived from a certain tax; since then, it is customary to append this tag to money earned in shady transactions.

I took over from my predecessor, Herbert Neumann, a number of sample certificates of health, with instructions that the first certificate cost twelve Marks, the second twenty, the third forty, the fourth fifty. Apart from this, more detailed certificates were drawn up, for which the prices varied, being fixed for each individual case.

In that short hour which had been left to instruct me in my new work as a doctor's clerk, I had to remember so much and learn so many new things, that I felt like the well-known scholar in Faust. As the short period of instruction was soon replaced by urgent tasks, it was not surprising that I paid no further attention to the sample certificates.

It was not long before I had to look for them among my pile of forms, samples and notes, because a Jewish fellow-prisoner asked for a certificate of health meant for the purpose of emigration. I was not well versed in the matter, but he pointed out which of the four samples was needed for Holland, which for England, which for America and which for Shanghai.

At that time it was still customary to allow the emigration from Germany of Jewish prisoners who were not politically implicated. Apart from other papers demanded by the Third Reich and the countries into which the Jew wished to emigrate, a certificate of health was invariably required, the receiving countries naturally not being inclined to accept sick people who would soon become a burden to them.

In those days, we prisoners would sometimes consider the question how the Nazis could permit prisoners to go abroad, knowing that they were aware, from personal experience, of the terrible conditions prevailing in the concentration camp of Buchenwald. We told ourselves that hardly one Jew, once

219

out in the free world, would trouble about the obligation not to spread atrocity stories enforced on him before he left the camp, and that the conscience of the world must be aroused by repeated reports from ex-prisoners of German concentration camps.

Of course, we realised that publication of conditions in Buchenwald would bring with it the danger that nobody more would be discharged from the camp and, in view of the Nazi mentality, retribution would be exerted against those still in camp.

We ourselves thought such a risk well worthwhile, in view of the flood of horror raging here, and which could only be combated by the roused conscience of the outside world.

We knew that newspapers abroad had occasionally published reports about Buchenwald and other German concentration camps. We knew that the camp management was aware of such reports, Ding having once told me himself that a fairly accurate report about the sick barracks had appeared abroad. And yet Jews were still discharged, with no retaliatory measures against them.

At the time we did not know how difficult it was to believe the veracity of such reports. The Nazis knew this. They knew that the conscience of the world, so slow to be aroused, was only too easily inclined to shrug off the unbelievable truth with the words, atrocity propaganda! They knew that even the Jew could not be particularly dangerous, however convincingly he cried aloud the horrible crimes of the Nazis, for they calculated, coldly and soberly, "The truth as stated by the Jew will not be believed, for the fact that he is allowed to go abroad makes his tale more incredible to believe."

Since the Nazi crimes have been revealed, we know that this Satanic calculation of theirs proved only too correct. The world's conscience slumbered on up to the very moment when the English and American troops entered these camps to witness for themselves the last weak reflection of the tremendous tragedy which had taken place there.

Only then did the world press report fully on Buchenwald, Belsen, Auschwitz and Dachau. Only then did the world realise the horror which had been concealed from the German people and the world under the term of National

Socialism. Only then did governments and responsible states-men raise their weighty words in accusation against Nazi crimes.

It will prove more difficult, however, to rouse the conscience of Germany itself—and keep it awake! For here truth is faced with a towering psychological obstacle which is almost im-passable. The man with a sense of responsibility only hesitat-ingly condemns his fellow-creatures, but in Germany some must condemn themselves! None will do so voluntarily and willingly! Yet it is urgent for the German people to open their eyes to the truth for all times, only then can a change of heart take place in them!

Today I clearly see before me tasks and difficulties; at the time, preparing the certificate of health my Jewish comrade wanted, I was still faced with the inconceivable. The matter seemed simple enough: the prisoner wanted to emigrate to Holland and needed the simplest health certificate, to prove that he was healthy and suffered from no infectious illness.

Although I assumed that the issuing of the certificate would cause no great difficulties, I was surprised at the speed with which the camp doctor conducted the examination. Indeed, it was literally carried out quicker than I can here describe the procedure. The prisoner undressed outside in the corridor; he was called in, Ding placed the stethoscope to his heart for two seconds, and sent him away again.

I prepared a certificate in accordance with the sample I had, and wrote a cash demand of twelve Reichsmarks for the cash office. I handed the demand to the prisoner, who duly obtained the money, which he gave to me in exchange for his certificate. I in turn paid the money to the doctor, and the case was closed.

Prisoners came every day with such requests; sometimes two, three or five, but often twenty, thirty, forty and more. In time, Ding did not even trouble to look at them, let alone examine them.

Certificates were issued right and left, everything being certified that the petitioner wanted certifying. The only dif-ference was in the fee which had to be paid, fixed as high as possible.

This was made all the easier because the amount did not

matter to the prisoners, nursing as they did vague hopes of escaping this hell.

I soon got to know the National Socialist differentiation between the camp doctor and the official medical officer of health, for they were one and the same person; yet if a certificate was requested from "the medical officer of health" it cost ten Reichsmarks more to get.

It happened sometimes that longer forms had to be filled in, to be sent to the Jewish prisoners by relatives of theirs who were endeavouring to collect the necessary emigration papers. On such forms questions were asked which could only be answered by doctors acquainted with medical terms. As doing this would have taken Dr. Ding probably half an hour or more, even without any medical examinations needed, he commissioned Jewish doctors to provide the answers, while collecting for himself the fifty or sixty Reichsmarks involved as fees.

Being an unsuspecting simpleton, I at first believed that Dr. Ding handed these fees to some cash office, not thinking that anybody with a fixed income could earn three hundred, four hundred, six hundred and even a thousand Reichsmarks daily in so simple a manner. However incredible this seemed, it did not take long to confirm what the camp doctor was doing.

On one occasion, when I handed him the few hundred Marks I had collected, he told me he intended to deliver the money to the S.S. assistance fund. This fund had sufficient money in hand, but every now and again, he said, he was obliged to pay it some fee because the camp management knew that fees for certificates were occasionally received by him.

On another occasion he asked me if I personally needed any money, but I refused to accept it, pointing out that I was only permitted to have ten Reichsmarks in my possession, that I had money of my own, and in any case would not know what to do with any I had, as it was no longer possible to make purchases from the canteen on account of a shortage of goods there.

He bowed to my refusal, although I had a strong feeling that he knew exactly why I had done so. I am sure he laughed at me to himself as an idealist. But then, I do not belong to those people who can, without reflection, say "non olet".

Ding may have sometimes wondered about the curious creatures who, with a knife at their throats, still retained their incomprehensible principles. He himself had often quite clearly indicated that he was prepared not to be over particular should one prisoner gain some personal advantage at the expense of another.

In order to give those prisoners who helped him some vitamin preparations and tonics, he sent for samples from firms who advertised their medicines in the medical weeklies. The men accepted these samples, but none touched the preparations which were in the camp apothecary.

Once a month orders for bandages, medicines and instruments were posted to the S.S. medical office in Berlin. At first, such orders were dealt with in a rather lax way, almost everything ordered being sent, what did not arrive one month being dispatched with the following month's delivery if Berlin had meanwhile obtained it.

Ding mainly agreed to the demands put forward by the senior nurse, who in turn was guided by the consumption reported by the camp chemist's store, in charge of a prisoner who was no chemist but who did his work excellently.

In view of the general conditions in the camp, we prisoner-nurses often regretted that we were not sufficiently medically educated to ensure that what we ordered was for the most suitable medicines we could use. Still, someone only had to call our attention to a medicament which had shown good results, and it was promptly included in our next monthly order, to be tried out. Sometimes it happened that Dr. Ding struck off or reduced the quantity of an expensive medicine on the list we had quoted too liberally, but we made allowances for this to happen.

At the outbreak of war, new instructions were issued, certain medicines for the sick ward being struck off altogether, and only small supplies of bandages could be ordered. To our dismay, Ding reduced the order list in a reckless and irresponsible fashion.

We found a way out of this predicament. We knew that we ourselves prepared the list ready for dispatch, and that nobody else troubled about it. Next month, then, after Ding had signed the list we had made out, we prefixed a figure here and added a nought there. To our relief, everything was right when the next cases arrived from Berlin.

It was only a pity, we thought, that we were not allowed at all to order certain medicines. Then we remembered that the new instructions did point out that certain medicines could be ordered in small quantities in cases of extreme emergency.

We studied these instructions carefully. Could we risk again listing at least those medicines which were in short supply? Ding had struck all those off, but we were acquainted with printing and knew what a space was, as well as a distance between printed lines. When, therefore, Dr. Ding had signed the order again, the list wandered through the typewriter, to emerge with some changes, allowances having previously been made for spaces. What we had to add fitted perfectly in the necessary column.

We did all this for our comrades. Had we been caught, we would all have suffered. We knew that quite well, but still we had to do it! Deep inside us existed a law so strong, so irresistible, so categorical, that there was nothing which did not subject itself to it!

Many a man gave his life in Buchenwald because his moral standards compelled him unselfishly to help his comrades. I know we must set up many monuments in Germany, in memory and honour of the dead; and also as a warning, for the number of Nazi victims is legion. We must not, however, forget a monument for those who tried to help their comrades in Buchenwald.

30. The Scientist

LITTLE power of observation is required to ascertain the fact that nature gives each person a different face and different characteristics. Even twins who can be mistaken for one another are readily recognised individually by their mother or by people who are in daily contact with them. There is also little power of observation required to judge a person's disposition from his face, clothing, hands or bearing.

A few weeks in Buchenwald, however, made it impossible to judge by anyone's appearance or face what he might have done in civilian life. The cruel, merciless fate which hung over everyone there crushed every distinguishing mark from every face and only the experienced psychologist could perhaps have been able, here and there, to detect faint signs to indicate a special character in someone.

Everywhere were the same torn, dirty uniforms, the shaven heads, the careworn faces, everywhere the same mixture of fear, horror and fatalism in the eyes of the prisoners; the same distress, the same poverty, the same way of life.

When they stood in rank and file, the scientist beside the labourers, the clergyman beside the habitual criminal, the teacher beside the craftsman, the artist beside the imbecile, the merchant beside the tramp, it would have been hard to distinguish one from another.

It was as if that which had previously constituted the whole essence of an individual personality had, with one blow, been completely destroyed. A person had to be a long time in the camp to know what this one or that had once been, and to possess a highly developed knowledge of human nature in order to separate by outward signs the chaff from the wheat, character from fickleness, wisdom from stupidity, idealism from materialism.

Life in the camp nearly always destroyed one's own values and sense of dignity. Those who knew how to retain their original personalities despite all they went through were the exception, not the rule. Buchenwald crushed any value of individual personality.

If an experienced observer could have looked down upon Germany from a lofty standpoint during those twelve years of horror, he would have noted throughout the whole country this same death of individual value; but in Buchenwald the death was carried to its uttermost limits. There was only one more stage in this levelling-down process—the grey-white ash of the cremated prisoners, sold to German farmers as fertiliser.

When the names of those who were murdered in German

225

concentration camps are chiselled in flaming letters on pillars which might reach to heaven, it will be seen how much nobleness, how much humanity, intelligence and knowledge, what spiritual and moral qualities, were brutally exterminated in this camp. Scientists were barbarically destroyed, as well as artists, educationalists, statesmen, politicians, leaders in all spheres of human life and famous the world over.

The name of Kreuzfuchs can be found in every dictionary which is not of National Socialist vintage. It is listed in the register of medical expressions, like the names of Basedow, Priesnitz or Billroth.

This man, whose name as a radiologist was written in the annals of history, lived in Vienna and was a Jew. He lived a quiet and retired life, existing only for his science, but he was a Jew. He was far too uninterested in current affairs to know what National Socialism was and had therefore never given an opinion on the matter; but he was a Jew. Why, I believe he was so completely wrapped up in his scientific tasks that he had even forgotten he was a Jew. Yet he was one! A Jew, nothing less than a Jew, and only a Jew! And that was his misfortune!

The day after Hitler had "liberated" Vienna, Kreuzfuchs was taken to Buchenwald because he was a Jew!

What I have to report of him amounts to little, and there are far more drastic examples of brutality to give, but I will confine myself to what I know of his fate.

In the camp, Kreuzfuchs had become an old shrivelled up little man, as thin as a skeleton. When I first saw him, I knew he would not have survived another day in the labour column outside the camp where he had been directed. But fellow-prisoners had contrived to find him work inside the camp environs. Nobody who saw him could have found any signs about him to indicate that he was a scientist, so completely had he been stripped of all personality.

Without question, his days were numbered. His Jewish friends knew this and thought up a scheme which would give him peace for however short a time.

The two or three Jewish doctors whom Dr. Ding had forced into his service had some peace in comparison with their Jewish fellow-prisoners. They exchanged this peace for the knowledge and experience they passed on to the Herr S.S. Doctor. They thought, then, that it would also be possible to interest Dr. Ding in an unparalleled discovery in radiology and thus save Kreuzfuchs.

Imperceptibly, step by step, Dr. Ding was prepared for this approach by the Jewish doctors. First, at a prognosis, the word "radiology" was dropped into the conversation, as if by accident. Then the results of radiology were discussed; later, its successes.

After a few days, Ding was so far prepared as to swallow, without resistance, the lapidary wisdom that radiology was the only means so far known to enable a doctor to diagnose certain illnesses with certainty.

A few days later still, of his own accord Ding expressed the wish to know this Kreuzfuchs who had done so much in the field of radiology.

Kreuzfuchs was so ignorant of the ways of the world that we had to convince him that he owed it to his life's work to answer the camp doctor's questions on radiology with promptitude and without hesitation.

Kreuzfuchs stood before the doctor at last, unassuming, reserved, clear in his answers and explanations. There, on the one side, was this shrivelled, emaciated man, already destined to die; and on the other, the all-powerful S.S. Sturmführer, the personification of exuberant health. They had nothing in common but their interest in the matter under discussion.

On the one side, the knowledge, the great knowledge; on the other, the splendid possibility of mobilising this knowledge for the benefit of the whole of mankind. On the one side, the scientist whose knowledge was so great that it no longer had the effect of pedantic education so much as the power of unobtrusive and unassuming instruction; on the other, the highly gifted S.S. officer who, possibly with the last dregs of decency still in him, could no doubt sense how great a thing was spread before him, something which was apart from human personality and individualism.

Ding conversed, asked questions, expressed opinions, and then dismissed the Jew without the usual malicious remarks, the gestures which might have indicated that he was no longer interested in him.

I wanted to know more. I therefore pretended ignorance, as I asked, "What kind of fellow was that?"

"That was Kreuzfuchs," Ding replied. "The man knows something."

Ding said no more, but even that little was water for our mill of confidence.

Some days later, Kreuzfuchs once more reported to the doctor. He had made a sketch and wanted to explain this to him. It dealt with the problem of aneurysma, a disease which causes enlargement of the aorta.

Ding was interested and had the drawing explained to him in detail. Carried away by his favourite subject, Kreuzfuchs made sweeping gestures, his eyes fixed on the sketch, occasionally emphasising his words by pointing to the drawing with shaking fingers. No longer able to follow his explanations, I confined myself to watching the two men.

Kreuzfuchs was completely absorbed in his explanation, while Ding himself could not at first take his eyes from the drawing. But then, he looked at Kreuzfuchs, back to the drawing, then again at Kreuzfuchs and back to the drawing once more.

There, what was causing Ding's eyes to flicker? I could see that he no longer followed the explanation, that something else stirred him. His chin moved forward, his lips tightened.

Kreuzfuchs saw nothing of this change, his eyes constantly on the drawing, his words quiet and clear, his shaking hand continually following the blue and red lines, the crosses and dots he had drawn.

For some time, however, Ding paid no attention to his words. I could see that he was getting worked up, and my heart pounded. I was petrified.

Ding drew up his right hand slowly, like a tiger lifting his claws. Then he hit out, tearing the drawing from the completely staggered Kreuzfuchs, crumpled it in his fist and hit the Jew brutally in the face.

At first Kreuzfuchs was absolutely stupefied, not realising what had happened; then, composing himself, he turned helplessly about, and ran through the door, as if for his life.

After Kreuzfuchs had left the room, Ding sneered in helpless rage, having lost all control over himself and devoid of shame. "What a swine! Such a Jew!" he muttered.

It took me some time to appreciate what had taken place before my eyes.

31. War

To us in the camp the 1st September, 1939, was a day similar to any other. The non-aggression and mutual assistance agreement with Russia, concluded a week before, was still the chief topic of our political conversation. Most had found it incredible to believe that the military alliance between Czechoslovakia and Russia had not been given effect to when German troops marched into that country. The enforced economic exchange of goods between Germany and Russia was considered to be unimportant because it was incomprehensible. But the announcement of a military agreement between the two most irreconcilable opponents in the world had flabbergasted everybody.

Now had dawned the 1st September, 1939, the day on which Hitler began his uninterrupted march to Narvik, Petsamo, Leningrad, Rshew, Wjasma, Stalingrad, Caucasus, el Alamein, Irun, Brest and Amsterdam. It was a day like any other, as I have said, for the mills of eternity still ground away in a twenty-four hour cycle and would do so, we thought, to the end of our days. The camp awakened and the tens of thousands still capable of working moved off for the roll-call.

I was in the surgery, doing my work. The medical orderlies arrived, followed by Ding.

An urgent call came from the gate. "Collect an important letter at once, but at once!" Seehausen went for the letter, which was a small packet, sealed twice. The word "Secret" was stamped on it several times, with exact instructions as to when the packet could be opened, and on whose orders.

It was as if the packet itself had stirred up a wasps' nest. Ding was excited, the medical orderlies dismayed. The papers were kept from me. But some forms had to be filled in, and

Seehausen himself sat down at the typewriter and, literally perspiring, struggled at his new task.

Ding stood beside him. The work went badly. Ding himself sat at the typewriter, and typed like a beginner, although he did better than Seehausen, whose job it really was to deal with all the writing in the sick ward.

I succeeded in reading the inscription on the envelope, which had been thrown carelessly on the table. Ding and Seehausen were far too busy filling in the forms to take notice of what I was doing. "Orders to the camp doctor of the concentration camp Buchenwald in the event of war."

Suddenly I realised the importance of this hour. As far back as 1930, I had taken part in meetings and had preached, "He who votes for Hitler, votes for war!" From then on I had never tired of standing firmly, with all the means at my disposal, against the madness which was approaching Germany like the darkest thunder clouds.

How I had struggled in 1932, making use of the spoken and written word in order to pull Germany back even at the last moment from the abyss into which she, and with her the whole of mankind, threatened to plunge. I had not been idle even when Hitler had gained power through lies and deception, terror, fear and crime. But the number of those who had thought as I had became ever fewer.

This sad realisation meant increased obligations for me, for I knew the real face of Fascism. In Italy in 1923 and 1924 I had experienced the brutal sadism with which Mussolini and his Black Shirts liquidated every opponent. I did not hesitate to continue my struggle even though Germany had adopted the same methods, if with a greater degree of brutality. I was forced underground, but knew that war, terrible war, faced us, the most horrid crime which could ever be committed against humanity.

I travelled willingly along the path I had taken, which led eventually to torture by the Gestapo, through the prisons of Münster, Berlin, Bremen and Celle, through the labour camps in East Friesland and the Lüneburg Heath to Buchenwald. Wherever I had gone I had not tired, using every opportunity to add my share of energy to the building up of a future dignified human society.

For a considerable time I had known that fate would not be avoided, that it must bring about the collapse of Nazism.

Now fate had at last taken its course and war was here. Still I was not disturbed. I was as calm as I would be on the last day of judgement. I left the room and informed my comrades of what I had learnt. "Attention! War against Poland! The world war has begun!"

We had discussed the question as to what would happen to us should war break out, and some had expressed the opinion that machine-guns and fat-squirters would probably liquidate us. Others thought that the strongest of us would be formed into labour columns in order to carry out work on fortifications and similar projects.

We who were politically active in the camp were, however, determined not to be liquidated without some resistance. This is why I gave my comrades the news, to pass on to others in our confidence.

By the early afternoon of the same day, the doctor and his orderlies had got themselves so tied up with their reports that they had to make use of me for the written work.

It was in this way that I obtained knowledge of the secret orders, which dealt mainly with the organisation of a concentration camp reinforcement, the C.C.-reinforcement. Two facts became evident to me. An immediate liquidation of the camp was not intended, an increase in the number of inmates being expected instead.

32. Concentration Camps Reinforcement

THE very next day the first members of the Concentration Camps Reinforcement arrived, and proved mainly to be elderly S.S. men with slight physical disabilities. Their task was to gradually take over the guard and other duties in the camp, leaving the younger ones available for front line service.

For more than eight months I watched this regrouping, one difficulty following another, so that it became obvious the new lot could never take over the running of the camp on their own responsibility.

The main cause of the trouble was to be found in the fact that not only did the S.S. men of the C.C.-reinforcement not know National Socialism but they had also lived through another era. Most of them had been in the front line during the first world war and had lived through the time of the Republic. Inherent in them, therefore, was still the ineradicable remains of a sense of justice. They were not yet free of those emotions of sympathy and compassion which nature and human upbringing instil in every human being. They had not gained the Buchenwald stamp. This meant that the camp management were obliged to place at least the main functions and the central control in the hands of tried S.S. men of the previous type.

I had two typical experiences a few days after the arrival of the C.C.-reinforcements.

There was the S.S. man Rose, a commercial representative from Berlin, who was attached to the sick ward as a medical orderly. Rose was fifty years old, married, with grown up children. He was good-natured and absolutely decent. At our first meeting I thought I noticed that he was uncertain and frightened, obviously belonging to that type of man who was really a forced rather than a voluntary member of the S.S.

The new prisoners were that day subjected to a medical examination in a barracks situated at the lower end of the square. Rose was present in order to acquaint himself with the procedure. I was also there. From one of the barracks windows we could overlook the whole square, right up to the gate and the adjoining buildings.

I noticed how Rose closely followed the examinations. Apparently he was as much impressed with what went on as were the unsuspecting prisoners, who kept perfectly still. He walked through the room on tiptoe, so as not to disturb Hans Rösler, our "doctor", who carried out the examinations with the dignity and authority of a distinguished medical man, tossing about Latin descriptions of illnesses as if he were as much at home in the medical faculty as a housewife in the kitchen.

I had to smile, knowing that in a few days Rose would

232

probably shuffle through the room just as awkwardly as did the old medical orderlies.

I saw him walk carefully and quietly through the room to look at the furniture. He approached the window which looked out on the square, and peered out attentively. I saw him move his head to and fro, as if he could not quite make out what he had first noticed out there, as if he wanted to observe what he saw from all sides. Only then did I notice that the stock at the gate was in use.

The cracking of the whips and the cries of pain from those being flogged penetrated into our barracks from the square. We ourselves were so accustomed to such sounds that we no longer heard them.

I stood beside Rose in a moment, curious to see his reactions to such brutality. He was certainly a shade paler than usual, his good-natured eyes betraying a strange mixture of tension and horror.

"What is this?" he inquired, his eyes never moving from the scene of the flogging, though it was not clearly visible from where we stood.

I tried to sound indifferent. "That there? Oh, someone is only getting the twenty-five allotted to him," I said.

"Twenty-five?" asked Rose, his voice slightly trembling.

"Yes, twenty-five lashes. He has been tied to the stock and is now receiving his twenty-five," I explained.

The man on the stock screamed pitifully, moans escaping from him between each blow he received—plaintive long drawn-out cries, the whip cracking like distant pistol-firing.

I saw Rose change colour, his knees shaking, and knew he was a man in whom feelings of humanity still remained.

He turned out to be a man, too. He could only help us in a limited way, but he did so as well as he was able to do. He provided us with cigarettes and gave us food; once he even smuggled a letter for my family out of the camp. Never did he participate in acts of torture. Of all the S.S. men I knew, he was the only one I cannot condemn for brutality.

With the first batch of C.C.-reinforcements there arrived a somewhat comical-looking Scharführer, perhaps fifty years old, who looked different from his comrades. He was a tall, stoutish man, in a very tight-fitting S.S. uniform. In ordinary jack-boots his legs looked like stilts thrust into boots too large for them.

On the left lower side of his chest was the Iron Cross, 1st Class, just above a funny barrel-like belly protruding from under his buckle, the face being slightly bloated, like that of a man who knows how to eat and drink well. He had all the characteristics of a person of sanguine temperament.

The scars on his jaw betrayed him as a former member of a students' association in which duels had been fought, the monocle, handled with assurance and in a casual manner, denoting the former officer of the monarchist stamp.

This was Dr. med. Blies from Offenbach on the Main who, as a result of mobilisation, had been ordered to join the C.C.-reinforcement for the concentration camp of Buchenwald.

Because of the mobilisation order, on the same day I had to send a report to the S.S. Chief Medical Office in Berlin, containing detailed personal data, S.S. rank, position in the camp and former army rank of all newly arrived C.C.-reinforcements. Added to the report were recommendations for promotion, so that it was only a few days later that, for example, S.S. man Rose became S.S. Oberscharführer and S.S. Scharführer Blies became S.S. Obersturmführer.

Once he was promoted, Dr. med. Blies's appearance became less comical. For the time being, however, he was still S.S. Scharführer and was introduced to his duties as assistant to the camp doctor. At first he was given a very favourable picture of what he had to do, but he certainly met with many surprises.

What probably astonished him most was the work carried out independently by the prisoners themselves, seeing that they had never received the slightest medical training to help them. He may have passed over their treatment of out-patients, but he could only be amazed by the fact that laymen dealt independently with the most difficult medical cases, carried out surgical operations and amputations and administered medicines and injections only a doctor should prescribe and do.

He had to acknowledge that a doctor could not have done better than the laymen did. Perhaps he soon realised that the latter were in fact better than the S.S. doctor, for although he slogged away like a farm horse in order to do justice to his own tasks, he never objected to the help of the laymen, nor in any way curtailed the independence of these prisoners, which he could have done at a moment's notice.

After conducting him through the sick ward, I had to briefly initiate him into the administration of the doctor's office. Apart from showing him various forms and reports, medical case histories and statistics, I also produced a death certificate which had just been completed. It contained an entirely fictitious report, according to which a prisoner had suddenly died of heat stroke, although he had actually simply starved to death like many other comrades. Still, "general physical weakness" as the cause of death was very seldom used in the files of the dead, however true.

Dr. Blies was surprised to note the competence with which the prisoner-nurses had treated this particular case, and I had once again to confirm the fact that we nurses treated such cases on our own initiative. When he read that a Cardiazol injection had been given to the prisoner as a last endeavour to save his life, he said, "Good gracious! You do that on your own here too?"

It did not take Dr. Blies long to recognise the inaccuracies of the death certificates, the medical case histories and other statements, and from then on he tried hard to avoid signing fictitious reports. He could not altogether evade doing so, unless he openly stated that he refused to do this task, for that would no doubt have meant his immediate liquidation.

Every time I submitted such papers to Dr. Blies for his signature, I could see how he gathered together all his energy, before jumping the hurdle his conscience set him. Once the first had been given the other signatures followed more easily, sometimes a little hesitantly, but never with quite as much a struggle as with the first.

Contrary to the habit of other S.S. doctors, he would first read any papers he had to sign, and gave his signature quickly and without hesitation to simple reports, orders and such, obviously not fictitious.

This observation of him repeatedly caused me to experiment by submitting to him papers which had previously been carefully placed in sequence. It intrigued me to learn how such a university scholar of the old school, now absorbed by

Nazism, would react psychologically. As sure as anything, it invariably happened that Dr. Blies always gave his signature to faked documents, even though he had first to undergo an inner struggle before he could force himself to do so.

The prisoners would have liked to have kept him in the camp, for there was not a single case he had where he ignored his duties as a doctor, and helped his patients as much as possible, without discrimination. But it was quite clear to us that Dr. Blies would endeavour to leave the camp as soon as possible, not being able to stomach what went on; and in fact, he was soon promoted and transferred to the Dachau S.S. Hospital, where he became Commander of the S.S. Office for Health and Application.

33. Dysentery in the Camp

THE declaration of war on Germany by England and France followed on 3rd September.

"Well, there we are again!" Dr. Ding received the news with such words. To my question as to what our ally Italy would now do, he said contemptuously, "Oh, they? They will let us down, of course. You cannot rely on them."

By the 2nd September new prisoners were already arriving in hundreds, followed by more and more in the days to come. Many were people who had been discharged from the camp during the mass release of the previous spring. The Communist deputy, Dr. Neubauer, was among them, although it was significant that he was again released after a fortnight, whereas the camp gates closed for ever behind many small officials and followers.

The outflanking battle in the Weichsel bend had not yet been fought when the first Polish transports came to Buchenwald. The special camp was again filled. All the new arrivals were subjected to a terrible procedure in order to prevent the supposed danger of spreading typhus and other epidemics.

Two large water barrels were placed in position, one filled

with a solution of lysol, the other with fresh water. The new prisoners had to undress in the open and were then literally thrown into the barrel of lysol, submerged several times, and brutally scrubbed with very rough brushes, in such a manner that their skins were often lacerated. They again had to rinse their bodies in the second barrel, and dress again without drying themselves.

It was great fun for all the Scharführer and S.S. officers of the camp, who enjoyed the procedure like care-free children love a Punch and Judy show. There was always an extra howl of delight from the row of spectators when a weak old man lost consciousness or a child wriggled unduly during the process of cleansing.

The special camp was again crowded in the most unbelievable manner. It was separated from us, so that we could not determine who or how many prisoners had been brought in.

We found later that at the time approximately two thousand prisoners were locked up in this hell-hole. Again, the daily food ration consisted of a pint of thin watery soup and one slice of bread. Again, the camp was strictly isolated from the rest. Again, death took its tremendous toll in a short space of time.

Then came dysentery in the camp. The passing of blood in cases of diarrhoea had been increasing for some time. Our comrade Rudolf Gottschalk, a former teacher, who had been given some training by a Jewish specialist in the laboratory and so had acquired considerable medical knowledge, had always examined excrements he suspected of abnormalities. When he stated, "No dysentery. No typhus. No tubercle," we could always note that he was right, from the course taken by the particular illness.

One day, however, he reported, "I have found dysentery germs." The sick person concerned was immediately isolated. Rudi reported a second, third and fourth case. These also were put into isolation. A few days later all their symptoms revealed that Rudi had made a correct diagnosis.

From what source had the dysentery entered the camp? we wondered. The prisoner-nurses themselves carried out the medical examination of new arrivals, doing, on their own initiative, everything possible from a hygienic point of view.

We realised that there were germ carriers in the camp, healthy people who contained the germ and secreted it in their bodies. Instant investigations were started in order to discover in which block the disease had first appeared. The initial cases were individual ones, and could not help us make a correct conjecture. All necessary measures were adopted to prevent the disease from spreading, but without success. The cases of dysentery began to increase.

I had drawn a plan of the camp, showing the individual blocks which were used as living quarters, and marking on it every new case. After a few days, the entries pointed like an arrow straight to the special camp.

The camp had been hermetically sealed, but Dr. Ding, Walter Krämer and I forced our way into it. We saw the same picture as that of four, five months before, perhaps still more horrible, still more dreadful, still more indescribable. Dysentery raged to an unimaginable extent.

There was no doubting this fact. The excretions of the sick, covering the ground in the tents as well as the entire yard, had been washed by the rain downhill into the main camp. The primitive latrine was a deep hole in the ground, a filthy tree trunk across it, and this was overflowing with blood, pus and excrement. We saw the horrible, simply unbearably stinking slime trickling down the gutters, into the main camp.

We tried to destroy this ideal breeding ground of the dangerous and murderous dysentery germ with hundredweights of chloride chalk. Not until months of struggle did we succeed in confining the epidemic within limits, and during that time how great was the toll of victims!

Within a few weeks the special camp was completely liquidated, for, after some time, during which the number of deaths from dysentery had decreased in the main camp, the Scharführer in charge of the food distribution for the special camp procured some artificially bred bacteria from the physiological institute and mixed these into the food. He wanted to be relieved of his special commission as soon as possible, and he was, too!

* * *

This pathological institute was established during the dysentery epidemic just described. One day, when we were struggling our hardest to combat the epidemic, two young S.S. doctors in smart uniforms arrived in the camp.

Despite the terrible lack of accommodation, they had one barracks cleared, and unpacked from countless cases and boxes, instruments, microscopes, breeding chambers, bottles, basins, phials and goodness knows what else. A bacteriological institute was thus established, the like of which the most modern university could not have had.

Then the two doctors set to work at their task. Our Rudi Gottschalk was only too pleased with their assistance, for he was already completely exhausted by his work. He had literally been working day and night without a break, and lately had not been feeling well. The first results soon came from the physiological institute, and the prisoner-nurses had their hands full trying to find accommodation for those reported by them to be suffering from dysentery.

Strangely enough, these sick people were actually quite different from those notified by Rudi! Still, perhaps they were less severe cases of dysentery than the others had been. Nevertheless, the matter developed still more strangely, for the excretions of those who had actually been affected by dysentery were reported from the institute as being free from germs!

During this time Dr. Zahel, the camp surgeon, was acting as doctor, and the prisoner-nurses submitted their observations to him. He walked through the isolation barracks and saw for himself how completely different the forms of the disease were. He went into the laboratory to Rudi, had dysentery preparations placed under a microscope, and looked repeatedly through the eye-piece. Then he returned to the physiological institute. He came back with some preparations which had just been certified there as positive. Rudi pushed them under the microscope, and could find no trace of dysentery bacteria.

I came into the laboratory just as Zahel sat down at the microscope. He stared and stared, pushed, adjusted and stared again. I could see small pearls of perspiration on his forehead as he lifted his head from the eye-piece. I knew what these pearls of perspiration meant, having seen him at work on operations. They always appeared if something was wrong.

I did not know much about microscopy, but at the time

when Rudi made his first report I had looked at the small
dangerous bacteria, had compared their shape with illustrations
in technical literature, and had later seen them many times
again. In looking through the microscope now I, too, could
find no trace of the little characteristic blobs to be found in the
dysentery bacteria.

Not a word did we three say, for each knew what the other
was thinking. It was just after one p.m. Zahel gazed out of the
window in thought for a moment, then, as if jerking himself
back to reality, he walked out, saying, "Stay here."

Rudi lit a cigarette. With my hands in my pockets, I walked
up and down the room, four paces this way, four paces that
way, having grown accustomed to this habit during the long
months of solitary confinement I had spent in prison. For the
time neither of us said a word to each other. Rudi was completely overworked, and did not look well.

"You look pale, Rudi," I said to him at last, but he waved
aside my remark.

That was all that was said between us until, about twenty
minutes later, Zahel re-entered the laboratory, holding in his
hand a porcelain saucer with a small amount of dried mucus.
Again nothing was said by any of us, but Rudi and I suddenly
realised that, during the absence at lunch of the two bacteriologists, from the breeding chamber of the physiological institute
Zahel had collected a section of the culture medium on which
the dysentery bacteria were bred.

Without a word, Zahel handed the dried mucus to Rudi, so
that he could make the usual preparations.

Rudi placed the glass plate on the platform, and with a
gesture invited Zahel to adjust the microscope. Just as silently,
Zahel bade him sit down to it. Involuntarily I said to myself,
"That is just like Zahel, quite like Zahel the distinguished
surgeon, whose knowledge and ability are extensive, a man
who once said to me, 'It was the darkest hour of my life when
I joined the S.S.'"

Rudi switched on the lamp, pressed his eyes against the eye-
piece, placed the mirror in position, set the eye-piece screw
and made his final adjustments. When he lifted his head again,
he uttered one word only, "Coli!"

Zahel walked up to the microscope, stared, adjusted the

preparation and stared again. He at last turned away, in silence.

Actually I did not belong with them, for what did I know of cocoons, bacillus and bacteriology? But Zahel indicated to me to sit down at the microscope. Even with my limited knowledge I established that I had never seen such a marvellously pure culture medium of coli bacillus, that completely harmless fission fungi which exists in the large intestine. Zahel silently walked up and down the laboratory.

As I got up from the microscope and nodded my head in agreement, Zahel said, "Tomorrow morning you will take test samples from all persons sick with dysentery; at three o'clock p.m. a van leaves for Jena."

The result of the tests in Jena confirmed that the new physiological institute had mistaken coli bacillus for dysentery bacillus!

Zahel dictated to me a sober and objective report for the Chief Medical Office in Berlin, informing his two colleagues that he had done so.

Any further mention of this matter would be superfluous, but for the sake of completion I must add that the two honourable bacteriologists from the physiological institute that evening produced several results which proved more conclusive, having previously obtained information from the prisoner-nurses as to which excretions came from persons sick with dysentery and which did not.

It was not necessary to inform Dr. Zahel of this new manoeuvre of theirs, for Berlin considered it advisable to recall the two bacteriologists for different duties elsewhere and replace them with other doctors.

Soon after, our Rudi himself was seriously ill with dysentery, and for weeks struggled between life and death; but he recovered. He had infected himself while working with the microscope—the two S.S. bacteriologists had not.

34. Experiments on the Living

DURING the fifth or sixth week of the dysentery epidemic, after the bacteriological institute had already been established, S.S. Untersturmführer Dr. Neumann suddenly appeared in the camp, bearing with him special powers of authority. It was said that he came from the closest circles around the Reich Chief Medical Officer, Gerhard Wagner. It was he who effected the further extension of the pathological institute and introduced a system of experiments on sick persons, on persons rendered sick by artificial means, and on healthy people.

He was a man in the thirties, erratic, very conceited, completely egotistical, who had no contact even with his S.S. colleagues. He possessed no particular characteristics to identify him as a doctor, a scientist or a personality above the average.

His complexion was a greyish-yellow, his features revealing signs of a hectic past, his eyes restless and piercing. By closely studying his face one came to the conclusion that he could, and probably would, commit atrocities, but perhaps only under certain conditions, in secret, behind closed doors.

The S.S. uniform he wore was slightly untidy, without the immaculate touch usually favoured by the S.S., but perhaps according to regulations, one would not quite know.

He limited his post-mortems at first to the bodies of people who had died from dysentery.

He was hardly in the camp half an hour before a corpse was ordered to be put on the table, as if corpses could run away, as if there were not enough material available for his studies! He had arrived in Buchenwald two hours before, had gone straight to the camp commandant, had there produced his authority, and had immediately had quarters allocated to him. He then went into the camp itself.

He acted as if he expected everybody to jump to attention for him, yet he did not have the stuff in him to command real authority, so that he was immediately cold-shouldered by the other S.S. Scharführer.

He needed assistance. The camp doctor and S.S. Scharführer regretted that they were overworked and unfortunately could not help him.

"Can prisoners be put at my disposal?" he demanded.

"Yes, certainly, Herr colleague," the camp doctor replied.

He did not even look at the prisoners sent to assist him. From his point of view, it was probable that anyone was good enough for the work he would give them to do.

"I have left my case with instruments up at the gate. Can a Scharführer collect my bag?" he asked.

"Why not send a prisoner, Herr colleague?" returned the doctor.

"Can that be done?"

"Yes, of course, Herr colleague."

"Where can I dissect?"

"Well, Herr colleague, there is only a barracks, the mortuary up at the gate; a little primitive, but it will do. We, too, carry out our dissections there."

"Are any corpses available?"

The doctor smiled. "Yes, of course, Herr colleague."

"Then I will begin at once."

"Just as you like, Herr colleague."

Neumann moved off with two prisoners, but considered it advisable to load his revolver before he went, an act which induced Seehausen to grin at the doctor.

After the lapse of about twenty minutes, Neumann returned to the doctor's room.

"Herr colleague, I have forgotten to pack a pair of rubber gloves. Can I have a pair?"

The doctor knew very well that there were a number of gloves available in the store. Despite this fact, he said, "Rubber gloves? Well, I am not sure—they are—hm—in short supply here, but—I'll get someone to have a look."

He then instructed me to look in the chemist's store. I understood quite well what was meant by this, and returned with a pair of rubber gloves which could only be used once more, but only just.

Somewhat taken aback, Neumann looked at them, but said nothing, although he obtained another pair from the S.S. sick ward the following day.

In the evening the prisoners detailed to work for Neumann

243

reported, "That's an odd customer. As close as an oyster, of boundless arrogance, and apparently of the opinion that we are stuffed full of wisdom. We were supposed to know on the spot how to handle parts of a body which had been cut out. When we were unable to do so, we were called the choicest names."

Realising that the newcomer had no support from the camp doctor and the Scharführer, the prisoners imagined he could be of little danger to us.

We were to find otherwise.

New cases full of numerous instruments arrived from Berlin, and the pathological institute was extended. Soon, Neumann had collected a number of preparations of all kinds. He had not only cut perforated intestines and other infected parts, but had prepared almost all other human internal organs in glasses and tubes—not only those affected by disease but also healthy ones; not only internal organs, but limbs on which sinews, nerves, veins, bones, joints and so on had been partly exposed; portions of skulls, genitals. One prisoner worked nearly all day on the cutting machines which produced the very thin slices needed for these preparations.

It was not exactly a comfortable prospect for us to know that we would perhaps swim around in one or several show glasses, or have our skins removed and tanned, as frequently happened. But we were at least certain we would feel nothing when the time came for us to fall victims to his experiments.

Neumann then suddenly appeared in our sick ward and in the emergency barracks which had been set up for the many dysentery cases. At first the nurses imagined he was on his rounds, but he soon exhibited an increasingly curious interest in individual sick persons.

The following day he began his own examinations and treatment.

Despite the fact that he did not tell any prisoner-nurse what he injected and what medicines he was prescribing, there was soon no doubt that he was experimenting on his patients.

None of the prisoners he personally attended ever regained their health. Now and again they showed some signs of improvement, after which they would be given new medicines and invariably became worse. Not one of his patients escaped death, and he dissected the majority of them instantly after death.

We were anxious to learn what medicines Neumann prescribed, but however hard we tried to do so, we could discover nothing, for he himself always gave the medicines to his patients.

The tubes with the liquid from the post-mortems bore no inscription, the powders and pills ordered for the sick, to swallow in his presence, were always wrapped in plain paper, or were taken from boxes without labels. He invariably put the wrapping paper in his pocket and he himself cleaned the syringe he had to use, immediately placing it in his instrument case, which he never let out of his sight and always carried with him.

He next proceeded to reserve a small room in the sick barracks for his sick. He would have eight patients at a time, there to undergo the most peculiar treatments. He repeatedly rubbed liquids and powder into the healthy skin of thighs, arms and backs of hands, until they produced complaints which sometimes spread over the whole body. At certain stages he would cut out the affected portions of the skin and take them to the pathological institute, where no one was allowed to disturb him at his work.

He inserted cannulae and tubes into the chests and abdomens of his wretched victims and sometimes kept them for weeks under observation. He injected long needles with some kind of liquid into internal organs, with and without narcotics.

As soon as these prisoners died, he carried out post-mortems on the bodies which were often still warm, nearly always examining single organs in detail, perhaps only superficially looking over the rest of the body. Every prisoner who died had at once to be replaced by another, selected by Neumann personally.

As I write these lines today I find it inconceivable that we prisoners were able to endure all that was going on at the time.*

* Neumann, later promoted to S.S. Hauptsturmführer, in 1948 during the "denazifications" was given a clean sheet by the Darmstadt Court although the author was heard as a witness. The Court considered the witness's testimony as invalid, presumably because his

35. Letters

APART from our philosophical conception of life and our political convictions, the strongest motive which gave us prisoners power to withstand the horrible things of which I have only recorded typical instances, was the feeling and knowledge that our loved ones were at home, waiting for us.

In the camp we were all intensely lonely, for a certain

Austrian fellow-prisoner, Gustav Wegerer (from 1938 to 1945 in Buchenwald, died 1954) did not appear as a witness. Wegerer was thoroughly disgusted with the scandalous judgements of that period, and did not answer several subpoenas because he was afraid of being arrested in the American zone. At that time the former concentration camp prisoners were considered by the American military authorities as being equally guilty with the Nazis. Wegerer, who had worked as a clerk under Neumann in the hospital, had—like the author—on 23rd April, 1945, accused Neumann in the strongest terms. The author saw Wegerer possibly twice and at most three times but never spoke to him up to his death. After the Darmstadt Court trial the author tried to get into touch with Wegerer in Vienna by letter. Wegerer did not reply, probably suspecting that this was an American trap.

The Darmstadt trial was conducted so much in favour of Neumann, on the premise that the testimony of concentration camp prisoners was invalid, that the witness Rudolf Gottschalk, realising the impossibility of making himself believed, lost his nerve and stamped from the courtroom, banging the door noisily. The President did not react to this gesture. The author had already foreseen this problem in April and May, 1945. Vide: p. 97. The Nazis mutually "whitewashed" each other and were given a clean bill by the courts since they testified on oath—some of them were even declared anti-Nazi, despite the fact that in public utterances the Nazis had declared exactly how much this oath meant to them. With what audacity the Nazis were operating once more, although they had at first grovelled can be explained by the fact that efforts were being made to allow the accused to bring a case against an honest witness for perjury. It is an interesting legal problem: by completely reversed legal practice the author would have gone to prison as the defendant, despite the fact that he was under oath to speak the whole truth, but had no witness to corroborate his evidence. As a witness on oath he should have obtained a more or less just sentence on Neumann.

amount of reserve remained even in our camp friendships. Our wives, our children, our friends at home, all those people with whom we were inextricably connected, were the most valuable possessions we could carry in our hearts.

We were again and again helped by the ever-recurring hope that one day a kind fate would once more unite us with our people. Our camp friendships were certainly strong sources of power, but it was only our unspeakable misery that brought us together. The loved ones at home were bound to us on another level, in surroundings which were more free, without the brutal compulsion of such misery.

Because of this, every line from home was the expression of this unity and was a soul-stirring experience precious and affecting to us who were surrounded by death and destined to die. The most blessed words, "feeling is all, names are just sound and smoke", could not describe the inner value of our hopes.

Every now and again we were allowed to write home brief letters, but anyone who wrote a careless word, either through ignorance or stupidity, was always terribly punished. It need hardly be mentioned that it was some time before he was again allowed to write. There was sometimes a general ban on writing, either to punish the whole camp, or because the Scharführer at the mail centre did not feel in the mood to censor our letters or postcards.

The mail we received from home was naturally also subjected to censorship. Letters written by quite unsuspecting relatives were at times the cause of punishment being meted out to prisoners. The censors cut out all sentences we were not allowed to see, and it was difficult for us to guess what they were. Perhaps they were passages of a political nature, or mention of efforts by relatives to effect our release, or sentences behind which the S.S. men imagined some kind of information in code to exist.

It frequently happened that one received the original addressed envelope with only two bits of paper, on which would appear the opening address and the signature of the sender; sometimes the envelope contained only one of the two.

But it did sometimes happen that letters came into the camp

uncensored, and these at times brought enlightening news from the outside world.

It is obvious that the censor was often fooled in the letters from and to the camp. Without previous arrangement, several prisoners and their relatives had developed such perfection in correspondence that there was hardly any forbidden news which was not unknowingly passed by the censor. Indeed, it was characteristic of the intelligence of the censors that they often passed passages which even a simple mind could have recognised as a very clumsy transcription of forbidden news.

I, too, had developed a system with my family, and was eventually able to give exact instructions as to the sort of efforts needed on their part to effect my release, although any references of this kind were strictly forbidden.

"The bright tomorrow may soon dawn and we'll be free!" These ambiguous lines of the Buchenwald song were perhaps the pole which time and again attracted our ideas. Even when, in our conversations, we convinced ourselves of the almost complete hopelessness of our release, we still held the slight subconscious hope that perhaps we would yet escape from this hell.

36. Release!

My friends had several times advised me to try and disappear from the sick barracks unperceived, and change over to a group of prisoners who led a fairly tolerable existence in a light labour column, unnoticed by the camp management.

My friends knew what knowledge I had gained through my activities as a doctor's clerk, and were of the opinion that because of this my release from the camp was entirely out of the question.

Their reasons weighed heavily on me, for I had myself experienced many instances of the frivolity with which S.S. men disposed of prisoners inconvenient to them.

There were two important reasons, however, why I could

not decide to follow the advice I was given. I thought that either the S.S. men had realised the danger which I could cause them, which meant they would not release me anyway, or they had not done so, in which case, because of their stupidity, they would release me as they had my predecessor, Herbert Neumann.

On the other hand, I told myself, because of my conception of life and convictions I was under an obligation to utilise to the last hour the possibilities which my position offered in the interests of many fellow-sufferers, as it became more and more influential.

My family secretly informed me that my son, who was at the front, had submitted an application for my release direct to the Security Head Office in Berlin. I had several times heard that this approach had led to success.

An application by a front-line soldier weighed more heavily with the National Socialists than one from a woman who had had to struggle through life for five long years without assistance. But a direct approach had meant that the Stapo Office (State Police Office) of my home town had been by-passed. There, Gestapo men sat who, from personal vindictiveness and in the knowledge that my presence alone would be unfavourable to them, had refused my release on principle. My family had now moved to northern Germany because they knew this to be true. I was sanguine of release because of these reasons.

Against this chance of success stood everything I had got to learn as a doctor's clerk. Yet I had not given the S.S. men any reason to suspect that I had witnessed too much against their conduct.

About two months after I had received the information from my family that I might be freed, I was ordered to the camp commandant Rödl for a so-called political interrogation. We prisoners knew quite well what this usually meant.

The interrogation was no more than a farce. Many a prisoner who had been ordered to these interrogations, and to whom the assurance had been given that he would soon go home, was, in fact, not released, however good his conduct had been.

When I entered Rödl's room he was sitting behind his desk,

my political file in front of him. After I had reported, he turned over the pages of my file and said:

"Have you any children?"

"Yes, Herr Obersturmbannführer."

"How many?"

"Three, Herr Obersturmbannführer."

"Your children will be pleased if you go home again?"

"Certainly, Herr Obersturmbannführer."

"The eldest has submitted an application for your release. You can thank him if you should be released, you understand?"

"Yes, Herr Obersturmbannführer."

"All right; get back to your work again."

"Very well, Herr Obersturmbannführer."

That was all. I was not asked in the usual way as to my possible camp punishments, my present political opinion and my views on the camp itself. I soon concluded that the political interrogation in my case was nothing but a meaningless gesture, especially when other prisoners, interrogated at a later date than I was, had meanwhile been released.

"Oh well, bad luck, that's that," I said to myself, and tried not to be too downhearted.

On an exceptionally fine, warm spring evening on the 9th May, 1940, I was in the nurses' quarters having my supper when, to my surprise, S.S. Oberscharführer Rose came to the sick ward, even though evening roll-call had been taken. No medical orderly had ever before, to my knowledge, been in the camp at such a late hour.

A comrade told me that Rose was in the doctor's room and wanted to see me.

It was obvious that Rose was very excited. He said to me, "You will be released tomorrow morning!"

Release? . . .

I remained calm. My heart beat no faster than normally.

Then Rose said, "Have you not some political file which I can take along with me? I must pretend to have been doing something here."

I unlocked the drawer of the desk and gave him one.

Then I was alone in the room. Released! I suddenly thought. What was the time? Seven p.m. Good! My future would have been decided by tomorrow this time. I would either be in the train on my way to the north or I would have been—shot while escaping.

Well, I thought, these few hours would also pass, after the last five years, six months, eight days and nineteen hours.

I went along to Richard Elsner.

"The time has come, Richard; tomorrow morning," I said.

"Good, Walter. I am sure it will work out all right."

I noticed that he, too, realised the uncertainty of my fate.

I then called on Walter Krämer, for he was the one intimate friend to whom I could speak of all those matters which had been assigned to me on account of my political function in the camp and which I wanted to settle. He, too, knew that I was finally leaving, in one way or the other.

I worked during the night, putting those files in order which needed most tidying. This caused no attention from the clerks on night duty and other prisoners, for I had often worked through the night. Only Walter Krämer and Richard Elsner knew why I now did this, and I was aware that both would observe silence. I did not want my departure from the camp to be known, knowing my friends would all come along to see me; and I did not want that.

Before the morning roll-call was taken, Hauptscharführer Strippel rang through to me. I had previously had many a duty conversation with him, and he always called me "You jolly type".

"Are you there, you jolly type?" he now inquired.

"Yes, Herr Hauptscharführer."

"When were you born?"

"On the 6th January, 1900."

"Right! Pack your things and be in the clothing depot at eight. I won't trouble to call your number through the loud-speaker. You are on your way home!"

I went at once to Walter Krämer. "I say, it's official. Strippel has just rung me up."

"Well, best of luck, old boy," he said. "Write some time when you are out so that we know if it went off all right."

I distributed the small private belongings I had organised during my time in the camp, my lighter, my cigarette holder, my fountain pen, my propelling pencil, my purse. I exchanged my good boots and my clean prison suit for old things, for at the clothing depot I had only to hand over one set of each item of clothing I possessed. A quick handshake with the prisoners with whom I had worked in the sick ward for more than a year.

A quarter of an hour remained before I went. Once more I looked through the doctor's room. There were the shelves with the fictitious death certificates, the desk with the castration and sterilisation files, the political files and the death poison; there, the typewriter on which I had typed health certificates and so many terrible things, the whole room with its four walls, within which I had had so many horrible experiences.

Ferdinand Röhmhild, a prisoner clerk, entered the room. He was an extremely quiet fellow who had always diligently carried out his work. I thought a lot of him, but I had hardly ever had any political or personal conversation with him.

"Walter," he said now, "I don't know whether they will release you. I hope they will; but anyway, I must tell you this in parting: what you have done here has restored my faith in the goodness of mankind."

Before I quite realised what he had said, he was out of the room. A stranger tells me that! I thought. A fellow whom I had hardly noticed! And he tells me that at a moment when I cannot return my thanks to him.

Right! Now I had gained the inner strength I needed for my last passage through Buchenwald!

I was soon standing in the passage of the Political Department, and with me were six or seven others who were to be released. We received a railway ticket to our home towns, together with certificates showing we were released on probation, and instructions to report within twenty-four hours after arrival there to the Gestapo of our home towns.

S.S. Obersturmführer Frerichs, the director of the Political Department, called me into the room in which at one time my personal data had been registered. There, the Scharführer sat at typewriters before large filing cabinets.

"Come with me," Frerichs said to me, and walked ahead into a second room which was almost empty. What was to happen? I wondered. I kept close behind him, determined not to die without a fight. He left the room for another beyond, which was his office. My nerves were strained to the limit.

I knew this method only too well! I was determined to act immediately against my liquidation.

"Close the door!" Frerichs said to me. I closed it without taking my eyes off him.

"You will be released today. I know you have seen things here which the public cannot quite understand yet. You must observe complete silence about it. You know that, don't you? You will soon be back here again if you don't, and what will happen to you then, you know too."

"I know that, Herr Obersturmführer," I said, and, through some inexplicable force which irresistibly overcame me and which even startled me, I added, "This is a hard camp, but I am convinced that its severity is necessary in the interests of the National Socialist State."

Then I walked backwards out of the room without once taking my eyes off him, as a lackey was prone to do before his master.

A guard took us along the Karacho Way as far as the barrier, on to the road to Weimar. The guards there did not even trouble to check our release papers.

Another ten paces. Then—I was suddenly seized by emotion. I could not walk on. My legs were shaking. My heart beat faster. I was breathless, until the tension ceased with one single free breath of air.

The sun shone wonderfully warm and friendly from the blue, cloudless sky, the pleasant breeze from the forest playing around my forehead and cheeks. I was free! The hardest journey of my life was now behind me.

A Necessary Epilogue

I WAS released from Buchenwald on 10th May, 1940—first on probation and then definitely. Before reporting as a precautionary measure to the Gestapo I got in touch with my friends who had formed a resistance group. This was the group which ultimately, in conjunction with the events of 20th July, 1944, became—unfortunately for too short a time—a focal point of world interest. As things stand this still holds good today, the influence of the other Germany—the better spiritual Germany —is the least known. Another purpose of this book is to make this known and to testify to that strength in which the world can have full confidence.

And something else must, in my opinion, be said, something which stands right at the beginning of this book and which possibly some readers may overlook. The human race is still threatened by the things in this book which arouse indignation and upon which it sits in judgement. The danger can only be averted if the methods of democracy are freely used and when mankind finally begins to learn the lessons of the past. Ignorance and indolence are the bitterest enemies of any progress towards a free, peaceloving, sensitive world of men. Since both the judicious and the perpetrators are drawn into the general destiny, as happened with the decent Germans during the Thousand Year Reich, every right-thinking man is challenged to be doubly attentive and to co-operate.

May this book prove a foundation stone for a better world.

WALTER POLLER.

London, 6th December, 1960.